Beginning Spring Data

Data Access and Persistence
for Spring Framework 6 and Boot 3

Andres Sacco

Apress®

Beginning Spring Data: Data Access and Persistence for Spring Framework 6 and Boot 3

Andres Sacco
Buenos Aires, Buenos Aires, Argentina

ISBN-13 (pbk): 978-1-4842-8763-7   ISBN-13 (electronic): 978-1-4842-8764-4
https://doi.org/10.1007/978-1-4842-8764-4

Managing Director, Apress Media LLC: Welmoed Spahr
Acquisitions Editor: Steve Anglin
Development Editor: Laura Berendson
Coordinating Editor: Jill Balzano
Copyeditor: Kim Burton

Cover designed by eStudioCalamar

Cover image by Mink Mingle on Unsplash (www.unsplash.com)

Distributed to the book trade worldwide by Apress Media, LLC, 1 New York Plaza, New York, NY 10004, U.S.A. Phone 1-800-SPRINGER, fax (201) 348-4505, e-mail orders-ny@springer-sbm.com, or visit www.springeronline.com. Apress Media, LLC is a California LLC and the sole member (owner) is Springer Science + Business Media Finance Inc (SSBM Finance Inc). SSBM Finance Inc is a **Delaware** corporation.

For information on translations, please e-mail booktranslations@springernature.com; for reprint, paperback, or audio rights, please e-mail bookpermissions@springernature.com.

Apress titles may be purchased in bulk for academic, corporate, or promotional use. eBook versions and licenses are also available for most titles. For more information, reference our Print and eBook Bulk Sales web page at http://www.apress.com/bulk-sales.

Any source code or other supplementary material referenced by the author in this book is available to readers on GitHub (https://github.com/Apress). For more detailed information, please visit http://www.apress.com/source-code.

Printed on acid-free paper

*To my grandparents, who taught me the importance
of always learning new things*

*To my wife and children for supporting me
while writing this book*

Table of Contents

About the Author

Andres Sacco has been a professional developer since 2007, working with a variety of languages, including Java, Scala, PHP, Node.js, and Kotlin. His background is mostly in Java and its libraries or frameworks, like Spring, JSF, iBATIS, Hibernate, and Spring Data. He is focused on researching new technologies to improve the performance, stability, and quality of the applications he develops.

In 2017 he started finding new ways to optimize data transference between applications to reduce infrastructure costs. He suggested actions applicable to microservices. As a result of these actions, the cost was reduced by 55%. Some of these actions are connected directly with the harmful use of databases.

About the Technical Reviewer

Manuel Jordan Elera is an autodidactic developer and researcher who enjoys learning new technologies for his experiments and creating new integrations. Manuel won the Springy Award 2013 Community Champion and Spring Champion. In his little free time, he reads the Bible and composes music on his guitar.

Manuel is known as dr_pompeii. He has tech-reviewed numerous books, including *Pro Spring MVC with WebFlux* (Apress, 2020), *Pro Spring Boot 2* (Apress, 2019), *Rapid Java Persistence and Microservices* (Apress, 2019), *Java Language Features* (Apress, 2018), *Spring Boot 2 Recipes* (Apress, 2018), and *Java APIs, Extensions and Libraries* (Apress, 2018).

You can read his detailed tutorials on Spring technologies and contact him through his blog at `www.manueljordanelera.blogspot.com`. You can follow Manuel on his Twitter account, @dr_pompeii.

Acknowledgments

I would like to thank my family members and friends for their encouragement and support during the process of writing this book.

- My wife, Gisela, was always patient when I spent long hours at my computer desk working on this book

- My little daughter, Francesca, who helped me to relax when I was writing each chapter

- My baby, Allegra, who is the new family member and my inspiration to write this book

- My friends, German Canale and Julian Delley, who always encouraged me to write a book and supported me when I doubted myself

- A special mention to Manuel Jordan for guiding me in improving the quality of my book

I sincerely thank the team at Apress for their support during the publication of this book. Thanks to Mark Powers for providing excellent support. Finally, thanks to Steve Anglin for suggesting and giving me the possibility to write a book about Spring Data.

Introduction

In the past, developers saved information in a relational database using conventional methods like JDBC. It worked for a time—when systems were small or not overly complex to maintain. Gradually, new technologies like Ibatis and Hibernate emerged to reduce the complexity of queries and facilitated access to different relational databases, allowing developers to focus on creating great applications instead of spending a lot of time figuring out how to connect to a database or reduce the number of connections.

Soon after, many non-relational databases appeared, solving certain problems even while others persisted. As a developer, one still needed to use a database client and struggle with myriad performance issues and/or bad practices.

Spring[1] proved to be the solution to multiple problems, be it related to dependency injection or how to intercept a method or class before/after another method calls it. It's no wonder the framework's developers created something to reduce the complexity involved in using multiple databases (relational and non-relational). Spring Data solves most of these issues, increasing developers' performance and ability to create new applications.

This book will cover the basics of creating an application that can access multiple databases and demonstrate how you can do things in different databases. Also, you will learn best practices to help reduce inefficiencies in your applications.

Why This Book

So, why write a book about Spring Data and how to persist information in different databases? Most developers use different databases to persist different types of information; for example, some use Redis (a possible mechanism of cache) or MongoDB (to save documents whose structure could change in the future). My purpose in writing this book was to explain Spring Data's power and its best practices.

---

[1] https://spring.io/

The following are some common questions associated with the use of databases.

- How can you optimize queries or the number of operations in a database?

- How do you create unit tests to validate that queries or changes work properly?

- How can you maintain a registry of all changes made to the database?

- How can you evaluate if there is a problem related to the performance of your query?

- Which database is the best option for the project you're working on?

These are just some of the questions I've tried to address throughout the book.

Who This Book Is For

This book is for developers with a programming background in Java who want to know how to persist information in different databases and how to create tests to validate whether their application performs as intended.

Note   It is beyond the scope of this book to explain in-depth *all* concepts related to the creation of queries.

You are not required to have previous experience using Spring or Spring Data because I will show you how to create a project from scratch with different layers, each with a specific purpose.

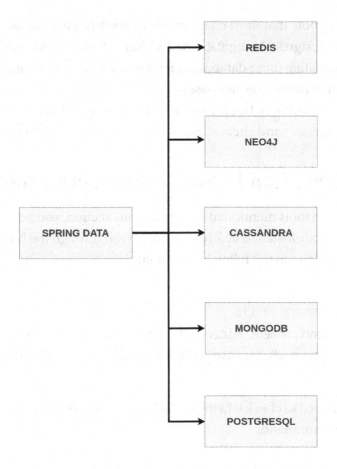

Prerequisites

You should have Java JDK[2] 17 or higher installed on your machine, Maven[3] 3.8.1 or higher, and an IDE you are comfortable with. IDE options include Eclipse,[4] IntelliJ IDEA,[5] and Visual Studio Code,[6] but many others exist. What matters is that you're comfortable with it.

---

[2] http://jdk.java.net/
[3] https://maven.apache.org/
[4] https://www.eclipse.org/downloads/
[5] https://www.jetbrains.com/es-es/idea/
[6] https://code.visualstudio.com/

It's important to note that most chapters of this book require different types of databases, such as Postgres,[7] MongoDB,[8] Redis,[9] Neo4j,[10] and Cassandra,[11] so to reduce the headache of installing these databases on your machine, I recommend you install Docker[12] and use it to run all the databases.

The use and installation of Docker are outside the scope of this book, but there are plenty of online tutorials[13] and cheat sheets[14] that show the most common commands.

How Do I Check That I Have the Right Prerequisites?

After installing all the tools mentioned in the previous section, you need to ensure that all of them are correctly installed before starting to read through the book.

In Java, you need to run the following command.

```
% java -version
openjdk 17.0.4 2022-07-19 LTS
OpenJDK Runtime Environment Microsoft-38107 (build 17.0.4+8-LTS)
OpenJDK 64-Bit Server VM Microsoft-38107 (build 17.0.4+8-LTS, mixed mode,
sharing)
```

After that, you need to check whether your installed version of Maven is correct by using the following command.

```
% mvn --version
Apache Maven 3.8.1
Maven home: /usr/share/maven
```

---

[7] https://www.postgresql.org/

[8] https://www.mongodb.com/es

[9] https://redis.io/

[10] https://neo4j.com/

[11] https://cassandra.apache.org/_/index.html

[12] https://www.docker.com/

[13] https://docker-curriculum.com/

[14] https://michaelhaar.dev/my-docker-compose-cheatsheet

Finally, check that Docker runs correctly on your machine. You can do so by running the following command.

```
% docker --version
 Docker version 20.10.12, build 20.10.12-0ubuntu2~20.04.1
```

To reiterate, I think Docker is optimal for this book, but only because it reduces the necessity to install different types of databases on your machine.

Why These Prerequisites?

There are several reasons to choose certain prerequisites for a book. Some of them are connected to a specific tool or version of Java that the reader will feel comfortable with or is likely to have a lot of experience using. In this book, the prerequisites are connected with an annual survey conducted by Synk.io.[15]

This survey suggests that most developers use only LTS versions of Java in production environments (i.e., Java 8/11/17). Also, the same survey mentions that 76% of developers use Maven to manage dependencies on at least some of their applications.

That said, note that all examples in this book can be translated into Gradle with minimum changes.

Source Code

The source code for this book is available for download at `github.com/apress/ beginning-spring-data`.

How This Book Is Structured

This book is structured into four parts.

- The first part (Chapters 1–3) surveys the history of Java persistence and the patterns connected to persistence, explains how to create a project in Spring, and briefly explains the different types of persistence available in Spring Data.

---

[15] https://snyk.io/jvm-ecosystem-report-2021/

- The second part (Chapters 4–6) gives a basic tour of key features of Spring Data with relational databases and presents tools for versioning changes in a database.

- The third part (Chapters 7–10) briefly explores how Spring Data interacts with non-relational databases like Cassandra, Redis, MongoDB, and Neo4j.

- The fourth part (Chapters 11–14) covers advanced topics like performing unit and performance tests using different libraries. The last chapter describes some best practices for using Spring Data.

PART I

Introduction

Spring Data is a vast topic that needs to be learned step by step. During this first part, you will learn the basic concepts of accessing a database without using a particular Spring module. The idea is that you see the pros and cons of each mechanism to better understand why Spring Data is a good solution. Also, you will see the different patterns and solutions that are language- and library-agnostic, and therefore can be applied to any framework or module.

The main goal of Part I is to teach you the basics of Spring and how to create a basic Spring Boot project using IDE, CLI, or the website. You will learn how to create a simple endpoint that persists information in a relational database and use this basic application throughout the book, changing only the type of database.

CHAPTER 1

Application Architecture

Persistence is typically one of the most important topics in any language because it provides a way to save information in the long term for the applications that consume or produce it. In the past, when developers created a single extensive application, problems tended to appear in one place. Perhaps most of the logic resided in stored procedures, but when microservices emerged and became an industry standard, most need to save their information. Hence, a topic's importance grows more than before with monoliths. Also, during the transition from monoliths to microservices, many non-relational databases are an alternative to solve specific problems, like the cache mechanism for saved information with a different structure.

Since Java was introduced, several ways to access information and other types of architecture have appeared. This chapter overviews the evolution of ways to access a database and the pros and cons.

Also, you learn some of the most relevant patterns associated with persistence in relational or non-relational databases.

Why Persistence Is So Important

Persistent information is one of the most important aspects of microservices and applications. You will lose everything if you don't preserve the data when you deploy or restart or if something happens to your system.

But there are other things you need to consider because they can affect the performance of the entire platform, adding latency or errors. The following are some problems associated with the inappropriate use or design of a database.

© Andres Sacco 2023
A. Sacco, *Beginning Spring Data*, https://doi.org/10.1007/978-1-4842-8764-4_1

- Incrementing the latency to execute the queries and obtain information for a database

- Incrementing the usage of CPU/memory for access to a database for a wrong design in the way to connect

- Choosing the old version or the incorrect type of database for the kind of information to persist

There are many problems associated with persistence, but this book does not require you to know all of them. A wrong decision or not understanding the pros/cons of each type of database and how access to the information could affect your entire system.

The History of Persistence

In the applications suffers an evolution since the JDBC appears in JDK 1.1 passing to ORM and now with the use of Spring Data which offers a standard interface to access different databases. Some of them are relational instead another one are not relational.

There are many ways to persist information in databases. Considering that at least 50% of developers use Spring Boot, according to Snyk reports,[1] it seems logical that many of them use Spring Data. Figure 1-1 shows the history of the persistence on Java until Spring Data appeared in 2011.

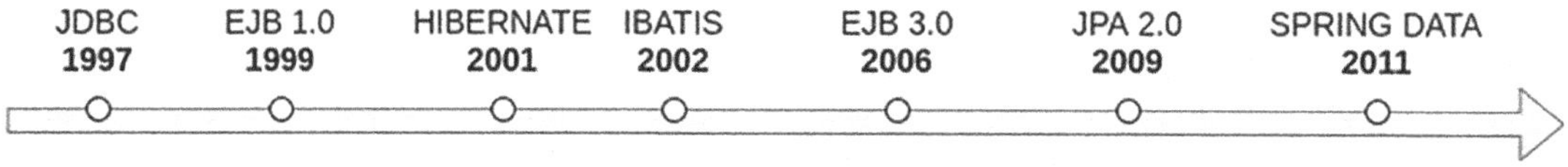

Figure 1-1. *History of persistence*

Most libraries that interact with databases are relevant today. All of them evolved over the years. Some interact with others; for example, Enterprise JavaBeans (EJB) and Java Persistence API (JPA) are two different things in Figure 1-1. The first versions of EJB contained all JPA specifications, which grew in relevance. EJB version 3.0 appears as two separate things that interact between them.

---

[1] https://snyk.io/jvm-ecosystem-report-2021/

JDBC

JDBC, or Java Database Connectivity, provides a common interface to communicate and interact with other databases. More concretely, JDBC offers a way to connect with a database, create and execute statements like creating/dropping/truncating tables, and execute queries like SELECT/INSERT/UPDATE/DELETE. Figure 1-2 shows a brief overview of the different components that interact in the communication with a database using JDBC.

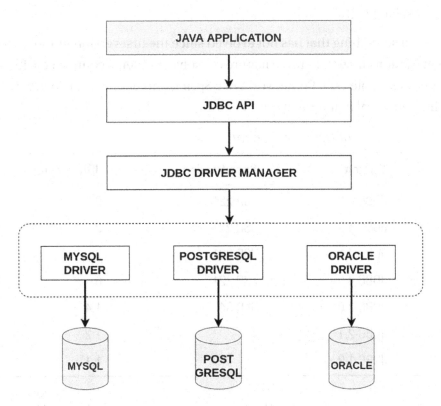

Figure 1-2. *Structure of JDBC*

Interacting with a database has a set of components or layers.

- **JDBC API**: This layer contains all the interfaces that all the drivers need to implement to allow the Java developers to use them. This layer is one of the most important because you can change from one database to another without changing many things, only the driver of the other database and little changes in the type of columns.

- **JDBC Driver Manager**: This set of classes acts as connectors between the drivers and the JDBC API, registering and deregistering the available databases, obtaining the connection with databases, and the information related to that connection.

- **Drivers**: To make the connection between databases, JDBC hides all the logic related to the way to interact with one database in a series of drivers, each of which contains the logic for one database. Typically, the companies that develop these databases create the drivers for most languages.

JDBC is not something that has not evolved since the first version in 1997. The subsequent versions try to add more features or solve problems connected with the performance (see Table 1-1). Frameworks like Spring implement a version of JDBC with some of the features of that framework.

Table 1-1. *Evolution of JDBC by Version*

Year	Version	Specification	JDK Version
2017	JDBC 4.3	JSR 221	9
2014	JDBC 4.2	JSR 221	8
2011	JDBC 4.1	JSR 221	7
2006	JDBC 4.0	JSR 221[2]	6
2001	JDBC 3.0	JSR 54[3]	1.4
1999	JDBC 2.1		1.2
1997	JDBC 1.2		1.1

This table shows the evolution of JDBC and the specifications that explain in detail which things introduce each version. Some of the first versions did not have concrete specifications.

---

[2] https://www.jcp.org/en/jsr/detail?id=221
[3] https://www.jcp.org/en/jsr/detail?id=54

JDBC Driver

The JDBC driver component implements the interfaces defined in the JDBC API to interact with a database. Think of this component as a client-side adapter to convert one database's specific elements or syntax into the standard that Java can understand.

JDBC offers four recommended types in different situations, as illustrated in Figure 1-3.

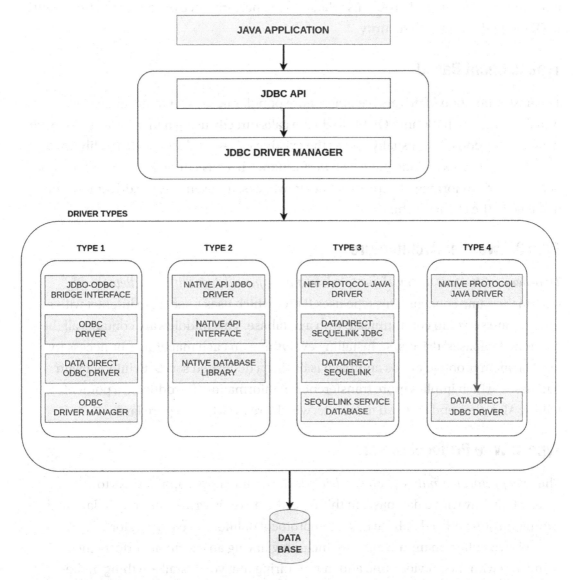

Figure 1-3. *Driver types that offer JDBC*

Type 1: The JDBC-ODBC Bridge

This type was adopted for the first JDBC drivers because most databases initially supported ODBC access. This driver converts JDBC into ODBC and vice versa acting as an adapter independent of the database. You can think of this as a universal driver that is part of the JDK, so you don't need to include any dependency in your project.

This type of driver is only used for developing or testing; it is not used in production environments because of problems related to the performance of converting from JDBC to ODBC and issues with security.

Type 2: Client Based

The next generation of drivers becomes more popular because it removes all the transformation of JDBC into ODBC to do the calls directly using native libraries for each database vendor, which usually reuses the existing C/C++ code to create the libraries.

The advantages include increased performance because there is no transformation between various formats. There are some drawbacks; for example, the driver must be installed in the client machine.

Type 3: Two-Tier Architecture

Two-tier architecture, *network protocol*, and *pure Java driver with middleware* all refer to the same concept. This type uses JDBC, which uses a socket to interact with a middleware server to communicate with a database. This middleware contains all the different databases' drivers, so installing everything on each machine is unnecessary.

The main problem of this approach is having a dedicated server to interact with databases, which implies more transference of information, introducing a point of failure. Also, the vendors need to rewrite, which are in C/C++ to pure Java.

Type 4: Wire Protocol Drivers

The *wire protocol* or *native protocol driver* is one of the most popular ways to connect directly with a database. In this type, the driver is written entirely in Java and communicates with a database using the protocol defined for each vendor.

This type offers many advantages, including having an excellent performance compared with the previous one and not requiring that you install anything in the client or the server. But, the main disadvantage is each database has a driver which uses different protocols.

How to Connect with a Database

There are several approaches, depending on the performance, like using a pool of connections. The basic process to connect with a database consists of the following steps.

1. **Import the classes.** You must include all the classes required to use JDBC and connect with a database. In most cases, all the classes exist in the java.sql.* package.

2. **Open a connection.** Create a connection using DriverManager. getConnection(), representing a physical connection with a database.

3. **Execute the query.** Create an object Statement that contains the query to execute in a database.

4. **Obtain the data.** After executing the query in a database, you need to use ResultSet.getXXX() method to retrieve the information of each column.

5. **Close the connection.** You need to explicitly close the connection to a database in all cases without considering if the application produces an exception or not.

Let's look at all the concepts related to accessing a database and obtaining certain information. The idea is to create a table structure that represents a catalog of countries/states/cities, which you use in the chapters on relational databases. Figure 1-4 shows the structure of the tables with the different relationships between them.

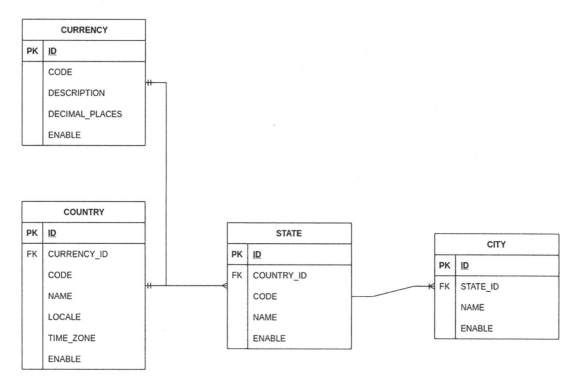

Figure 1-4. *The structure of the catalog database*

Note   You can find the structure and the insert to populate the information of these tables, along with all other source code, at github.com/apress/beginning-spring-data.

When everything looks fairly similar in your database, as in Figure 1-4, you can connect to a database and obtain a list of the countries that exist using a block of code similar to the following.

```
package com.apress.jdbc;

import java.sql.Connection;
import java.sql.DriverManager;
import java.sql.Statement;
import java.sql.ResultSet;
import java.sql.SQLException;
```

```java
public class App {

    static final String DB_URL = "jdbc:postgresql://localhost:5432/catalog";
    static final String USER = "postgres";
    static final String PASS = "postgres";
    static final String QUERY = "SELECT id, code, name FROM country";

    public static void main(String[] args) {

        // Open a connection and close it when finish the execution
        // The use of try/catch in this way autoclose the resources
        try(Connection conn = DriverManager.getConnection(DB_URL,
        USER, PASS);
            Statement stmt = conn.createStatement();
            ResultSet rs = stmt.executeQuery(QUERY);) {

            // Obtain the information of one row
            while (rs.next()) {

                // Retrieve the data by column
                int id = rs.getInt("id");
                String code = rs.getString("code");
                String name = rs.getString("name");

                System.out.println(String.format("ID: %s, Code: %s, Name:
                %s", id, code, name));
            }
        } catch (SQLException e) {
            e.printStackTrace();
        }
    }
}
```

The **DB_URL** has a specific format connected to each database type. Each URL type is defined in the specific database driver you need to include in your project before running the application. Table 1-2 lists common JDBC URLs by database. If you don't like to test this example with Postgres, you can try with others for the list.

Table 1-2. *JDBC URL by Database*

Database	JDBC URL
PostgreSQL	jdbc:postgresql://host:port/database?properties
SQL Server	jdbc:sqlserver://[serverName[\instanceName][:portNumber]][;property= value[;property=value]]
Oracle	jdbc:oracle:thin:[<user>/<password>]@//<host>[:<port>]/<service>
MYSQL	jdbc:mysql://host:port/database?properties

EJB

Enterprise JavaBeans, or EJB, is a specification for building portable, scalable, and reusable business applications without reinventing the way to do certain common things like security, access to a database, sending messages across different applications, and many more. In the first versions of Java, some of these features existed in other libraries or a basic version inside the JDK, so when EJB emerged, unify all these features in the same framework.

One of the biggest differences with the previous approach of using JDBC to access a database is you need an EJB container that runs inside an application server like Glassfish,[4] Wildfly,[5] and Jetty.[6] Figure 1-5 shows some of the most relevant features that EJB provides.

---

[4] https://javaee.github.io/glassfish/
[5] https://www.wildfly.org/
[6] https://www.eclipse.org/jetty/

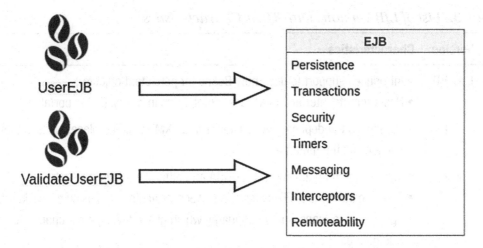

Figure 1-5. *Features that provide EJB*

EJB has had multiple versions since 1999, introducing many new features, improving performance, and fixing bugs from the previous version. Recently, EJB was adopted in Jakarta EE in versions 8 and 9. Table 1-3 describes the most relevant things in[7] each version.

---

[7]https://jakarta.ee/about/working-group/

Table 1-3. *List of EJB Versions with Their Characteristics*

Year	Version	Characteristics
1998/ 1999	EJB 1.0	• Introduces support to use Entity Beans for persistent objects • Has a remote interface to access remotely, so in a way, EJB is portable
1999	EJB 1.1	• Introduces the deployment descriptor in an XML which replaces a class that contains all the metadata
2001	EJB 2.0[8]	• Introduces compatibility with CORBA and other Java APIs • Clients in the same J2EE container could access another EJB using a local interface • Appears JavaBeans Query Language, which gives developers a chance to do SQL queries
2003	EJB 2.1[9]	• Adds support to create web services using SOAP • Introduces the possibility of having a timer service to have a cron to invoke certain services in a period of time • Adds support to use ORDER BY, AVG, MIN, MAX, SUM, and COUNT operations in the EJB query
2006	EJB 3.0[10]	• Appears the POJO (Plain Old Java Objects) as a replacement for the EJB Bean class • Rewrites most of the code to use annotations instead of having a big file with the configuration • The remote and local interfaces no longer necessary to be implemented • JPA entities were decoupled from the EJB container to use independently
2009	EJB 3.1[11]	• EJB Lite runs multiple components in the same VM as an EJB client
2013	EJB 3.2[12]	• Autocloseable interfaces • Adds more control over the transactionality of life-cycle interceptor methods.
2020	EJB 4.0[13]	• Deprecation of the ***EJBContext.getEnvironment()*** method • Removes methods relying on ***JAX-RPC*** • Most packages in ***javax.ejb*** moved to ***jakarta.ejb***

---

[8] https://www.jcp.org/en/jsr/detail?id=19

[9] https://www.jcp.org/en/jsr/detail?id=153

[10] https://www.jcp.org/en/jsr/detail?id=220

[11] https://www.jcp.org/en/jsr/detail?id=318

[12] https://www.jcp.org/en/jsr/detail?id=345

[13] https://jakarta.ee/specifications/enterprise-beans/4.0/

EJB Types

The architecture of EJB has three main components: the EJB container, the application server, and the Enterprise JavaBeans (EJB), which are split into various types.

- **Session beans**: These components contain all the logic related to a user task or use case. The session bean is available during the execution of that task or uses case like a conversation. But, if the server crashes or restarts, all the information that resides inside the session bean is lost.

  There are two types of session beans: stateful and stateless. The main difference is that the first saves the states after someone calls it, and the second (stateless) does not save any information after the invocating.

- **Message-driven beans**: The previous beans work fine when you want synchronous communication between applications, but message-driven beans are the correct option if you need asynchronous communication. The most common implementation uses JMS (Java Message Service)[14]. This type of EJB acts as a listener in a topic of a queue waiting for a message and doing something when the message arrives. This type of communication became popular when microservices appeared.

- **Entities**: This component has classes that represent tables and provide an interface for CRUD (create, retrieve/read, update, delete) operations in a database. EJB 3.0 introduced a change in this type of component to use JPA instead of the previous entities-beans, which are part of the EJB specification.

Figure 1-6 shows the interaction between the components forming part of the EJB.

---

[14] https://docs.oracle.com/cd/B19306_01/server.102/b14257/jm_create.htm

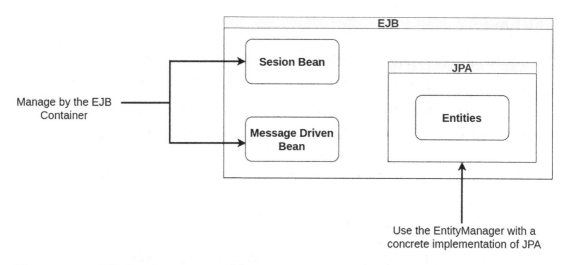

Figure 1-6. *EJB Components and how to interact with JPA*

JPA

The Java Persistence API, or JPA, is a specification[15] connected directly with the persistence into databases. To be more specific, JPA provides a set of interfaces that all the providers need to follow to guarantee that there are following the standard so you can change the provider without too much effort.

Using JPA, developers can access the information in a database and execute certain operations like insert, update, delete and retrieve using a Java class that represents the structure of the tables. To do these operations, you need to annotate the classes with annotations representing the most common things in a table, such as the table name, column size, and the relationship between tables.

JPA offers several ways to do the queries to retrieve the information. One is using a SQL statement directly like JDBC with classes to help construct the sentence, and another introduces an abstraction so that you don't need to write the entire sentence because the provider of JPA generates the sentence dynamically. Figure 1-7 shows the different layers or the structure of JPA with an application.

---

[15] https://www.jcp.org/en/jsr/detail?id=338

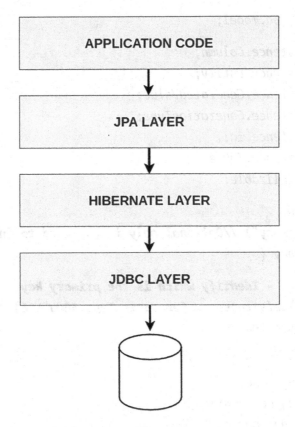

Figure 1-7. *Example of the structure of layers using JPA*

This specification has many implementations, but the most relevant are Hibernate,[16] EclipseLink,[17] Apache OpenJPA,[18] and Spring Data JPA.[19] Each of them implements the specification of JPA but differently, prioritizing things like the performance or the developer experience.

Let's look at an example where you can declare a class representing one table in a database.

---

[16] https://hibernate.org/

[17] https://www.eclipse.org/eclipselink/

[18] https://openjpa.apache.org/

[19] https://spring.io/projects/spring-data

```
package com.apress.jpa.model;

import javax.persistence.Column;
import javax.persistence.Entity;
import javax.persistence.GeneratedValue;
import javax.persistence.GenerationType;
import javax.persistence.Id;
import javax.persistence.Table;
import java.io.Serializable;

@Entity // Required
@Table(name = "currency") //Optional only if you need to indicate the name
public class Currency {

    @Id //Required - Identify which is the primary key
    @GeneratedValue(strategy = GenerationType.SEQUENCE) //Indicate the
    way to generate the ID
    private Long id;

    private String code;
    private String description;
    private Boolean enable;

    @Column(name = "decimal_places", length = 5) //Optional: Indicate the
    name and the lenght of the column
    private String decimalPlaces;

    public Currency(Long id, String code, String description, Boolean
    enable, String decimalPlaces) {
        this.id = id;
        this.code = code;
        this.description = description;
        this.enable = enable;
        this.decimalPlaces = decimalPlaces;
    }

    // Setters and getters for all the attributes
    //Override the hashCode and equals methods
}
```

The way to indicate the name and the length of the columns is not so complicated. If you do not indicate the name and the size by default, the implementation of JPA defines the values, which is 255 in the string.

Note   You learn more about JPA in Part II of this book.

Spring Data

The main problem with all the previous mechanisms of persistence is you don't have the chance to access both types of databases, relational or non-relational. But Spring Data solves this problem, allowing you to access databases using repositories with an interface to do CRUD operations. Also, you can create concrete that implements the repository interfaces with the idea of doing specific operations not covered by the Spring Data framework. These repositories are available in almost all implementations to access databases to reduce the complexity of using multiple databases in the same application. There are basic repositories that you use to extend the functionality of your repositories. In particular, two are most relevant. CrudRepository has the basic operations for all the entities. PagingAndSortingRepository contains all the logic to obtain the information of one structure in a database using the criteria of pagination and sorting.

Figure 1-8 illustrates that Spring Data supports MongoDB, Redis, Neo4j, Cassandra, and all the relational databases. Others, like ElasticSearch[20] and Couchbase,[21] are not covered in this book because they have a similar structure for saving information.

---

[20] https://www.elastic.co/
[21] https://www.couchbase.com/

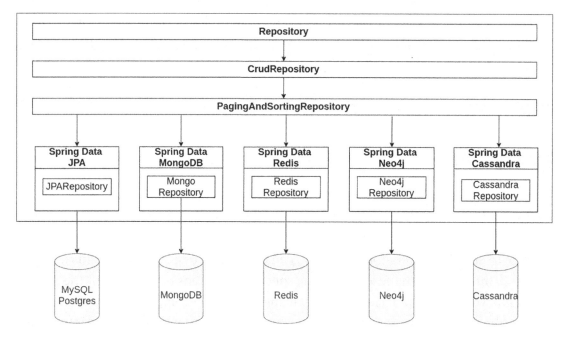

Figure 1-8. *The structure of repositories depends on the database*

Note   In some databases, Spring Data provides a way to allocate and translate exceptions in a database using templates used behind the scenes for the repositories or DAO to do certain operations like insert or retrieve information. Spring Data JPA is excluded from the use of Templates because it's an abstraction to access all the RDBMS databases.

You can think of these templates to create custom repositories outside the basics that Spring Data provides. For example, you can introduce security or a compression mechanism in Redis before inserting or retrieving the information.

Object Mapping

One of the most significant advantages that JPA offers developers is the possibility to map a table with a particular class considering all the possible types of columns and the relationship between tables. Spring Data extends this approach to all NoSQL databases. Each type of database offers its annotations to represent the information to map databases with Java classes. Table 1-4 shows that each object could be represented in other databases without significant changes in the fields' names and types. You only need to change the annotations related to each database.

Table 1-4. *Declaring Entities in Various Databases*

JPA	MongoDB	Neo4j
@Entity **@Table(name =** **"currency")** public class Currency { **@Id** **@GeneratedValue** **(strategy =** **GenerationType.** **SEQUENCE)** private Long id; **@Column(name =** **"decimal_places",** **length = 5)** private String decimalPlaces; //Other attributes and set/get }	**@Document(** **collection="currency)** public class Currency { **@Id** private Long id; **@Field("decimal_places")** private String decimalPlaces; //Other attributes and set/get }	**@NodeEntity**public class Currency { **@GraphId** private Long id; private String decimalPlaces; //Other attributes and set/get }

JPA and Spring Data support mapping relationships between an object that could be stored in another object (table, document, node). The annotations in Table 1-5 tell Spring Data about the relationships among these objects and how to retrieve information.

Table 1-5. *Declaring Relationships Among Objects in a Database*

JPA	MongoDB	Neo4j
| ```
@Entity
@Table(name =
"country")
public class Country {
    @Id
@GeneratedValue
(strategy =
GenerationType.
SEQUENCE)
    private Long id;
    @OneToMany
    private
List<Currency>
currencies;
    //Other attributes
and set/get
}
``` | ```
@Document(
collection="country)
public class Country {
    @Id
    private Long id;
    private
List<Currency>
currencies;
    //Other attributes and
set/get
}
``` | ```
@NodeEntity
public class Country {
    @GraphId
    private Long id;
    @RelatedTo( type =
"has", direction =
Direction.OUTGOING)
    private List<Currency>
currencies;
    //Other attributes
and set/get
}
``` |

Some databases do not have relationships, like Mongo in its first versions, but since version 3, you can relate different entities. The idea behind this type of database is to reduce duplicate information in entities.

Repository Support

When you write an application that needs to persist/retrieve information from a database, you create a class or layer that contains all these operations in most cases. There are multiples ways to group these operations: all together in the same class, one class per table, but the most common way to do it is to create a class that represents the DAO pattern, which is discussed more in the next section, with all the operations of one table. This means that you can have multiple classes to access the database, where the main difference is the table you access. To reduce the complexity of having multiple
```

classes with the same code, Spring Data offers the possibility to use an abstraction that contains all these operations, and you only need to indicate the name of the entity/table that you access.

Spring Data offers interfaces that provide common database operations. You need to create an interface that extends from one of that common interfaces and indicate which table or structure you want to access. Behind the scenes, Spring Data transforms this interface into one query to save/retrieve the information depending on the type of database. Figure 1-9 illustrates combining interfaces to have more operations available which is covered in more detail in Part II of this book.

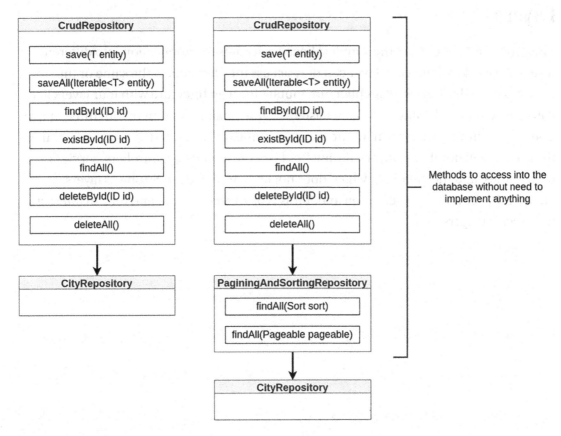

Figure 1-9. *Example repositories that extend default Spring Data methods*

Architectures Types

The applications generally have a structure that helps you to understand where you can find logic, such as validations, business logic, entities, and the interfaces/classes to access a database. All of them are important to understand the hierarchy of the layers and which rules you need to follow to create a new feature or application.

In Java, tools like Archunit[22] allow you to define and check if everything in your project follows your defined structure.

Layers

This type of architecture is the simplest because it splits the application into different layers like a cake where each layer can only access the elements to the same or the inferior level. These types of architecture mutate from architecture with four layers like view/presentation, business logic, persistence, and database to others with three or five. There is no universal criterion for the correct number of layers. But, if you consider that three is a small number of layers, Spring Boot is represented by controllers, services, repositories, and the database, which does not appear directly in Spring as layers. Figure 1-10 shows a representation about this type of architecture and how to interact the different layers.

---

[22] https://www.archunit.org/

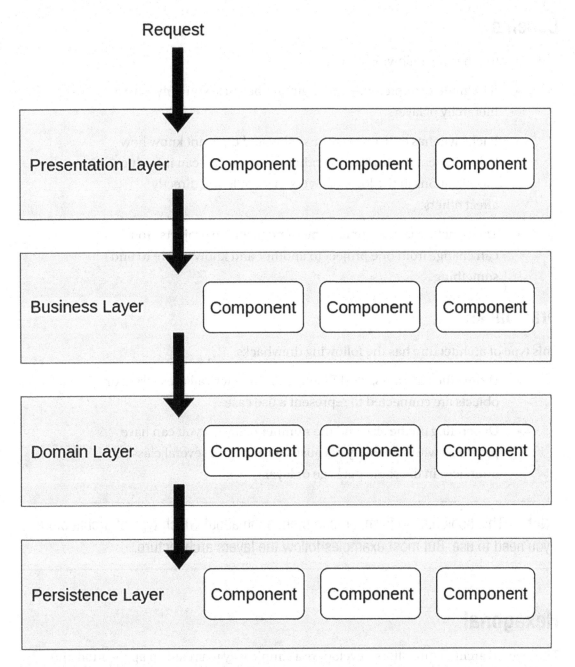

Figure 1-10. *The basic structure of layers*

Benefits

This structure has the following benefits.

- It's simple to implement and maintain because you only have a hierarchy of layers.

- Each layer has only one responsibility and does not know how to implement the logic of the other layers, so you can introduce modifications in the logic of layers that could not directly affect others.

- The structure is more or less the same in all the projects. You can change from one project to another and know where to find something.

Drawbacks

This type of architecture has the following drawbacks.

- Hiding the use cases, it's difficult to know where all the classes or objects are connected to represent a use case.

- Depending on the size and the number of layers, you can have problems with scalability because you can have several classes/interfaces in the same package or layer.

Note   This book has no formal recommendation about which type of architecture you need to use. But most examples follow the layers architecture.

Hexagonal

The layered architecture offers developers a simple way to create an application and understand the separation of roles or responsibilities. In 2005, Alistar Cockburn[23] proposed a new alternative that encapsulates or keeps all external communication with

---

[23] https://alistair.cockburn.us/hexagonal-architecture/

databases or external systems agnostic. To this, he created the concept of input/output in the architecture to represent communication with external resources like databases or external systems.

The main idea of this type of architecture is to create all the business logic that isolates it from the external tools and technologies that are irrelevant to how the application works. Figures 1-11 shows the different elements that have the hexagonal architecture and how to interact with external resources like databases or other applications.

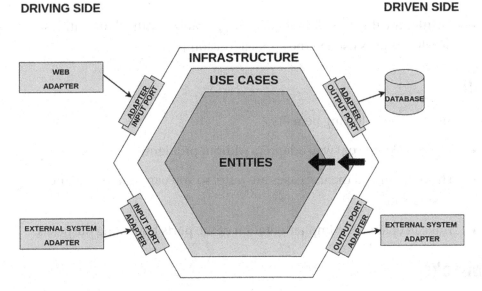

Figure 1-11. *Hexagonal architecture with the most relevant layers*

This architecture splits the hexagon into two parts. One part is called the "driving side," where the actors start the interaction, such as external systems and web/mobile systems. The other part is the "driven side," where the actors receive a request to obtain certain information from a database or other external systems.

Components

The hexagonal architecture has several components inside each part of the structure, but I mention only the most relevant for understanding the basic idea.

- **Infrastructure** contains the port and adapters responsible for connecting with external systems or databases using different protocols. The *ports* are interfaces agnostic to the technology defining the methods to access the application or other systems. The *adapters* are the implementation of the ports related to a specific technology, like a query to a database or a REST controller.

- **Use cases** are the core of the systems because it contains all the logic related to various scenarios and how they are related. Depending on the author, this component receives other names like *application* or *domain layer* and combines the use cases with the domain component.

- **Entities** are the pure domain of the application, with all the entities of value objects used in the application component.

Benefits

This structure has the following benefits.

- You can change or swap adapters without problems.

- The domain and the use cases are pure, so you can understand the business logic.

- You can change the implementation of the ports for testing purposes.

Drawbacks

This type of architecture has the following drawbacks.

- Implementing some frameworks is difficult because you can make mistakes with what you consider adapters/ports.

- Introduce indirection to find the implementation of each port.

- No guideline explains all the things about the organization of the projects, so anyone can introduce something wrong.

Persistence Design Patterns

Throughout this book, some code responds to the same structure because patterns are associated with access to a database. This section introduces the most relevant of these patterns, but there are other ones this book does not cover, most of which are mentioned on Martin Fowler's website.[24]

Data Access Object (DAO)

A data access object (DAO) pattern persists and retrieves information for databases. It allows developers to isolate the business layer for the persistence layer, which in most cases is associated with a database but could be anything that has the responsibility of access to the information.

This pattern hides the complexity of performing all the CRUD operations into a database so you can change or introduce modifications without significantly affecting all the rest of the layers. It is not common in Spring Data because most developers use the repository pattern. But some cases related to the performance or operations are not supported for that pattern, so the DAO patterns appear to rescue us from the problem.

Figure 1-12 show how the different interfaces/classes interact to access the database following this pattern.

---

[24] https://martinfowler.com/

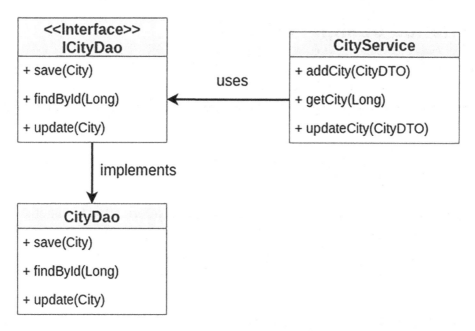

Figure 1-12. *DAO interface with the implementation and how to interact with the service layer*

When they start to use this pattern, most developers create a generic interface with all the possible methods and create one class to access a specific table and reduce the number of files connected with access to a database. Listing 1-1 shows the different methods that a common DAO could have, of course, you can create other ones but most of the frameworks implement these methods.

Listing 1-1. A Common Interface to Access a Database

```
public interface CommonDao<T> {

    Optional<T> get(long id);

    List<T> getAll();

    void save(T t);

    void delete(T t);
}
```

Now that you have seen a common interface, the implementation is more or less similar in all cases. The difference relates to the name of the table and the queries to access a database, but all the DAO respects the same format.

Listing 1-2 shows a possible implementation of the interface that appears on Listing 1-1; take into consideration that there are other ways to do it.

Listing 1-2. Implementation of a Common DAO

```java
public class CityDao implements CommonDao<City> {

    private List<City> cities = new ArrayList<>();

    public CityDao() {
        cities.add(new City("BUE", "Buenos Aires"));
        cities.add(new City("SCL", "Santiago de Chile"));
    }

    public Optional<City> get(long id) {
        return Optional.ofNullable(cities.get((int) id));
    }

    public List<City> getAll() {
        return cities;
    }

    public void save(City city) {
        cities.add(city);
    }

    public void delete(City city) {
        cities.remove(city);
    }

}
```

Note   Focusing only on the pattern example, there is no real connection between a database and creating cities in the application's memory, but the concept is the same.

Repository Pattern

The repository pattern accesses a database to obtain certain information introducing an abstraction for the rest of the layers. The spirit of the repository pattern is to emulate or mediate between the domain and data mapping using interfaces to access the domain objects.

The main difference between the DAO and repository patterns is the repositories are next to the business logic and try to hide all the logic related to the queries to a database. The most common use is to create an interface containing certain methods; frameworks like Spring Boot and Quakus transform the methods into specific queries to a database. In contraposition, the DAOs implement all the logic using queries to access a database. See Table 1-6 to check the main differences between the approaches.

Table 1-6. *Main Differences Between DAOs and Repositories*

DAO Pattern	Repository Pattern
It's closer to the database because dealing queries and tables.	It's closer to the business/domain layer because it uses abstraction to hide the implementation.
DAOs could not contain repositories because they are in different layers.	Repositories could contain or implement DAOs.
It's an abstraction of the data.	It's an abstraction of a collection of objects.

Spring Data offers developers a basic interface to implement the logic of pagination and CRUD operations without needing extra work. Listing 1-3 shows an example of an interface that follows the repository pattern

Listing 1-3. Example of a Repository

```
interface CityRepository {

    Optional<City> get(long id);

    List<City> getAll();

    void save(City city);

    void delete(City city);
}
```

You can use a repository with one or multiple repositories to hide the logic to access the information. You can take the interface from Listing 1-3 and create a concrete class that uses the Repository in the same way that Listing 1-2.

Listing 1-4. Example of a Repository with a DAO

```
public class CityRepositoryImpl implements CityRepository {

    private CityDao cityDao;

    public CityRepositoryImpl(CityDao cityDao) {
        this.cityDao = cityDao;
    }

    public Optional<City> get(long id) {
        return cityDao.get(id);
    }

    public List<City> getAll() {
        return cityDao.getAll();
    }

    public void save(City city) {
        cityDao.save(city);
    }

    public void delete(City city) {
        cityDao.delete(city);
    }
}
```

This combination is very infrequently seen because most developers use one or another. Spring Data offers a huge set of elements for repositories to solve using only the repository interfaces.

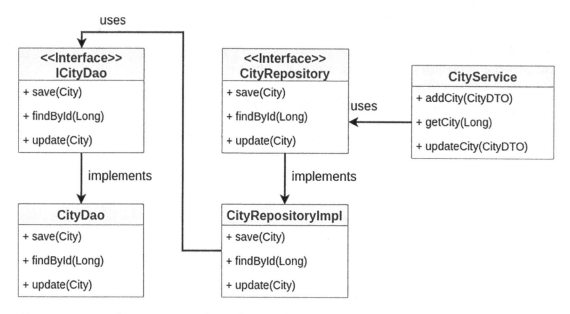

Figure 1-13. *The structure of combining both patterns*

Data Transfer Object (DTO)

The data transfer object (DTO) pattern is used in multiple languages, aggregated, and encapsulates data for transfer between the layers of your application or applications. You can think of this pattern as a data structure that does not contain any business logic and could represent a combination of structures.

This pattern is not something that has appeared recently. Martin Fowler mentioned it in 2002 in his book *Patterns of Enterprise Application Architecture*. It's also discussed on his webpage.[25]

This pattern helps to reduce the number of calls to different endpoints or processes to obtain all the information necessary to do a certain task, which is expensive in terms of time or the size of the information to transfer.

---

[25] https://martinfowler.com/eaaCatalog/dataTransferObject.html

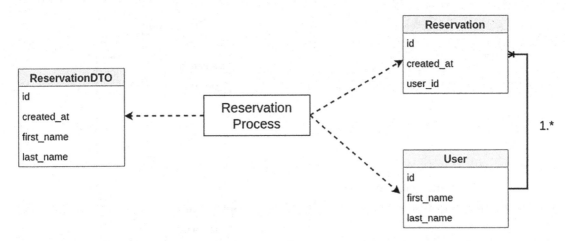

Figure 1-14. Example of DTO that combines two different objects

---

Note   This pattern appears in examples when classes transform the entities used to persist the information into a database and the other application layers.

There are a variety of ways to map objects; some are done manually and imply creating a class that receives an object and returns another. Another approach is to use libraries like MapStruct,[26] Orika,[27] Dozer,[28] JMapper,[29] and ModelMapper[30], to do most of the translation automatically. There are a lot of analyses and benchmarking[31] about which library is the best option according to the use of CPU, memory, or complexity to implement it.

Specification Pattern

The specification pattern filters or selects a subset of objects based on criteria. For example, think that you want to know all the users that have at least two reservations at your travel agency, so you create a class that receives each user and checks if that user satisfies the conditions or not.

---

[26] https://mapstruct.org/

[27] https://orika-mapper.github.io/orika-docs/

[28] http://dozer.sourceforge.net/

[29] https://jmapper-framework.github.io/jmapper-core/

[30] http://modelmapper.org/

[31] https://www.baeldung.com/java-performance-mapping-frameworks

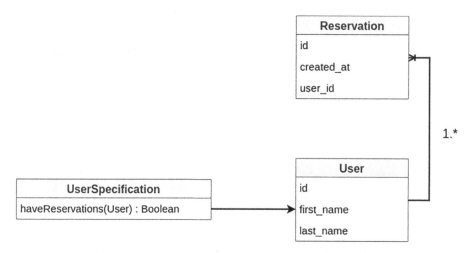

Figure 1-15. *Specification example*

Martin Fowler[32] first discussed the specification pattern a long time ago. Now it's associated directly with the repository pattern, which is in Spring Data to filter the results of the table into a database.

Other Patterns

I covered the patterns most relevant to this book to better explain access to databases or transferring information between different layers. Other patterns solve particular problems, like filtering the results or saving historical data.

Summary

This chapter covered the evolution of persistence into Java databases using technologies like JDBC, which offer an essential way to access the information with the chance to introduce multiple problems in the execution of the SQL query. Once JDBC appeared, there were a lot of ways to access and execute queries in a database. The most relevant is JPA, specifications that all libraries can follow.

Spring Data allows developers to make changes between relational and non-relational databases without introducing significant changes.

You also learned about the types of architecture and the most common patterns associated with persistence.

---

[32] https://martinfowler.com/apsupp/spec.pdf

CHAPTER 2

Spring Basics and Beyond

In Chapter 1, you read about ways to persist the information in databases. Spring Data is the only one that offers the possibility to use relational and non-relational databases. Before discussing how the framework works behind the scenes, you need to know how Spring Framework works. In this chapter, you learn how to create a small project, which you use throughout this book.

According to the survey that Synk[1] does each year, Spring is used by 58% of developers because it offers the possibility to create an application without a lot of effort. Also, this framework offers a lot of integration with other tools like Vault, Kubernetes, Apache Kafka, and many more.

Note This book does not cover all topics related to the Spring Framework and Spring Boot because many other Apress books do. The following is only a brief overview of the concepts.

Spring Basics

The first version of Spring was released in 2004, and after that, this framework grew in the number of developers that adopted it and the number of features/technologies that are supported. Nowadays, a big community of developers gives support to issues that each version of Spring has. There is an annual conference with the most important topic showing developers the latest features of the newest version.

This framework offers a container that creates and manages the existing components. The way to define these components is using annotations or XML, which

---

[1] https://snyk.io/jvm-ecosystem-report-2021/?utm_campaign=JVM-SC-2021&utm_medium=Report-Link#spring-dominates

A. Sacco, *Beginning Spring Data*, https://doi.org/10.1007/978-1-4842-8764-4_2

nowadays is not so popular when the components are defined. The Spring application context is the responsibility to manage the life cycle of each of them. Spring applies a pattern called dependency injection (DI), a technique in which an object receives other objects that it depends on. The status of the other object is managed by Spring without any intervention from the developer, Figure 2-1 shows how the different component on Spring interact between them.

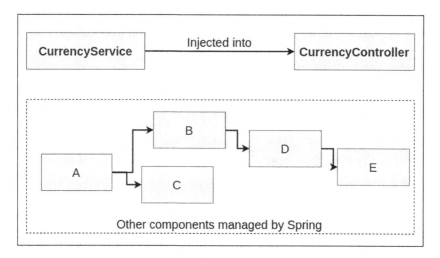

Figure 2-1. *Interaction between components*

Spring is an ecosystem of modules that interact to provide functionality. This ecosystem contains the following elements.

- **Core** contains all the core functionalities that Spring uses across the modules, like the dependency injection or how to manage the life cycle of the components.

- **Web** is a group that supports developing web applications that serve HTTP requests.

- **Data Access** provides a set of basic tools to persist the information in places like databases, relational and non-relational.

- **Testing** is a group that offers support to create a test to check whether everything you develop using Spring works fine or not.

Figure 2-2 show the different modules that compose the Spring framework.

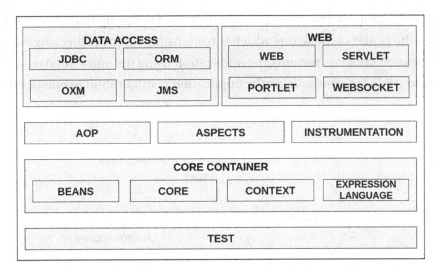

Figure 2-2. Spring modules

Spring Boot

Spring Boot is a project released in 2014 to reduce the complexity of creating and developing Java Web Applications, which behind the scenes uses Spring. Some of the key features of Spring Boot include autoconfiguring all the components to quickly get started without the need to deploy an artifact on a web server and provide ways to monitor and check if everything works fine or not.

Figure 2-3 illustrates some of the modules that exist in Spring Boot. The most relevant is in the center of the figure, which is responsible for providing support to the other modules and creating/running the application using the embedded web server. Also, it's responsible for externalizing the application configuration in one or more files.

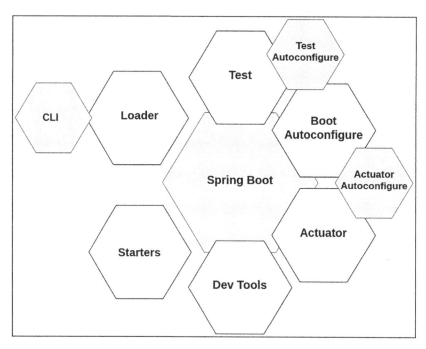

Figure 2-3. *Spring Boot modules*

One of the dependencies of Spring Boot that interact directly with the topic of this book is the actuator. The actuator is responsible for checking and informing if the application is healthy or not. Typically, Spring Boot internally checks that everything in the application context is okay. But when your application interacts with a database, you can explicitly indicate that you check the status and send the information as part of the response.

Basic Application Setup

Let's create a catalog microservice that contains all the information about cities, states, and countries. To do this, you define a set of endpoints for each resource. Most operations are common in a CRUD (create, retrieve/read, update, delete) operation.

First, you must create a basic skeleton that allows you to add different databases in the following chapters to persist the information. For simplicity, let's use examples of databases applying the restrictions or having the ability to persist the information.

There are several ways to create an application that uses Spring Boot. Remember that you use Spring Boot with the idea of creating web applications easily. Some imply creating a project manually and adding all the necessary dependencies to run the applications. In some cases, this approach could not be the best option and produced a lot of errors for missing dependencies. To solve this problem, Spring Boot offers a different mechanism to create a project and all the necessary dependencies simply. There are two that are the most popular.

- Using Spring Initializr[2] from the webpage

- Using IDE plugins like Eclipse, IntelliJ, or Visual Studio Code

This book teaches you how to create a project using both options but only covers the IntelliJ IDE.

Creating an API Using Spring Initialzr

First, let's create a project using Spring Initalizr, an intuitive interface to understand how to configure the project. When you go to the webpage, you find something similar to Figure 2-4, where you need to indicate: the configuration management, language, version of Spring Boot, and all the project metadata (group, artifact, name, and version of Java).

---

[2]https://start.spring.io/

Figure 2-4. *Using Spring Initializr, you can create a new application.*

Note   All the examples in this book use Maven instead of Gradle.

For this book, fill in the input with the information in Table 2-1.

Table 2-1. *Project Metadata to Generate a New Project*

Attribute	Value	Description
Project	Maven Project	The kind of project to generate: either maven-project or gradle-project
Language	Java	The programming language to use: java, groovy, or kotlin
Spring Boot	3.0.0-M4	The version of Spring Boot to build against
Group	com.apress	The project's group ID, for the sake of organization in a Maven repository
Artifact	api-catalog	The project's artifact ID, as it would appear in a Maven repository
Name	api-catalog	The project name; also determines the names of the application's main class
Description	Microservices that contain all the information in the catalog	The project description
Package name	com.apress.catalog	The project's base package name
Packaging	Jar	How the project should be packaged: either jar or war
Java	17	The version of Java to build with

After that, you need to add the dependencies to support basic operations like creating the endpoints of the microservices and processing the configuration files, so you need to click the ADD DEPENDENCIES... button, which shows a page similar to Figure 2-5.

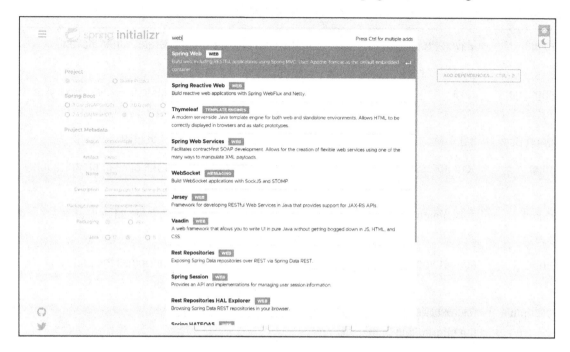

Figure 2-5. *You can add dependencies from the webpage.*

For this project, add the following dependencies.

- **Spring Boot Actuator**[3] provides endpoints that give specific information, like if the application is healthy or not, the caches in the application, and more. Also, you can create custom endpoints that can extend or not an existing endpoint.

- **Spring Configuration Processor**[4] generates the metadata for developers to use in the configuration files like YML or properties, so it's simpler for you to know which are the properties available for one configuration because you start to type and the IDE helps you with options to use in the file.

---

[3] https://docs.spring.io/spring-boot/docs/current/reference/html/actuator.html
[4] https://docs.spring.io/spring-boot/docs/current/reference/html/configuration-metadata.html

- **Spring Web** allows you to add support to your application to create a RESTful API with an embeddable server like Tomcat.

- **Spring Boot Devtools**[5] is a library that provides helpful features for developers, like a fast application restart and debugging an application remotely.

You don't add any dependency connected with Spring Data because this chapter focuses on creating a basic project that exposes endpoints in which you include a level of logic to access databases using Spring Data.

After you include the dependencies, you only need to click the Generate button, which packages the application in a ZIP file. You only need to decompress the file in any directory you want and continue with the step in the "How to Run the Application" section.

Creating an API in the IDE

Let's create an application using your IDE. In this book, IntelliJ is the default IDE. You need to open IntelliJ and go to the top menu by selecting **File ➤ New ➤ Project.** After selecting the option to create a new project, you get a window like the one shown in Figure 2-3. Select a JDK version and where Spring Boot's generator will create the application. In recent versions of this plugin, you need to complete information on the Java version, the name of the group/artifact, and other details in Spring Initalizr, as shown in Figure 2-6.

---

[5] https://docs.spring.io/spring-boot/docs/current/reference/html/using.html#using.devtools

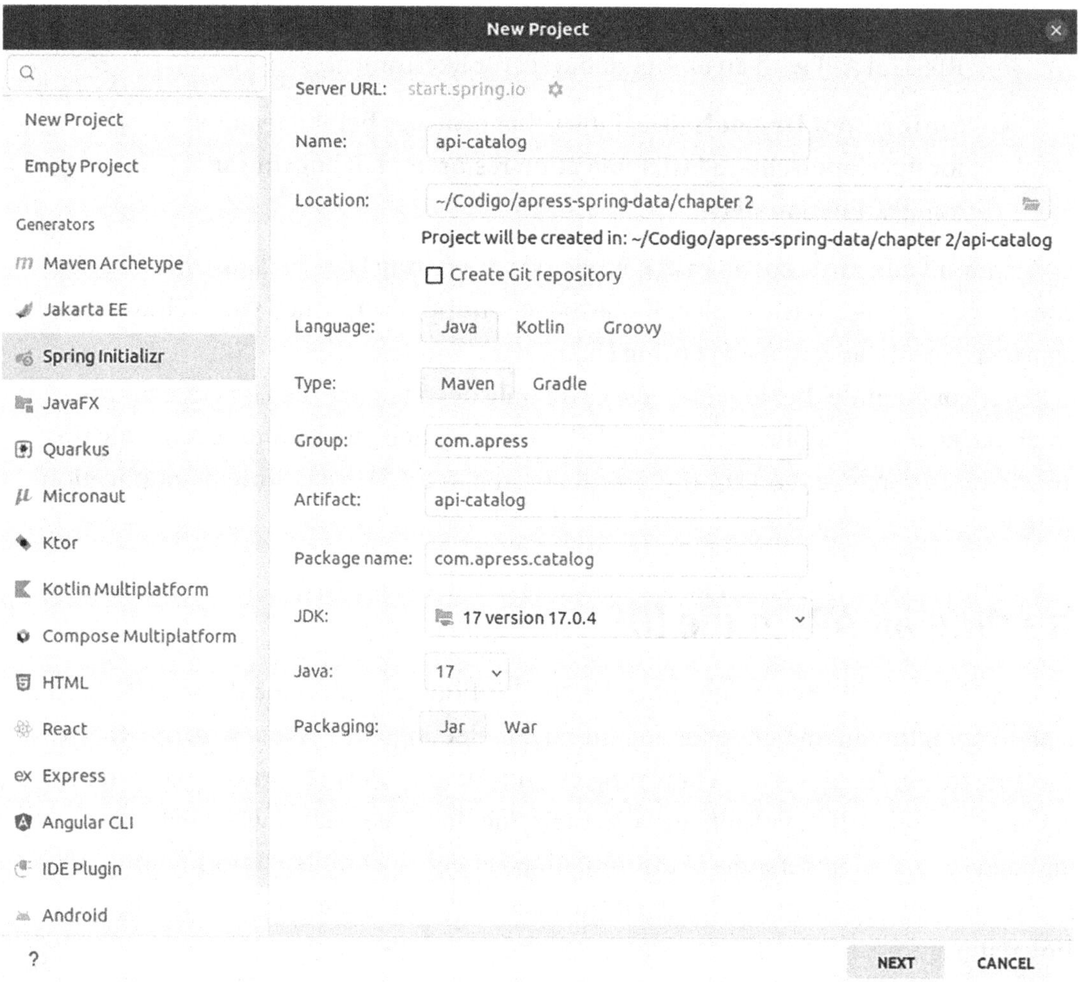

Figure 2-6. *Modal to create a new project in IntelliJ*

The next step is to include all your project's dependencies. Include Spring Boot Actuator, Spring Dev Tools, Spring Configuration Processor, and Spring Web. The main difference between Spring Initalizr and this option is that the dependencies are organized in groups to facilitate finding them as you can see on the Figure 2-7.

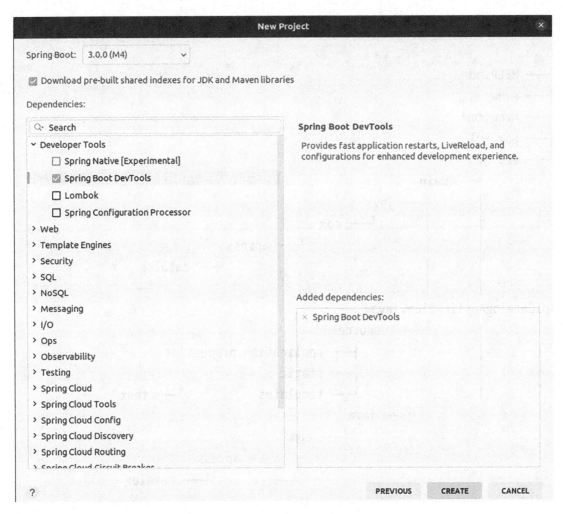

Figure 2-7. *Modal to add all the project's dependencies*

After this entire process, the result is the same as that using Spring Initalizr.

How to Run the Application

Listing 2-1 shows the project's basic structure.

Listing 2-1. Structure of the Project That You Created Using Spring Initializr

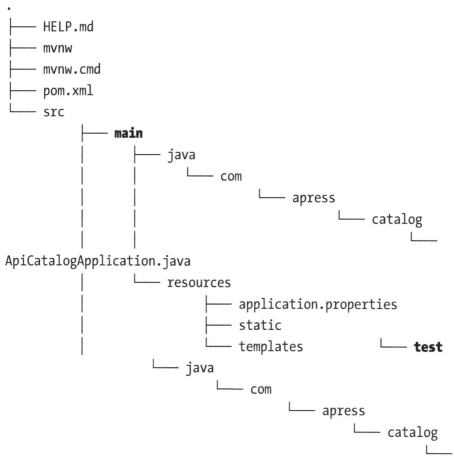

```
.
├── HELP.md
├── mvnw
├── mvnw.cmd
├── pom.xml
└── src
            ├── main
            │       ├── java
            │       │       └── com
            │       │               └── apress
            │       │                       └── catalog
            │       │                               └──
ApiCatalogApplication.java
            │       └── resources
            │                       ├── application.properties
            │                       ├── static
            │                       └── templates          └── test
                        └── java
                                └── com
                                        └── apress
                                                └── catalog
                                                        └──
ApiCatalogApplicationTests.java
```

The folder structure is similar to any Maven or Gradle project, but there are small changes. Let's go over the project's parts.

- **mvnw** and **mvnw.cmd** are scripts that act as a wrapper if you don't have Maven installed on your machine.

- **pom.xml** contains all the specifications Maven needs to build the project, like dependencies, plugins, and repositories.

- **ApiCatalogApplication** is the main class of the application.

- **ApiCatalogApplicationTests** is a simple test class that checks that the application runs fine.

- **application.properties** is a file that is initially empty but offers the chance to load all the configurations related to the application. You can also create a file with the same name but with the YML extension to configure the application.

Now that you know the components within the project, it's time to see what the pom.xml file looks like and which are the most relevant sections. Listing 2-2 contains a parent pom that solves all the problems related to the different versions of the libraries that Spring Boot needs; for that reason, you don't see any declaration of version in the dependencies.

Listing 2-2. The Initial Maven Build Specification

```
<?xml version="1.0" encoding="UTF-8"?>
<project xmlns="http://maven.apache.org/POM/4.0.0" xmlns:xsi="http://www.
w3.org/2001/XMLSchema-instance"
    xsi:schemaLocation="http://maven.apache.org/POM/4.0.0 https://maven.
    apache.org/xsd/maven-4.0.0.xsd">
    <modelVersion>4.0.0</modelVersion>
    <parent>
        <groupId>org.springframework.boot</groupId>
        <artifactId>spring-boot-starter-parent</artifactId>
        <version>3.0.0-M4</version>
        <relativePath/> <!-- lookup parent from repository -->
    </parent>
    <groupId>com.apress </groupId>
    <artifactId>api-catalog </artifactId>
    <version>0.0.1-SNAPSHOT</version>
    <name>api-catalog </name>
    <description>Microservices which contain all the information of the
    catalog </description>
    <properties>
        <java.version>17</java.version>
    </properties>
    <dependencies>
        <dependency>
            <groupId>org.springframework.boot</groupId>
```

```
            <artifactId>spring-boot-starter-actuator</artifactId>
        </dependency>
        <dependency>
            <groupId>org.springframework.boot</groupId>
            <artifactId>spring-boot-starter-web</artifactId>
        </dependency>

        <dependency>
            <groupId>org.springframework.boot</groupId>
            <artifactId>spring-boot-devtools</artifactId>
            <scope>runtime</scope>
            <optional>true</optional>
        </dependency>
        <dependency>
            <groupId>org.springframework.boot</groupId>
            <artifactId>spring-boot-configuration-processor</
            artifactId>
            <optional>true</optional>
        </dependency>
        <dependency>
            <groupId>org.springframework.boot</groupId>
            <artifactId>spring-boot-starter-test</artifactId>
            <scope>test</scope>
        </dependency>
    </dependencies>

    <build>
        <plugins>
            <plugin>
                <groupId>org.springframework.boot</groupId>
                <artifactId>spring-boot-maven-plugin</artifactId>
            </plugin>
        </plugins>
    </build>
    <repositories>
        <repository>
            <id>spring-milestones</id>
```

```
            <name>Spring Milestones</name>
            <url>https://repo.spring.io/milestone</url>
            <snapshots>
                    <enabled>false</enabled>
            </snapshots>
        </repository>
    </repositories>
    <pluginRepositories>
        <pluginRepository>
            <id>spring-milestones</id>
            <name>Spring Milestones</name>
            <url>https://repo.spring.io/milestone</url>
            <snapshots>
                    <enabled>false</enabled>
            </snapshots>
        </pluginRepository>
    </pluginRepositories>
</project>
```

As before, **application.properties** is empty. The idea is to remove that file and create a new file, **application.yml**, with the content in Listing 2-3, which defines the endpoints of the actuator that the application exposes, the port, and the default URL. The reason for doing this is that you reduce the complexity of the configuration file to understand the hierarchy of properties, but you can do the same with application.properties without problems.

Listing 2-3. The Configuration with the Default URL and the Exposed Endpoints

```
management:
    endpoints:
        web:
            base-path: /
            exposure:
                include: "*" # Indicates that all the endpoints expose it.
server:
    port: 8080 # Indicate the default port of the application
    servlet:
        context-path: /api/catalog # Indicate the default url
```

It's time to run the application. There are two ways to do it. You can use the IDE or the command line, which is the option shown on Listing 2-4.

Listing 2-4. The Command to Run the Application

```
./mvnw spring-boot:run
```

Next, run the command. You see an output similar to Listing 2-5 with all the information about the location of the application that starts, the container server that the application uses, and other additional details. The most relevant information of this output is the port, and the default URL (/api/catalog), which you need to always check in case something could be wrong.

Listing 2-5. Console Output

```
  .   ____          _            __ _ _
 /\\ / ___'_ __ _ _(_)_ __  __ _ \ \ \ \
( ( )\___ | '_ | '_| | '_ \/ _` | \ \ \ \
 \\/  ___)| |_)| | | | | || (_| |  ) ) ) )
  '  |____| .__|_| |_|_| |_\__, | / / / /
 =========|_|==============|___/=/_/_/_/
 :: Spring Boot ::                (v3.0.0-M4)

2022-09-19T11:05:12.370-03:00  INFO 1172745 --- [  restartedMain] c.apress.
catalog.ApiCatalogApplication   : Starting ApiCatalogApplication using Java
17.0.4 on asacco with PID 1172745 (/home/asacco/Codigo/api-catalog/target/
classes started by asacco in /home/asacco/Codigo/api-catalog)
2022-09-19T11:05:12.375-03:00  INFO 1172745 --- [  restartedMain] c.apress.
catalog.ApiCatalogApplication   : No active profile set, falling back to 1
default profile: "default"
2022-09-19T11:05:12.425-03:00  INFO 1172745 --- [  restartedMain] .e.DevTo
olsPropertyDefaultsPostProcessor : Devtools property defaults active! Set
'spring.devtools.add-properties' to 'false' to disable
2022-09-19T11:05:12.426-03:00  INFO 1172745 --- [  restartedMain] .e.Dev
ToolsPropertyDefaultsPostProcessor : For additional web related logging
consider setting the 'logging.level.web' property to 'DEBUG'
2022-09-19T11:05:13.297-03:00  INFO 1172745 --- [  restartedMain] o.s.b.w.
embedded.tomcat.TomcatWebServer  : Tomcat initialized with port(s): 8080 (http)
```

```
2022-09-19T11:05:13.304-03:00  INFO 1172745 --- [  restartedMain] o.apache.
catalina.core.StandardService   : Starting service [Tomcat]
2022-09-19T11:05:13.304-03:00  INFO 1172745 --- [  restartedMain] org.
apache.catalina.core.StandardEngine  : Starting Servlet engine: [Apache
Tomcat/10.0.22]
2022-09-19T11:05:13.344-03:00  INFO 1172745 --- [  restartedMain]
o.a.c.c.C.[.[localhost].[/api/catalog]   : Initializing Spring embedded
WebApplicationContext
2022-09-19T11:05:13.346-03:00  INFO 1172745 --- [  restartedMain] w.
s.c.ServletWebServerApplicationContext : Root WebApplicationContext:
initialization completed in 919 ms
2022-09-19T11:05:13.817-03:00  INFO 1172745 --- [  restartedMain] o.s.
b.d.a.OptionalLiveReloadServer        : LiveReload server is running on
port 35729
2022-09-19T11:05:13.831-03:00  INFO 1172745 --- [  restartedMain]
o.s.b.a.e.web.EndpointLinksResolver      : Exposing 13 endpoint(s) beneath
base path ''
2022-09-19T11:05:13.861-03:00  INFO 1172745 --- [  restartedMain]
o.s.b.w.embedded.tomcat.TomcatWebServer  : Tomcat started on port(s): 8080
(http) with context path '/api/catalog'
2022-09-19T11:05:13.879-03:00  INFO 1172745 --- [  restartedMain] c.apress.
catalog.ApiCatalogApplication    : Started ApiCatalogApplication in 1.837
seconds (process running for 2.137)
```

The application is running, and the only thing that you need to do is check if the application responds fine or not. To do this, you can check the status of the health endpoint, which is exposed by the actuator, as shown in Figure 2-8. If everything works fine, JSON shows the application status as **UP**.

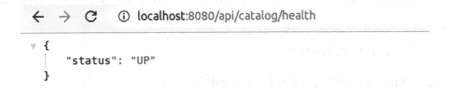

Figure 2-8. *The result of the health endpoint of the application*

Now it's time to create the endpoints used throughout this book. In this section, the endpoints only return a fake response.

The first task is to define a DTO class, which is the object that most endpoints receive and contains all the information about a currency. Listing 2-6 is a simple class that contains variables and setter/getter methods.

Listing 2-6. This Class Contains All the Information About a Particular Currency

```
public class CurrencyDTO {
    private Long id;
    private String code;
    private String description;
    private Boolean enable;
    private Integer decimalPlaces;

    public CurrencyDTO(Long id, String code, String description, Boolean
    enable, Integer decimalPlaces) {
        this.id = id;
        this.code = code;
        this.description = description;
        this.enable = enable;
        this.decimalPlaces = decimalPlaces;
    }
    //All the setters and getters
}
```

Listing 2-7 defines **CurrencyService,** which contains all the business logic related to the CRUD operations of currency. Include the @Service annotation, which allows you to delegate the creation and the injection in other classes in Spring Boot.

Listing 2-7. This Class Contains All the Business Logic of the CRUD Operations

```
@Service
public class CurrrencyService {

    public CurrencyDTO getById(Long id) {
        return new CurrencyDTO(id, "USD", "Dollar", true, 2);
    }
```

```
    public CurrencyDTO save(CurrencyDTO currencyDTO) {
        return currencyDTO;
    }

    public CurrencyDTO update(CurrencyDTO currencyDTO) {
        return currencyDTO;
    }

    public void delete(Long id) {
        // TODO Auto-generated method stub
    }
}
```

The Service class does not contain much logic because there is no persistence mechanism at this point in the book, but this class needs to interact with different repositories in the future. After that, you need to define a RestController that exposes each of the operations you can do with the currencies (see Listing 2-8).

Listing 2-8. Currency Controller with the Endpoints That Expose

```
@RestController
@RequestMapping("/currency")
public class CurrencyController {

    private CurrrencyService currrencyService;

    @Autowired
    public CurrencyController(CurrrencyService currrencyService) {
        this.currrencyService = currrencyService;
    }

    @GetMapping(value = "/{id}")
    public ResponseEntity<CurrencyDTO> getById(@PathVariable Long id) {
        CurrencyDTO response = currrencyService.getById(id);
        return new ResponseEntity<>(response, HttpStatus.OK);
    }

    @PostMapping
```

```java
    public ResponseEntity<CurrencyDTO> save(@RequestBody CurrencyDTO
    currencyDTO) {
        CurrencyDTO response = currrencyService.save(currencyDTO);
        return new ResponseEntity<>(response, HttpStatus.CREATED);
    }

    @PutMapping(value = "/{id}")
    public ResponseEntity<CurrencyDTO> update(@RequestBody CurrencyDTO
    currencyDTO) {
        CurrencyDTO response = currrencyService.update(currencyDTO);
        return new ResponseEntity<>(response, HttpStatus.OK);
    }

    @DeleteMapping(value = "/{id}")
    public ResponseEntity<Void> delete(@PathVariable Long id) {
        currrencyService.delete(id);
        return ResponseEntity.accepted().build();
    }
}
```

When you finish all the modifications in the source code, run the application and try to obtain any currency information to check if the mapping is okay. The response needs to be similar to what's shown in Figure 2-9, where you invoke localhost:8080/api/catalog/currency/1.

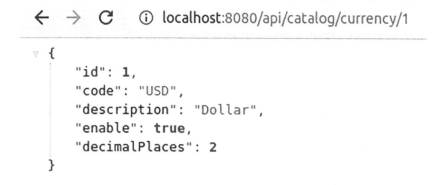

Figure 2-9. *The result of invoking the GET endpoint for currencies*

> **Note**   The scope of this book does not cover all the aspects of creating a REST API using Spring Boot. For that reason, only basic examples of creating an application are provided to give you the chance to see an entire flow from a REST endpoint to the database.

Best Practices

During the creation of a new application using Spring Boot, best practices are helpful to developers to reduce common problems, such as determining the available endpoints or why the application works fine on the IDE but poorly in other environments. This section discusses a few best practices.

Preventing Conflicts with the Dependencies

Most developers include dependencies in their projects without thinking about possible conflicts between different versions of the same library. Dependency management tools like Gradle or Maven solve conflicts using particular strategies. This approach works fine until an error appears when you try to deploy your application in some environments; during the build or the execution, you can find exceptions like ClassNotFoundException, NoClassDefNotFound, or MethodNotSupportedException.

To solve this type of problem or restrict the use of the application to certain versions of JDK or Maven, you can use the Enforcer plugin, which has support in Maven[6] or Gradle[7]. The dependencies associated with Spring Boot do not have this problem, but if you add other dependencies, the problem could appear, so just in case, add the plugin.

Figure 2-10 shows how the conflicts with different versions of the same dependency appear on the console.

---

[6] https://maven.apache.org/enforcer/maven-enforcer-plugin/index.html
[7] https://kordamp.org/enforcer-gradle-plugin/#_introduction

```
[INFO] Deleting /home/asacco/Codigo/api-catalog/target
[INFO]
[INFO] --- maven-enforcer-plugin:3.0.0-M3:enforce (enforce-versions) @ api-catalog ---
[WARNING]
Dependency convergence error for org.junit.jupiter:junit-jupiter-engine:5.8.2 paths to dependency are:
+-com.apress:api-catalog:0.0.1-SNAPSHOT
  +-org.springframework.boot:spring-boot-starter-test:3.0.0-M4
    +-org.junit.jupiter:junit-jupiter:5.8.2
      +-org.junit.jupiter:junit-jupiter-engine:5.8.2

and

+-com.apress:api-catalog:0.0.1-SNAPSHOT
  +-org.junit.jupiter:junit-jupiter-engine:5.3.2

[WARNING] Rule 0: org.apache.maven.plugins.enforcer.DependencyConvergence failed with message:
Failed while enforcing releasability. See above detailed error message.
[INFO] ------------------------------------------------------------------------
[INFO] BUILD FAILURE
```

Figure 2-10. *Enforcer plugin showing a conflict of dependencies*

Documenting the Endpoints

One of the biggest problems when using another REST API is knowing information about the endpoints like the URL, request/response, and HTTP method. There are different methods to document all this information. The default standard is OpenAPI Specification.[8] Frameworks like Spring Boot and Quarkus offer libraries to document the endpoints and dynamically generate the documentation like appears on the Figure 2-11.

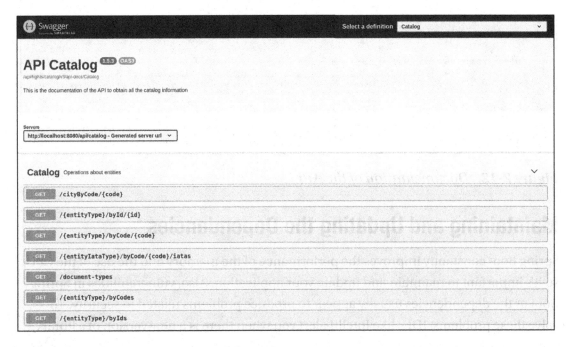

Figure 2-11. *Documentation of the API*

Logging All the Details

Logging is one of the most relevant features to find and solve problems in pre-productive or productive environments because it gives you information that helps you reproduce or understand the problem.

---

[8] https://swagger.io/specification/

There are different ways to implement logging depending on your budget. Tools like ELK (Elastic Logstash[9] and Kibana[10]) or CloudWatch[11] from AWS are alternatives to having all your application's logs of the instances in one place.

Figure 2-12 shows how the ELK stack presents the different logs of the application.

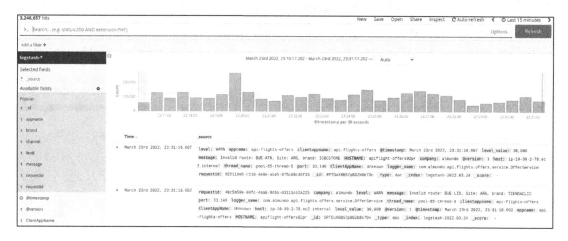

Figure 2-12. *Documentation of the API*

Maintaining and Updating the Dependencies

Spring Boot constantly improves the performance of the memory and the use of the CPU, so it's important to maintain and update your application. Also, vulnerabilities in Spring Boot or the dependencies usually appear to produce problems related to security. To solve these problems, IDEs like IntelliJ alert you when there is a new version of a library.

Summary

In this chapter, you learned how to create a Spring Boot project using tools like Spring Initializr or your IDE. Both strategies return the same result, but the IDE depends on the plugins, which could not be updated and did not appear in the previous versions.

The definition of endpoints and running the application is used throughout this book to check if everything is okay with accessing the database.

---

[9] https://www.elastic.co//logstash/
[10] https://www.elastic.co//what-is/kibana
[11] https://aws.amazon.com//cloudwatch/

CHAPTER 3

Spring Data and Different Types of Persistence

Chapter 1 discussed mechanisms to persist the information. One of them is Spring Data which offers the possibility to persist the information using different databases with a certain level of abstraction and solve most of the common operations without requiring many lines of code.

This chapter covers the basics of Spring Data, including how the repositories work and define custom implementations. These topics are relevant because most of them are used in the remaining chapters.

What Is Spring Data?

Spring Data is a family of projects supported by Spring to simplify access to databases like MongoDB, Redis, Cassandra, Neo4j, Memcached, and all the relational databases. In relational databases, Spring Data provides simplified access compared with other alternatives like JDBC, Hibernate, JPA, JDO, or MyBatis, reducing the number of classes, layers, and configurations necessary for any database operation.

Spring Data[1] first appeared at the 2010 Spring One conference. Rod Johnson (SpringSource) and Emil Eifrem (Neo Technologies) tried to connect a Neo4j database with an application using Spring. They created classes to generate a connection between the application and the database; these classes became the base of Spring Data. After that, the project family grows to provide support for different databases following the spirit of reducing the complexity and creating a certain level of abstraction between the application and the database.

Now let's think about why you need to move to Spring Data instead of using a database driver. Imagine that you have an application that uses Redis. The cost associated with maintaining this database is high, so the infrastructure team suggests

---

[1] https://spring.io/projects/spring-data

© Andres Sacco 2023
A. Sacco, *Beginning Spring Data*, https://doi.org/10.1007/978-1-4842-8764-4_3

moving the information to Cassandra, which is highly optimized. The problem with his scenario is if you have all the logic to persist and retrieve the information using only the database driver, you need to change numerous lines of code related to the CRUD operations, the connection, and all the configuration. But if you use Spring Data changing the database implies changing annotations in the entities, the configuration properties, perhaps information in the repositories, and nothing more. The time to migrate from one database to another is shorter using Spring Data, and you have a unique way to access databases.

Spring Data has groups of modules; some are across all types of databases, and others are for certain types. Let's look at the most relevant of these modules.

- **Spring Data Commons** provides a metadata model for persisting Java classes in a specific database using the repositories interfaces in the next section.

- **Spring Data REST**[2] is on top of Spring Data modules and helps you to create a RESTful API using the repositories associated with the entities.

- **Spring Data JPA**[3] provides an implementation of JPA using repositories which are an interface with support for all the CRUD operations in most cases. Creating a custom repository with a specific logic to access the database is possible if you need it.

- **Spring Data JDBC**[4] provides an implementation for accessing a database using JDBC using repositories without more JPA capabilities, like lazy-loading and cache.

- **Spring Data for Apache Cassandra**[5] supports all the CRUD operations and TTL definitions in the Cassandra entities. It also supports the configuration of multiple instances of a database.

- **Spring Data MongoDB**[6] offers the possibility to execute all the operations in a MongoDB database using the repositories or MongoTemplate, which is another way to execute the CRUD operations.

---

[2] https://spring.io/projects/spring-data-rest
[3] https://spring.io/projects/spring-data-jpa
[4] https://spring.io/projects/spring-data-jdbc
[5] https://spring.io/projects/spring-data-cassandra
[6] https://spring.io/projects/spring-data-mongodb

- **Spring Data Neo4j**[7] supports reactive and imperative applications using Neo4j Graph Database.

- **Spring Data Redis**[8] supports accessing Redis databases to save a simple value or something more complex like an object. Also, it supports using the Redis with a Sentinel mechanism responsible for monitoring and exposing a service with high availability.

Figure 3-1 shows other modules not covered in the previous explanation but connected with Spring Data. These modules are covered in more detail later in this book.

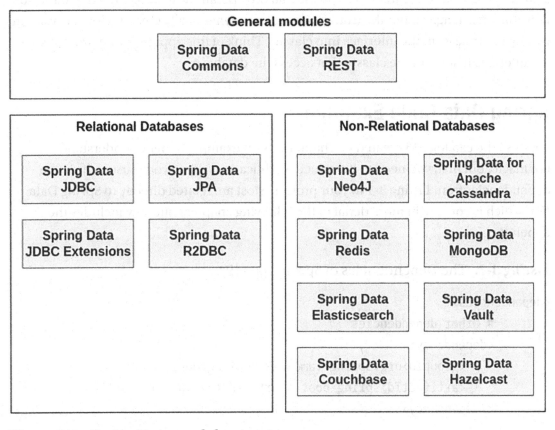

Figure 3-1. Spring Data modules structure

[7]https://spring.io/projects/spring-data-neo4j
[8]https://spring.io/projects/spring-data-redis

The source code of all the projects of Spring Data is available to download from the Spring GitHub repository[9].

How Does Spring Data Work?

Chapter 1 discussed the repository pattern, which provides a way to access the database and execute any CRUD operations, but what does Spring Data do behind the scenes? How to translate the result of the query into an object? If it's the first time you use Spring Data and read that some interfaces provide all the operations to access the database, you may think it is magical. But the truth is Spring Data dynamically creates a lot of classes in runtime to transform the interface into classes. Think of this approach as a proxy, using the interface instead of the classes that access the database.

Spring Data Code Example

Let's use the catalog API created in Chapter 2 as an example to better understand the magic. But first, you need to introduce modifications. First, you must include the dependencies from Listing 3-1 in your project. Most are related directly to Spring Data JPA, which is covered in more detail in the following chapters but only includes the dependencies.

Listing 3-1. The Dependencies of Spring Data JPA

```
<dependencies>
        # Other dependencies
        <dependency>
            <groupId>org.springframework.boot</groupId>
            <artifactId>spring-boot-starter-data-jpa</artifactId>
        </dependency>

        <dependency>
            <groupId>org.postgresql</groupId>
            <artifactId>postgresql</artifactId>
        </dependency>
```

---

[9] https://github.com/spring-projects?q=data&type=all

```
    <!-- This library will help you to transform an entity into a DTO
    and vice-versa -->
    <dependency>
        <groupId>org.mapstruct</groupId>
        <artifactId>mapstruct</artifactId>
        <version>${mapstruct.version}</version><!-- check the latest
        version on the Maven repository[10] -->
    </dependency>

    <dependency>
        <groupId>jakarta.persistence</groupId>
        <artifactId>jakarta.persistence-api</artifactId>
    </dependency>

</dependencies>


<build>
    <plugins>
        <plugin>
            <groupId>org.springframework.boot</groupId>
            <artifactId>spring-boot-maven-plugin</artifactId>
        </plugin>
        <plugin>
            <groupId>org.apache.maven.plugins</groupId>
            <artifactId>maven-compiler-plugin</artifactId>
            <version>3.8.1</version>
            <configuration>
                <source>${java.version}</source>
                <source>${java.version}</source>
                <annotationProcessorPaths>
                    <path>
                        <groupId>org.mapstruct</
                        groupId>
```

[10] https://mvnrepository.com/artifact/org.mapstruct/mapstruct

```
                                       <artifactId>mapstruct-
                                       processor</artifactId>
                                       <version>${mapstruct.
                                       version}</version>
                                </path>
                          </annotationProcessorPaths>
                    </configuration>
              </plugin>
        </plugins>
</build>
```

After that, you introduce all the necessary settings to connect with the database. Listing 3-2 introduces the configuration in application.yml. The example uses PostgreSQL, but you can use any relational database. If you need the instructions to install the database, go to Appendix D.

Listing 3-2. Configuration to Include in application.yml

```
spring:
  datasource:
    url: "jdbc:postgresql://localhost:5432/catalog?autoReconnect=true"
    username: postgres
    password: postgres
    driverClassName: org.postgresql.Driver
    validation-query: select 1;
    maxActive: 100
  jpa:
    show-sql: false
    generate-ddl: false
```

Now that you have all the dependencies and completed the configuration, the application will not fail, but it does not do anything with the database. So the next step is to create an entity. This happens because, in the configuration, you don't indicate that you generate the database structure when the application is starting. In this case, you use the entity in Chapter 1, which represents the currency table. For now, do not put much effort into understanding all the annotations because they are covered in more detail in

Part II of this book. Listing 3-3 contains the entity to persist the information with all the annotation to transform the columns on the database and the attributes on the class.

Listing 3-3. An Entity to Persist and Retrieve Information in the Currency Table

```
import  jakarta.persistence.Column;
import  jakarta.persistence.Entity;
import  jakarta.persistence.GeneratedValue;
import  jakarta.persistence.GenerationType;
import  jakarta.persistence.Id;
import  jakarta.persistence.Table;

@Entity
@Table(name = "currency") //Optional only if you need to indicate the
table's  name
public class Currency {

        @Id //Identify which is the primary key
        @GeneratedValue(strategy = GenerationType.SEQUENCE) //Indicate the
        way to generate the ID
        private Long id;

        private String code;
        private String description;
        private Boolean enabled;

        @Column(name = "decimal_places") //Optional: Indicate the name and
        the length of the column
        private int decimalPlaces;

        public Currency() {}
                // Setters and getters of all the attributes
                //  Override hashCode and equals

}
```

The next step is to create an interface that accesses the currency's table and executes the different operations. Chapter 1 discusses the repository pattern, which has a hierarchy of interfaces, each supporting different operations. Listing 3-4 uses one of the most basic repositories for CRUD operations.

Listing 3-4. Repository to Access the Database

```
import org.springframework.data.repository.CrudRepository;
import org.springframework.stereotype.Repository;

import com.apress.catalog.model.Currency;

public interface CurrencyRepository extends
CrudRepository<Currency, Long> {

}
```

Chapter 1 also discussed the DTO pattern, which is a way to transfer/move information into different layers without exposing the design of our database. But, one of the problems with this pattern is how you can map the attributes from one class to another without writing many lines of code. To solve this problem, Java offers libraries to do this mapping operation, reducing the number of code lines. Listing 3-5 uses Mapstruct[11].

Listing 3-5. Mapper Configuration to Convert an Entity into a DTO

```
import com.apress.catalog.dto.CurrencyDTO;
import com.apress.catalog.model.Currency;
import org.mapstruct.Mapper;
import org.mapstruct.factory.Mappers;

@Mapper(componentModel = "spring")
public interface ApiMapper {

    ApiMapper INSTANCE = Mappers.getMapper( ApiMapper.class );

    CurrencyDTO entityToDTO(Currency currency);

    Currency DTOToEntity(CurrencyDTO currency);
}
```

---

[11] https://mapstruct.org/

> **Note**   An analysis of the libraries that do mapping is beyond the scope of this
> book; however, options include ModelMapper,[12] JMapper,[13] and Orika.[14]

The last step is to modify CurrencyService to use the repository defined in Listing 3-4
and MapperFacade to do the transformation between the entity and the DTO (see
Listing 3-6).

Listing 3-6. CurrencyService with Modifications to Retrieve Information

```
import com.apress.catalog.dto.CurrencyDTO;
import com.apress.catalog.mapper.ApiMapper;
import com.apress.catalog.model.Currency;
import com.apress.catalog.repository.CurrencyRepository;
import org.springframework.beans.factory.annotation.Autowired;
import org.springframework.stereotype.Service;

import java.util.Optional;

@Service
public class CurrencyService {

    CurrencyRepository repository;

    @Autowired
    public CurrencyService(CurrencyRepository repository) {
        this.repository = repository;
    }

    public CurrencyDTO getById(Long id) {
        CurrencyDTO response = null;
        Optional<Currency> currency = repository.findById(id);

        if(currency.isPresent()) {
            response = ApiMapper.INSTANCE.entityToDTO(currency.get());
        }
```

----

[12] http://modelmapper.org/

[13] https://jmapper-framework.github.io/jmapper-core/

[14] https://orika-mapper.github.io/orika-docs/

```
        return response;
    }

//Other existent methods without changes
}
```

The final step is to run the application and make a request to the API at `http://localhost:8080/api/catalog/currency/1`. Before running the application, you should create the database with tables and rows. You can find all these things in a SQL script in the source repository of the book. If everything works fine when you run the application you will see a response more or less similar to the Figure 3-2.

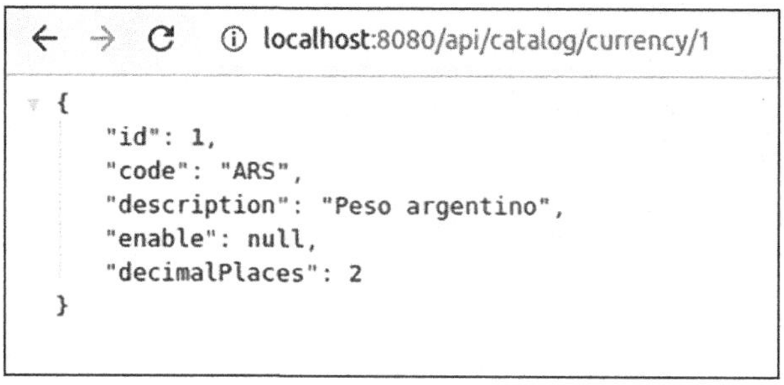

Figure 3-2. *Response to executing a request to the API*

Now that you have a working that returns results from your database, it's time to learn what happens behind the scenes.

Core Concepts

This section covers two of the most relevant aspects of how Spring Data works behind the scenes and how you can extend the default repositories to do other custom operations.

Object Mapping

Object mapping is the part of Spring Data responsible for creating property access and mapping. The flow consists of creating a new object using the class's public constructor and populating all the exposed properties.

Note   Typically, variations depend on the database used to persist the information, such as customizing columns or the name of the fields.

Let's start with the creation of objects using Spring Data. For this topic, the core module detects all the persistent entities interacting with the database and generates a factory class at runtime to create a new instance. Why create a class to instantiate the class instead of using reflection to create the instance and populate all the attributes? The main problem with this approach is related to issues associated with performance. Now it's time to see what happens with the Currency entity defined in Listing 3-3. Behind the scenes, Spring Data takes the entity a creates a new class that implements from ObjectInstantiator, as shown in Listing 3-7.

Listing 3-7. Class Created at Runtime to Instantiate an Entity

```
public class CurrencyObjectInstantiator implements ObjectInstantiator {

    Object newInstance(Object... args) {
        return new Currency((Long) args[0], (String) args[1], (String)
        args[2], (Boolean) args[3], (Integer) args[4]);
    }
}
```

This approach works fine if you follow some rules for all your entities.

- The class needs to have at least one public constructor. You don't need to create a public constructor that could be the default constructor.

- When you have more than one public constructor, you need to indicate which is the primary using the @PersistenceCreator annotation.

- The class isn't private or a static inner class.

There are a few rules or constraints to obtain more or less a 10% increase in performance but remember that all these classes are only visible at runtime, and Spring Data is in charge of orchestrating, so you don't have control over them.

The next step is to populate the information that Spring Data obtains from the database. Following the principle of reducing the blocks of code in your application, the core module generates a class in charge at runtime to set all the entity's attributes. Listing 3-8 uses the class from Listing 3-3 to see what creates Spring Data behind the scenes.

Listing 3-8. Class Created At Runtime to Set the Properties of an Entity

```java
public class CurrencyPropertyAccessor implements
PersistentPropertyAccessor {

    private Currency currency;

    public void setProperty(PersistentProperty property, Object value) {
        String name = property.getName();

        if ("id".equals(name)) {
            this.currency.setId((Long) value);
        } else if ("code".equals(name)) {
            this.currency.setCode((String) value);
        } else if ("description".equals(name)) {
            this.currency.setDescription((String) value);
        }
        //Others else if conditions, one per each attribute of the entity
    }
}
```

The property population rules are the same as the object instantiation; if you follow the previous constraints, you should not have any problem with Spring Data. If Spring Data cannot use it this way, try to use reflection so that you do not lose the performance improvements.

Note   This approach is only used when you have a constructor that does not receive all the parameters of the persistent entity or when you have an empty constructor.

Repositories

The repositories are the abstraction that Spring Data uses to interact with databases reducing the number of code blocks in your application. If you have experience with some of the old frameworks or libraries to access the database, perhaps remember the size of the DAO classes which interact with the database and map the results all in the same layer was too big and complex to follow the logic. But if you check the interface in Listing 3-4, you can see that there is no logic inside—just an interface that extends from another. So, what happens behind the scenes?

Spring Data offers a list of repositories (all of which are interfaces you can extend), indicating the entity and its ID type. At runtime, the framework creates a proxy class with all the logic necessary to access the database. In Listing 3-4, the repository extends from **CrudRepository<T, ID>**,[15] which provides a set of methods to execute the CRUD operations in the database. Listing 3-9 features some of this interface's operations.

Listing 3-9. CrudRepository Methods

```
package org.springframework.data.repository;

import java.util.Optional;

@NoRepositoryBean
public interface CrudRepository<T, ID> extends Repository<T, ID> {

  <S extends T> S save(S entity); //Save or update the entity

  Optional<T> findById(ID primaryKey);

  Iterable<T> findAll();

  long count();

  void delete(T entity);

  boolean existsById(ID primaryKey);

  // ... other methods omitted.
}
```

---

[15] https://docs.spring.io/spring-data/commons/docs/current/api/org/springframework/data/repository/CrudRepository.html

Other interfaces are PagingAndSortingRepository<T, ID>[16] which extends from CrudRepository, JpaRepository, and MongoRepository. Each of the two latest repositories is used for a specific type of database instead of CrudRepository and PagingAndSortingRepository, which are generic interfaces for all databases. In Spring Data 3.0.0, a new repository appeared. ListCrudRepository<T, ID> ID>[17] includes extra methods to retrieve a list of elements instead of an Iterable interface.

The methods that provide the most common repositories are useful in most cases. But what happens if you need to find an element for another property, not just for the ID? Spring Data provides a mechanism to create custom queries without creating extra classes.

Automatic Custom Queries

Spring Data analyzes each repository, searching all the defined methods to generate a particular query for each of them. If you need a particular query, you can define a new method in the interface using keywords that Spring Data uses to create the query. In this case, you need to create a method that uses **findBy** or **existBy**, followed by the field name you want to search in the table. Spring throws an exception if the attribute does not exist in the table (see Listing 3-10).

Listing 3-10. Custom method to Create a Specific Query

```
@Repository
public interface CurrencyRepository extends
CrudRepository<Currency, Long> {
    List<Currency> findByCode(String code);
}
```

Other keywords permit creating a set of queries combing attributes, limiting the quantity of the results, or ordering in a particular way (see Table 3-3). The structure of the query is split into two parts: the first one defines the subject of the query and the second one is the predicate. The subject of the query defines which type of operation the query needs to execute instead. The predicate is the attributes part of the clause that filters, orders, or is distinct.

---

[16] https://docs.spring.io/spring-data/commons/docs/current/api/org/springframework/data/repository/PagingAndSortingRepository.html

[17] https://spring.io/blog/2022/02/22/announcing-listcrudrepository-friends-for-spring-data-3-0

Let's look at examples of other queries in the CurrencyRepository filter for attributes and order the results. Listing 3-11 uses a List interface instead of a Set interface to show you can have duplicate elements. But if you want to change to a Set interface, the query continues working without problems.

Listing 3-11. Examples of Custom Queries That Find and Order the Results

```
public interface CurrencyRepository extends
CrudRepository<Currency, Long> {
    // General queries
    List<Currency> findByCode(String code);
    List<Currency> findByCodeAndDescription(String code, String
    description);

    // Order queries
    List<Currency> findByDescriptionOrderByCodeAsc(String description);
    List<Currency> findByDescriptionOrderByCodeDesc(String description);
}
```

The examples look fairly simple but let's see what Spring Data generates as a query to access the database. All the applications change the value of the show-sql property from false to true in application.yml. If you run the application and make a request you will see on the console queries like the Table 3-1.

Table 3-1. *Equivalence Between Methods and Queries in the Database*

Method	Query
List<Currency> findByCode(String code);	select currency0_.id as id1_0_, currency0_.code as code2_0_, currency0_.decimal_places as decimal_3_0_, currency0_.description as descript4_0_, currency0_.enabled as enabled5_0_ from currency currency0_ where currency0_.code=?
List<Currency> findByCodeAndDescription(String code, String description);	select currency0_.id as id1_0_, currency0_.code as code2_0_, currency0_.decimal_places as decimal_3_0_, currency0_.description as descript4_0_, currency0_.enabled as enabled5_0_ from currency currency0_ where currency0_.code=? and currency0_.description=?

(*continued*)

Table 3-1. (*continued*)

Method	Query
List<Currency> findByDescri ptionOrderByCodeAsc(String description);	select currency0_.id as id1_0_, currency0_.code as code2_0_, currency0_.decimal_places as decimal_3_0_, currency0_.description as descript4_0_, currency0_.enabled as enabled5_0_ from currency currency0_ where currency0_.description=? order by currency0_.code asc
List<Currency> findByDescri ptionOrderByCodeDesc(String description);	select currency0_.id as id1_0_, currency0_.code as code2_0_, currency0_.decimal_places as decimal_3_0_, currency0_.description as descript4_0_, currency0_.enabled as enabled5_0_ from currency currency0_ where currency0_.description=? order by currency0_.code desc

Table 3-2 describes the most relevant subject keywords. Some of these keywords could not be supported for specific non-relational databases.

Table 3-2. *Query Subject Keywords*

Keyword	Description
findBy… getBy… queryBy…	These keywords are generally associated with a select query and return an element or set of elements that can be a Collection or Streamable subtype.
countBy…	Returns the number of elements that match the query.
existBy…	Returns a boolean type with true if there is something that matches the query.
deleteBy…	Removes a set of elements that matches the query but does not return anything.

Table 3-3 shows the equivalence between predicate keywords and the database keyword. There are more keywords in the official Spring Data documentation[18].

Table 3-3. *Query Predicate Keywords*

Logical Keyword	Keyword expressions
LIKE	Like
IS_NULL	Null or IsNull
LESS_THAN	LessThan
GREATER_THAN	GreaterThan
AND	And
OR	Or
AFTER	After or IsAfter
BEFORE	Before or IsBefore

Part II of the book shows how to create queries to access relational databases.

---

[18] https://docs.spring.io/spring-data/commons/docs/current/reference/html/#appendix.query.method.predicate

Manual Custom Queries

The second way to create queries to access a database is the classical way—writing the query you need to execute in a format similar to SQL and defining a method in the interface. Listing 3-12 modifies the previous repository to include a manual query that finds an element using the code.

Listing 3-12. Example Manual Query

```
import com.apress.catalog.model.Currency;
import org.springframework.data.jpa.repository.Query;
import org.springframework.data.repository.CrudRepository;
import org.springframework.data.repository.query.Param;

public interface CurrencyRepository extends
CrudRepository<Currency, Long> {
    // General queries
    List<Currency> findByCode(String code);
    List<Currency> findByCodeAndDescription(String code, String
    description);

    // Order queries
    List<Currency> findByDescriptionOrderByCodeAsc(String description);
    List<Currency> findByDescriptionOrderByCodeDesc(String description);

    // Manual query
    @Query("SELECT c FROM Currency c where c.code = :code")
    Currency retrieveByCode(@Param("code") String code);
}
```

There are many ways to declare a query.

- Declare it as constant at the top of the interface so that you have all the declarations of methods to understand each of them.

- Externalize all the queries into a properties file and import them dynamically into each repository. One of the cons of this approach is that you need to have a good organization to know which file contains the queries of each repository.

- Lastly, have a class that contains all the queries of a specific repository. This approach is useful when you have a lot of queries that are too long. You clear your repository to have only the methods in one place and all the queries in another place. Also, define naming patterns to identify the idea behind each query.

There are many pros and cons with each of these approaches, but it depends on you which of them is the best for you.

Why do you need to create a manual query if there is a way to do it automatically? One answer is that you need to improve the performance of the query that Spring Data generates, or you don't need all the attributes of the table. You cover a specific scenario. This situation has the name of Projections[19]. Another answer is that the query is so complex that not exist keyword to express it. No rule explains all the potential scenarios when you need to use one mechanism instead of another. But if you know that your application has a problem with the performance of the query, the best alternative could be to check to write the query manually and see what happens.

Note   This book does not cover all the sentences or syntax of SQL because it's out of scope. Appendix F recommends books and websites with more information.

Implementing Repository Methods

Spring Data repositories offer methods that cover common scenarios, but you can extend them by adding methods. However, some scenarios require you to implement logic. Listing 3-13 creates an interface and a class that extends the interface with all the logic.

---

[19] https://docs.spring.io/spring-data/jpa/docs/current/reference/html/#projections

Listing 3-13. Example Custom Repository

```
public interface CustomCurrencyJPARepository {
    List<Currency> myCustomFindMethod(String code);
}

@Repository
@Transactional
public class CustomCurrencyJPARepositoryImpl extends
CustomCurrencyJPARepository {
            // Include all the dependencies necessary to access the
            database

    List<Currency> myCustomFindMethod(String code) {
                //Here all the logic related to your custom method
            }
}
```

Listing 3-13 has a block where you must inject all the dependencies you need to access the database in the constructor. For example, in a relational database, you need to include EntityManager. One last thing you need to know about the example is you have the chance to return any class that extends the Iterable, List, and Set interfaces. But, in this case, you return a list because it is not a constraint about whether the elements are duplicated.

After seeing the block of code in the previous example, you can consider what to include in this section. The answer to that question is that another approach exists in the middle between writing the entire query manually or delegating all the responsibility to create the query to Spring Data. The Criteria API offers a way to create queries in a programmatic way preventing errors in the syntaxis. To implement this approach, you must create a custom repository containing all the logic to create the query.

Let's look at the Criteria API as an example. Listing 3-14 transforms a simple method that finds currency by code into a custom method.

Listing 3-14. Example of a Custom Query Using the Criteria API

```
public interface CustomCurrencyJPARepository {
    List<Currency> myCustomFindMethod(String code);
}
```

```
@Repository
@Transactional
public class CustomCurrencyJPARepositoryImpl extends
CustomCurrencyJPARepository {
    EntityManager em;

    public CustomCurrencyRepositoryImpl(EntityManager em) {
        this.em = em;
    }

    List<Currency> myCustomFindMethod(String code) {
        CriteriaBuilder cb = em.getCriteriaBuilder();
        CriteriaQuery<Currency> cq = cb.createQuery(Currency.class);

        // You need to define the main entity
        Root<Currency> currency = cq.from(Currency.class);

        // Define all the conditions of the query
        Predicate codePredicate = cb.equal(currency.get("code"), code);

        //You can have more than one where clause
        cq.where(codePredicate);

        // Create the query and after that executed
        TypedQuery<Currency> query = em.createQuery(cq);
        return query.getResultList();
        }
}
```

The flow of this method is first to create a criteria builder responsible for creating the elements of the query. After that, you need to indicate which entity you want to obtain as part of the response, in this case, Currency. The next step is to define the root of the query: the table that appears in the FROM XXXX block in the SQL sentence. Also, you can include all the conditions the query needs to match using the predicate conditions, which do not necessarily need to be only one. You can create as many as you want. Lastly, you need to create the query and indicate which type of response you want, which could be a list or one element.

For JPA, Spring Data offers another possibility to encapsulate all this logic to create the query using classes. The specifications are classes you can create to extend from the Specification interface, which encapsulates the logic of custom queries but does not create an implementation of a repository. This approach helps you only have interfaces representing the layer to access a database (see Listing 3-15).

Listing 3-15. Example of Criteria Using a Specification

```java
public class CurrencySpecification implements Specification<Currency> {

    private static final long serialVersionUID = 27534733999996931822L;

    Currency entity;

     public CurrencySpecification(Currency entity) {
        this.entity = entity;
    }

    @Override
    public Predicate toPredicate(Root<Currency> root, CriteriaQuery<?>
    query, CriteriaBuilder builder) {

        //create a new predicate list
        List<Predicate> predicates = new ArrayList<>();

        CriteriaQuery<Currency> cq = builder.createQuery(Currency.class);

        // You need to define the main entity
        Root<Currency> currency = cq.from(Currency.class);

        // Define all the conditions of the query
        Predicate codePredicate = builder.equal(currency.get("code"),
        entity.getCode());

        predicates.add(codePredicate);

        return builder.and(predicates.toArray(new Predicate[0]));
    }
}
```

I don't want to introduce more complexity to this chapter. More in-depth examples are given in Part II of this book.

Summary

In this chapter, you learned about the types of access to databases using the features that offer Spring Data, like the repositories which create abstraction where you cannot define the logic to execute a query. You can also create a custom repository and define the entire logic.

PART II

SQL Persistence

Part II discusses the aspects of persistence using Spring Data with relational databases like MySQL and Postgres. You learn the basics of persisting information in a database with some validations in the schema, like column size and relationships between entities. With this approach, you can reduce the number of transactions in the database that can produce an error. You also learn about working with transactions and concepts related to ACID (atomicity, consistency, isolation, and durability).

Finally, you learn different mechanisms to reduce the impact of the changes in the database using tools for versioning scripts, like Liquibase and Flyway, running scripts manually, or using Spring's auto-update feature.

Persistence and Domain Model

In the previous chapter, you learned the basics of Spring and how to build a project that exposes an endpoint that persists information into a database using an architecture of layers with Spring Data. Still, the endpoint only obtains the knowledge of one entity without any connection or relationship with another. This type of situation in the relational database is not so common.

This chapter explains the relationships between the entities and how to use inherence to reduce duplicate code in Java. To do this, let's use the catalog's database model you saw in Figure 1-4 in Chapter 1, which represents a catalog's list of countries, states, cities, and currencies.

Lastly, you learn how to validate the values of the entities before persisting the information into the database because you could send something to the database that produces an exception. This type of situation, in most cases, implies cost associated with the transference of information across the network in most of the relevant cloud providers. Hence, validating the data before sending it to the database is essential.

JPA Configuration Using Annotations

JPA offers a set of annotations that provide the metadata in the entities with the idea that a library/framework that extends this specification uses the information to execute certain operations, like creating a table or validating if the model in the database matches the entities.

This concept sounds abstract, but JPA uses annotations to represent in the classes the different types of elements and relationships that exist in the database; for example, the name of the columns could not be the same in a table as in an entity, or you want

© Andres Sacco 2023
A. Sacco, *Beginning Spring Data*, https://doi.org/10.1007/978-1-4842-8764-4_4

to indicate that if a row in a table is removed, all the tables that have a relationship with this row need to be removed too. You can find most annotations related to the JPA API in the **jakarta.persistence** package. It's important to check the package when you import a class because many classes have the same name in different libraries.

Annotations are not a unique way to map attributes in classes with entities. JPA offers it using XML descriptor files, which were used in the early versions of Hibernate. Nowadays, using XML to declare mapping is unusual, but retro-compatibility lets most JPA implementations use it.

Before learning the annotations, you created one of the entities representing a table in the database. As shown in Figure 4-1, the table with the gray background is the only one in your application so let's create all the entities as a common POJO class without any annotation because you include it in the sections of this chapter.

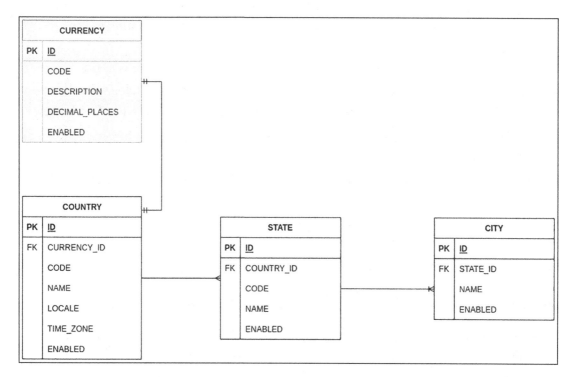

Figure 4-1. *Recap of the entire database structure*

This database model is familiar. You can see this type of information in most of the site's e-commerce when the user completes the checkout to indicate the shipping address or travel agency when the user needs to find a flight. The idea is to represent a real scenario but is not complex because the goal of this book is that you understand the concepts behind Spring Data.

Remember that the database structure with all the inserts to populate the database exists in the repository that contains all the source code of this book.

Note   It is not in the scope of this book to explain how to normalize a database and the pros/cons of having a schema that reduces the duplicate elements or information between other tables. Many books cover these concepts in a lot of detail.

Also, this book does not explain the cost associated with the transference of information across the network by cloud providers because It's a vast topic that needs a particular book for each cloud provider. Many resources on the Internet explain this topic in detail.

Let's create a Country class without representing the relationship between the other entities; include a basic Java attribute (e.g., Long, String, Boolean), as shown in Listing 4-1.

Listing 4-1. Country Class in the Database

```
public class Country implements Serializable {
    private Long id;
    private String code;
    private String name;
    private String locale;
    private String timezone;
    private Boolean enabled;

    // Constructors, setters, and getters for all the attributes
    // Override the hashcode and equals
}
```

Now replicate the same with the State to have a representation of the table in Java objects (see Listing 4-2).

Listing 4-2. State Class in the Database

```
public class State implements Serializable {
    private Long id;
    private String code;
    private String name;
    private Boolean enabled;

    // Constructors, setters, and getters for all the attributes
    // Override the hashcode and equals
}
```

Note Modifications are introduced throughout this book to improve and reduce the duplicate code. For now, the relationship between the entities is not relevant, so no association between the classes appears.

Lastly, do the same with the City class to have the representation of all the tables.

Listing 4-3. City Class in the Database

```
public class City implements Serializable {
    private Long id;
    private String name;
    private Boolean enabled;

  // Constructors, setters, and getters for all the attributes
   // Override the hashcode and equals

}
```

The last thing to do is create the DTOs with the same structure as the entity classes but with the prefix DTO, for example, CountryDTO. Remember that the purpose of using DTO classes is to keep your application's domain private from the consumer.

Only the attributes appear in the blocks of code without any methods. The idea is to reduce the number of lines that do not show something relevant so that, for that reason, you don't see all the setters, getters, and constructors.

Entity

Tables are a key element of databases. They are responsible for containing specific types of information, such as product data, users, or invoices. JPA offers a simple way to translate a Java class into a table in the database using different types of annotations. The most important are **@Entity** and **@Table** because both help JPA understand all the attributes inside the class that need to be persisted in a table. Another thing to consider with entities is the override of the hashCode and equals methods to prevent any conflicts with the object's content.

Listing 4-4 shows where you need to include both annotations to transform a simple Java class into an entity with a persistent state.

Listing 4-4. Definition of an Entity That Represents a Table

```
@Entity //This annotation indicates to JPA that it's something that has a
persistent state
@Table(name = "country") //This annotation is optionally
public class Country implements Serializable {
    // Attributes, constructors, setters, and getters for all the
    attributes
    // Override the hashcode and equals
}
```

The definition of the name in the **@Table** annotation is optional when the table's name is the same in the database with the same letters in the lower or uppercase. In the @Entity annotation, this is not optional because the only way that Spring Data detects that the class has information that needs to persist. Still, it's a good practice to indicate the name table in all cases because if you decide to change the class name, the application could not work, so with the definition of the table name, the class name is agnostic. You can change it for everything that you want.

Also, you can define the schema that contains the table because you can use multiple schemas in JPA. The most common use is to define only one schema for the entire group of tables.

```
@Table(name = "country", schema = "catalog")
```

Now let's run the application following the instructions in Chapter 2 and check what happens if you only define the **@Entity** and **@Table** in the Country class without anything else.

```
2022-04-26 16:17:43.372  INFO 39331 --- [  restartedMain] o.apache.
catalina.core.StandardService    : Stopping service [Tomcat]
2022-04-26 16:17:43.390  INFO 39331 --- [  restartedMain]
ConditionEvaluationReportLoggingListener :

Error starting ApplicationContext. To display the conditions report re-run
your application with 'debug' enabled.
2022-04-26 16:17:43.405 ERROR 39331 --- [  restartedMain] o.s.boot.
SpringApplication                 : Application run failed

org.springframework.beans.factory.BeanCreationException: Error creating
bean with name 'entityManagerFactory' defined in class path resource [org/
springframework/boot/autoconfigure/orm/jpa/HibernateJpaConfiguration.
class]: Invocation of init method failed; nested exception is org.
hibernate.AnnotationException: No identifier specified for entity: com.
apress.catalog.model.Country
```

Two things appear when you run the application, one of them is connected directly with the entity not yet defined, which is the primary key or main attribute. The other thing that appears in the implementation behind the scenes is Hibernate. It's not necessary to use Hibernate directly because behind the scenes, Spring Data includes an abstraction layer to hide the real implementation.

The exception that appears in the console is one of the possible exceptions. Each entity needs to follow the rules to be considered valid.

- Each entity needs to have an attribute/class with the **@Id** annotation to indicate the primary key or the main attribute for search.

- The entities need to have a constructor without arguments that cannot be defined. JPA uses the default constructor that has all the Java classes, but if you create a constructor with an argument, you need to define it.

- The classes must not be declared final.

- All the attributes need to have a setter and getter. Also, it is good practice to include overriding the hashCode and equals methods.

To solve the problem in Listing 4-4, you only need to add the **@Id** annotation in the id attribute in the Country class. Now, if you run the application and the microservice again, everything works fine without any problem. You can run the application in the IDE or execute the **./mvnw spring-boot:run** command. Listing 4-5 show the Country entity with the @Id annotation.

Listing 4-5. Adding the Table ID

```
@Entity //This indicates to JPA that it's something that has a
persistent state
@Table(name = "country") //This is optionally
public class Country implements Serializable {

    @Id
    private Long id;

    // Attributes, constructors, setters, and getters for all the
    attributes
    // Override the hashcode and equals

}
```

Considering that the attribute that you declare as **@Id** is not a good practice to modify the value after you persist the first time because you could have problems with the cache mechanism that provides Spring Data and Hibernate behind the scenes. Another thing to consider is that **@Id** must have a value because you set the value when you create the object, or you delegate the responsibility to generate the value to the database using one of the key generators in the next section.

Tip   Define the hashCode and equals methods in all your entities because it helps you to know if two instances of an entity are identical, so refer to the same row of a table. If you don't declare all the comparisons between two or more instances of an entity, compare the position in memory, which could be different. Each instance could have the same information.

When two objects have the same values and refer to the same row in a database, it is known as database identity; instead, when two objects do not share the same location in the memory but do not have the same values are known as object identity.

Before continuing with the rest of the explanation about the annotations related to the columns, replicate the same logic of the previous chapter to expose an endpoint for obtaining the information of one **Country**. If you prefer, you can check the folder in the repository of Github to obtain the source code of the previous chapter and add the new changes to this chapter.

Columns

After you declare the table's name in your class, the next step is to declare the name and the type of each table column that matches each class attribute. Also, you can define each column's length, minimum, and maximum and use these definitions to validate if the values in one particular instance are valid or not to persist. And if the column accepts null values or not.

To indicate the name, length, maximum, and minimum, whether it supports null values or not, JPA offers the @Column annotation, in which you can only use one type over each class attribute.

Tip   Is it necessary to include the **@Column** annotation in all the attributes? The answer is no because JPA supposes that the name of the attribute and the column in the database are the same. A good practice is defined in all cases, including the annotation and defining the name if it allows null values, and all the possible things you can use to validate the entity before persisting it. Also, consider adding the String columns to the correct length of the attributes.

Some vendors of relational databases differentiate between words in lower cases and uppercases, so a good practice is to try to indicate the name of the columns in all cases.

Let's modify the previous entity to include the @Column annotation and properties you can define inside (see Listing 4-6).

Listing 4-6. Definition of the Columns in the Entity

```
import jakarta.persistence.Column;
import jakarta.persistence.Entity;
import jakarta.persistence.Table;
```

```
import jakarta.persistence.Id;

@Entity //This indicates to JPA that it's something that has a
persistent state
@Table(name = "country") //This is optionally
public class Country implements Serializable {
    @Id
    private Long id;

    @Column(name = "code", nullable = false, length = 4)
    private String code;

    @Column(name = "name", nullable = false, length = 30)
    private String name;

    @Column(name = "locale", nullable = false, length = 6)
    private String locale;

    @Column(name = "time_zone", nullable = false, length = 10)
    private String timezone;

    @Column(name = "enabled",  nullable = false)
    private Boolean enabled = Boolean.TRUE;

    // Attributes, constructors, setters, and getters for all the
    attributes
    // Override the hashcode and equals

}
```

Listing 4-6 reveals the following.

- The name of the columns could be the same or not; for example, the timezone attribute in the table is declared differently.

- If you want to declare a default value in the column, you can do it as the attribute enabled assigned a value in the declaration. Another option is to use the columnDefinition property with the specification of the default value.

Table 4-1. *Definition of the Default Value*

The Default Value in the Attribute	The Default Value in the Annotation
`@Column(name = "enabled", nullable = false)` `private Boolean enabled = Boolean.TRUE;`	`@Column(name = "enabled", nullable = false,` `columnDefinition = "boolean default true")` `private Boolean enabled;`

The @ColumnDefinition annotation does the same, but it is directly connected with Hibernate. I recommend always using the annotations that JPA provides because if Spring Data JPA uses another vendor in the future, parts of your code may no longer compile.

- The length property is only valid with the columns that save a string. The columns are numeric, so you can indicate the minimum and maximum values that support using the annotations connected with Spring Validator.

- The nullable property is valid only with the primitive's wrappers.

Tip   If you need to declare that a column has a unique value, there is an attribute "unique" in the annotation. By default, the property's value is false, so you need to declare explicitly that the column is unique. For example, the code of a country could be unique because it represents unambiguously and only one country. For now, you do not include this property because this case is used to see how to introduce changes in an existing table.

The main problem when you define an entity of an existing table is which is the correct type so let's discuss how to define each ANSI SQL type in a Java class.

Primitive Types

Table 4-2 describes the basic correlations between the SQL types and Java types. In Java, you can use the primitive type or the wrapper; for example, instead of using **long,** you can use **java.lang.Long**.

Table 4-2. Equivalence Between the SQL Type and Java Type

ANSI SQL Type	Java Type
BIGINT	long, java.lang.Long
BIT	boolean, java.lang.Boolean
CHAR	char, java.lang.Character
CHAR (e.g. 'N', 'n', 'Y', 'y')	boolean, java.lang.Boolean
DOUBLE	double, java.lang.Double
FLOAT	float, java.lang.Float
INTEGER	int, java.lang.Integer
INTEGER (e.g. 0 or 1)	boolean, java.lang.Boolean
SMALLINT	short, java.lang.Short
TINYINT	byte, java.lang.Byte

There is no rule about how a boolean type needs to be represented. Many databases use various types of columns, like BIT, BYTE, BOOLEAN, or CHAR, to refer to the boolean type, so check which of these types of columns your database supports.

Note   As a recommendation, try to use primitive wrappers (Double, Float, etc.) instead of primitive variables (double, float) when you have a column that allows null values because JPA vendors could have other behavior to try to map null values in a primitive variable (e.g., in Hibernate, a null value in the database could be translated into a 0 if the class has an int variable).

Now let's explore why defining the correct Java type is important. First, introduce the validation of the DDL in the database. This property indicates that the application needs to check if the entity map structure matches the table in the database.

```
jpa:
    show-sql: true #Show the queries that are created for Spring Data
    generate-ddl: false # Switches the feature on and off and is vendor
    independent
    hibernate:
```

ddl-auto: validate #Check if the entities have the same structure in the database the entities have the same structure in the database

Next, change the attribute type from a string to an integer, such as the Country entity's time zone.

```
import jakarta.persistence.Column;
import jakarta.persistence.Entity;
import jakarta.persistence.Table;

@Entity //This indicates to JPA that it's something that has a persistent state
@Table(name = "country") //This is optionally
public class Country implements Serializable {

    @Column(name = "time_zone", nullable = false)
    private Integer timezone;

    // Attributes, constructors, setters, and getters for all the
    attributes
    // Override the hashcode and equals
}
```

Finally, run the application with these modifications and check if something like the following output appears in the console.

```
org.springframework.beans.factory.BeanCreationException: Error creating
bean with name 'entityManagerFactory' defined in class path resource [org/
springframework/boot/autoconfigure/orm/jpa/HibernateJpaConfiguration.
class]: Invocation of init method failed; nested exception is javax.
persistence.PersistenceException: [PersistenceUnit: default] Unable to
build Hibernate SessionFactory; nested exception is org.hibernate.tool.
schema.spi.SchemaManagementException: Schema-validation: wrong column
type encountered in column [time_zone] in table [country]; found [varchar
(Types#VARCHAR)], but expecting [int4 (Types#INTEGER)]
    at org.springframework.beans.factory.support.
AbstractAutowireCapableBeanFactory.initializeBean(AbstractAutowireCapableBe
anFactory.java:1804) ~[spring-beans-5.3.16.jar:5.3.16]
```

Character Types

When you need to represent a string with more than one character, there are many SQL types that you can use depending on the element size you need to save. Table 4-3 shows the equivalence between the different SQL types and Java classes; many SQL types could use the same class.

Table 4-3. *Equivalence Between the SQL Type and Java Type Character*

ANSI SQL Type	Java Type
CLOB	java.lang.String
NCLOB	java.lang.String
CHAR	java.lang.String
VARCHAR	java.lang.String
NVARCHAR	java.lang.String
LONGVARCHAR	java.lang.String
LONGNVARCHAR	java.lang.String

Date and time types

If you need to save something connected with a date in a column, there are many SQL types and Java types depending on the precision you need to save it. Table 4-4 shows the equivalence between the different date SQL types and Java classes; many SQL types could use the same class.

Table 4-4. *Equivalence Between Date/Time Types*

ANSI SQL Type	Java Type
DATE	java.util.Date
	java.sql.Date
	java.util.Calendar
	java.time.LocalDate
TIME	java.util.Date
	java.sql.Time
	java.time.OffsetTime
	java.time.LocalTime
TIMESTAMP	java.util.Date
	java.sql.Timestamp
	java.util.Calendar
	java.time.Instant
	java.time.LocalDateTime java.time.ZonedDateTime
BIGINT	java.time.Duration

JPA 2.2 supports all the new classes in the **java.time** Java 8 package. It provides many new methods that previously existed in the Joda library. Still, if you use an old version of JPA, you can find in your code a conversion between **java.sql.Date** and **java.util.Date.**

Binary Types

When you need to save a large volume of data, like a book, video, audio, or photo, there are many formats in SQL Type to solve the situation. Table 4-5 shows the equivalence between the different SQL types and Java classes.

Table 4-5. *Equivalence Between Binary Types*

ANSI SQL Type	Java Type
VARBINARY	byte[ ], java.lang.Byte[ ], java.io.Serializable
BLOB	java.sql.Blob
CLOB	java.sql.Clob
NCLOB	java.sql.Clob
LONGVARBINARY	byte[ ], java.lang.Byte[ ]

Note   BLOB and CLOB are known as LOBs (large object types). Each has the responsibility to save something, but the main idea of both is to save large volumes of information. The following describes each of them.

- A BLOB (binary large object) stores binary files like videos, gifs, and audio files.

- A CLOB (character large object) stores large files that contain text like PDF documents, text files, and JSON files.

- Depending on the database, there are several formats; for example, in MySQL, type TEXT represents a CLOB.

Other Types

Other types are not the group for criteria. In most cases, it is convenient to use it to reduce any conversion after obtaining the information from the database. Table 4-6 show some of the most relevant of SQL types and the equivalence with the Java classes.

Table 4-6. *Equivalence Between Other Types*

ANSI SQL Type	Java Type
NUMERIC	java.math.BigInteger java.math.BigDecimal
INTEGER, NUMERIC, SMALLINT, TINYINT, BIGINT, DECIMAL, DOUBLE, FLOAT, CHAR, LONGVARCHAR, VARCHAR	Enum
VARCHAR	java.util.Currency
	java.lang.Class
	java.util.Locale
	java.net.URL

The enumeration could be saved as many types and mapped directly to an enum in the Java class. The explanation is that you can save the enumeration as a string or an ordinal type like a number and delegate to the framework the responsibility to transform a column's information into a value of the enumeration. To see this concept practically, let's create a continent enumeration and include an attribute in the Country entity.

```
import jakarta.persistence.Enumerated;
import jakarta.persistence. EnumType;

public enum Continent {
    SOUTH_AMERICA, NORTH_AMERICA, EUROPE, ASIA, AFRICA, ANTARCTIC;
}

@Entity //This indicates to JPA that it's something that has a
persistent state
@Table(name = "country") //This is optionally
public class Country implements Serializable {

    @Enumerated(EnumType.STRING)
    private Continent continent;
```

```
// Attributes, constructors, setters, and getters for all the
attributes
// Override the hashcode and equals
}
```

Let's not include the continent attribute in the Country class for now. Chapter 6 explains how to introduce modifications to a database by versioning the changes on the tables or columns using some tools like Flyway or Liquibase.

Non-Persistent Attributes

JPA offers the possibility to indicate attributes that do not need to be persisted in the database. It's not the best practice, but there are many reasons to do it, for example, an old application with logic inside the entity.

Let's go back to your Country entity and map the relationship between the entities but include the **@Transient** annotation over the attribute. If you run the application including this annotation, the application works without any problem because JPA ignores the attribute and does not create a relationship between the table and the entity. Listing 4-7 shows how the Country entity looks like with some transient attributes.

Listing 4-7. Definition of Non-Persistent Attributes

```
import jakarta.persistence. Transient;
import jakarta.persistence.Entity;
import jakarta.persistence.Table;

@Entity //This annotation indicates to JPA that it's something that has a
persistent state
@Table(name= "country") //This annotation is optionally
public class Country {

    @Transient
    private Currency currency;
    // Attributes, constructors, setters, and getters for all the
    attributes
    // Override the hashcode and equals

}
```

Primary Key and Generators

The primary key is one of the most discussed topics because there are many ways or approaches to decide which is the best type to use as a primary key. Sometimes, the best option is to use a Long key because you save a short number of rows in the database. On the other hand, you can have an entity with a huge number of rows, so a good option could use a UUID. Also, another reason to use a UUID is for security because if your application exposes an endpoint that gives all the information of an entity using the ID, you can increment or decrement the ID and obtain the rows of a table instead if you use a UUID reduces the risk that someone knows which are valid UUIDs that exist in the database.

Note   Using a VARCHAR, which is the way to represent a UUID in the database, is less efficient than using a numerical type like BIGINT or INTEGER. Also, the numerical types use less space than VARCHAR.

If you use VARCHAR to save a UUID, consider the length of the column because sometimes this column has a small size. When you try to persist the information, an exception appears.

It is within the scope of this book to explain scenarios when one approach is better than another. Consider this explanation as a way that no existing correct answer for all cases, so you can find an old application that could not follow any of the approaches you read in this section's first part.

After you select the primary key of an entity, the next thing to do is define the strategy to generate the value. To do this, you need to indicate over the declaration of attribute that acts as the primary key the @GeneratedValue annotation and indicates the generation mechanism. Doing this, JPA completes this value before persisting the entity.

Let's modify the Country entity to include the strategy to generate the value, delegating the responsibility to indicate the next value to the database (see Listing 4-8).

Listing 4-8. Definition of the Strategy To Generate the Primary Key

```
import jakarta.persistence.Column;
import jakarta.persistence.Entity;
import jakarta.persistence.GeneratedValue;
```

```
import jakarta.persistence.GenerationType;
import jakarta.persistence.Id;
import jakarta.persistence.Table;

@Entity //This annotation indicates to JPA that it's something that has a
persistent state
@Table(name= "country") //This annotation is optionally
public class Country implements Serializable {
    @Id
    @GeneratedValue(strategy = GenerationType.SEQUENCE)
    private Long id;

    // Attributes, constructors, setters, and getters for all the
attributes
    // Override the hashcode and equals

}
```

Listing 4-8 shows a strategy to generate the value of the primary key, but JPA offers an enumeration with multiple options. Let's look at each of the available options.

- **GenerationType.SEQUENCE** defines a numeric sequence in the database, so before persisting the information in the JPA table, call the sequence to obtain the next number to insert into the table. The main benefit of using the sequence is that you can use it in any column in multiple tables connected directly by one table, but it's a common practice to use it for a specific purpose. Some databases that support the use of SEQUENCE are Oracle and PostgreSQL.

Note   Each database has a particular way of indicating the strategy to generate the sequence. Let's look at how to declare in PostgreSQL.

```
CREATE TABLE IF NOT EXISTS city
(
    id      bigint GENERATED ALWAYS AS IDENTITY PRIMARY KEY,
    name  varchar(80)            NOT NULL,
    enabled    BOOLEAN      DEFAULT true        NOT NULL,
    state_id bigint NOT NULL REFERENCES state(id)
);
```

Note   Depending on the database version, an alternative could be declared in the generator outside the table's structure.

```
CREATE SEQUENCE city_id_seq;
CREATE TABLE IF NOT EXISTS city
(
    id      bigint DEFAULT NEXTVAL('city_id_seq') NOT NULL,
    name  varchar(80)            NOT NULL,
    enabled    BOOLEAN      DEFAULT true        NOT NULL,
    state_id bigint NOT NULL REFERENCES state(id)
);
```

- **GenerationType.IDENTITY** is a special behind-the-scenes column that does the same as the SEQUENCE check, which is the next available value. Some databases do not support the definition of a SEQUENCE, so they have an alternative special column like this that is an auto-incremented value.

Let's examine the definition of the City table in MySQL.

```
CREATE TABLE IF NOT EXISTS city
(
    id      bigint NOT NULL  AUTO_INCREMENT,
    name  varchar(80)            NOT NULL,
    enabled    BOOLEAN      DEFAULT true        NOT NULL,
    state_id bigint NOT NULL state(id),
    PRIMARY KEY (id)
);
```

- **GenerationType.TABLE** is an alternative approach when you have a database that does not support using SEQUENCE; for example, MySQL 5.7 and lower do not have it. The goal is to have a table in your schema containing one row per entity that needs to generate an ID, which is the next available value.

- **GenerationType.AUTO** is a strategy that considers the database you used and defines which is the best option to use. You can indicate this strategy in the annotation or without anything **@GeneratedValue()** because both cases indicate the same.

Note   There are many implementations of table generators to optimize and reduce the risk of collision. Examples include Hilo and Pooled optimizer, which is part of the Hibernate. A detailed explanation of these implementations is beyond the scope of this book, but you can find a great explanation on Vlad Mihalcea's blog.[1]

Always indicate which strategy generates the value because it is a good way to have control and not delegate to Spring Data, which delegates to Hibernate, which is the best strategy for you.

Types of Relationships

When you define the structure of your database, many tables have a relationship with others to reduce the number of redundant information. You can see the relationship between tables when you have a foreign key in one table and the primary key in another.

JPA has a set of annotations to declare the types of relationships between the entities. The relationship could be unidirectional if you can access the information of both entities from one of them; for example, you have the information about the Currency of a Country but not vice versa; in the other hand, exists a bidirectional relationship when you can navigate from any entity to the other one.

---

[1] https://vladmihalcea.com/migrate-hilo-hibernate-pooled/

The following describes the types of relationships between the entities.

- **@ManyToOne** is the most common type of relationship where many
  entities reference one another; for example, many countries could
  have the same currency in the catalog's application. Spring Data uses
  the foreign key in one table to join with the other; for example, the
  country's table uses currency_id to join with the column id in the
  currency table.

  An alternative to this is **@OneToMany** which is used when you try to
  have a bidirectional relationship, but in your tables, both types are the
  same. To do a bidirectional relationship, both entities need to have
  an attribute that refers to the other entity where one is @ManyToOne,
  and the other is @OneToMany. For example, in the catalog's
  application, there are multiple @ManyToOne relationships. Let's
  make the connection between the Country and Currency entities.

  In the Country entity, there is a Currency attribute with the
  @ManyToOne annotation, and in Currency, you can include adding
  a Country attribute with the @OneToMany annotation. This is the
  way to generate a bidirectional relationship. An example of a one to
  many relationship appears on Figure 4-2.

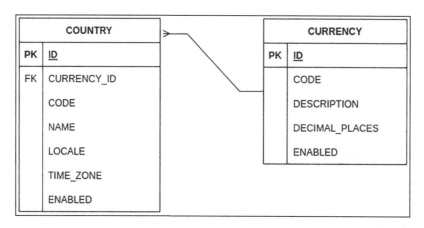

Figure 4-2. *Two tables of the catalog's application*

- **@OneToOne** is not the most frequent type of relationship. One table
  has a foreign key associated with the table's primary key without
  having the chance to refer to multiple rows. One problem with this

type of problem is when you create a bidirectional relation, so both entities refer to the other with a non-null value. This could produce an exception because one entity needs that the other exists in the database, and vice versa is like a deadlock. To solve this problem, one of the entities needs to have the possibility to allow null values so you have a way to persist an entity and, after that, use it to put the reference in the other one.

- **@ManyToMany** is one of the most complex relationships. If you have previously worked with databases, you know that this type of relation implies creating an intermediate table that contains the primary key of both tables. In the JPA world, these three tables become two entities, and the specific implementation of JPA has the responsibility to understand how the query and hide or abstract how it is implemented in the database.

For example, let's transform the relationship between Country and Currency into many-to-many so one country could have multiple currencies, and one currency could have multiple countries associated with it. The database has a structure similar to Figure 4-3, but in your catalog's application, there are only two entities: Country and Currency.

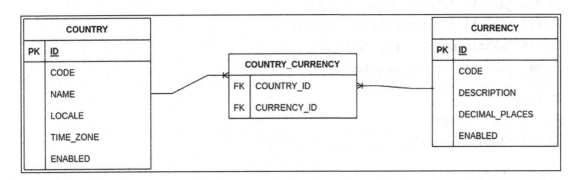

Figure 4-3. *A hypothetical situation of transforming the relation in many-to-many*

In all the types of relationships, you can indicate if you accept null values or not, which is a way to say that the column in the database could or couldn't have a value. When you indicate this information in the relationship, it impacts the query that Hibernate generates to obtain the information. For example, in a **@ManyToOne** relation, if you allow null values, the query uses a **LEFT JOIN** instead, which indicates the opposite query contains an **INNER JOIN**. If you don't indicate anything in the annotation, the column accepts null values.

Note   In some cases, the relationship between the entities does not directly correlate with the number of tables in the database; for example, if you have a relationship with many-to-many between two entities could be transformed into three tables. This "strange" situation has a simple explanation; JPA and most of the implementation hide from the developer the details about the structure of the database.

The scripts you run to populate the database in previous chapters, the relationship between tables exists but is not mapping in the entities. Now it's the type to map the entities' relationship, so let's remove the @Transient annotation in Country and include the **@ManyToOne** annotation, a variant of one-to-many (see Listing 4-9).

Listing 4-9. Definition of the Relationship Between Two Entities

```
import jakarta.persistence.Column;
import jakarta.persistence.Entity;
import jakarta.persistence.FetchType;
import jakarta.persistence.JoinColumn;
import jakarta.persistence.ManyToOne;
import jakarta.persistence.Table;

@Entity
@Table(name= "country")
public class Country {

    @ManyToOne
    @JoinColumn(name = "currency_id", nullable = false)
    private Currency currency;

    // Attributes, constructors, setters, and getters for all the
    attributes
    // Override the hashcode and equals

}
```

It's important to define the name of the column in the Country table that acts as the foreign key to indicate to Spring Data how to match tables.

Let's run the application and invoke the country endpoint using a particular ID. If you didn't create all the classes with the same logic as the Currency entity to access the information, it's time to do it. The best way to check if everything works fine is to invoke the endpoint and check the response as you can see on the Figure 4-4.

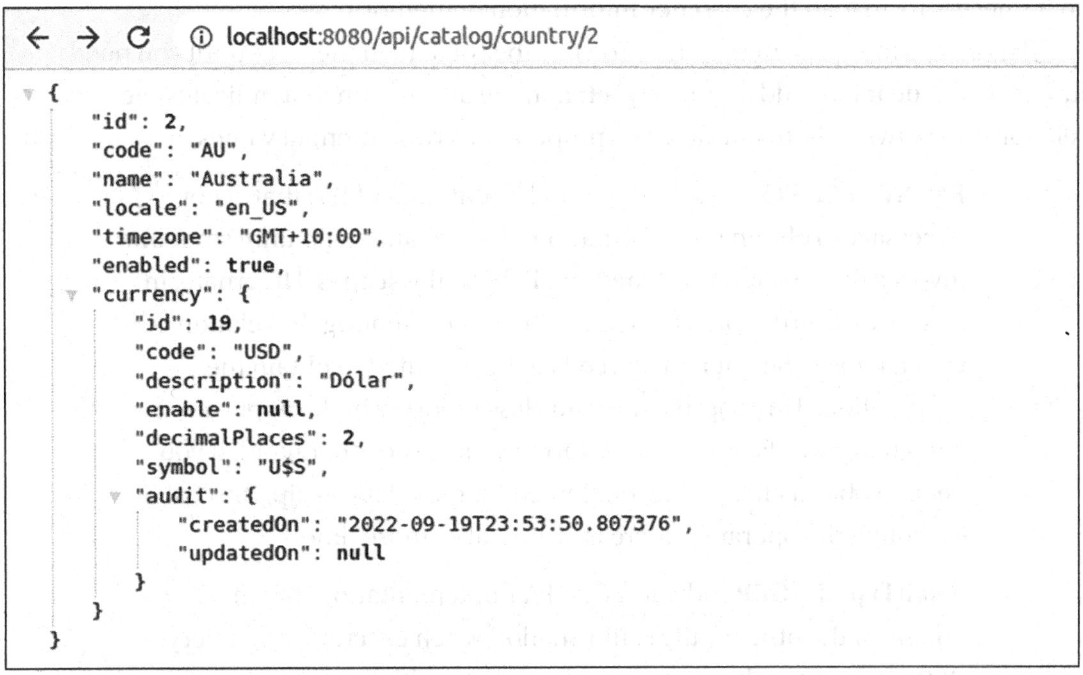

```
←  →  C      ⓘ  localhost:8080/api/catalog/country/2

▼ {
      "id": 2,
      "code": "AU",
      "name": "Australia",
      "locale": "en_US",
      "timezone": "GMT+10:00",
      "enabled": true,
    ▼ "currency": {
          "id": 19,
          "code": "USD",
          "description": "Dólar",
          "enable": null,
          "decimalPlaces": 2,
          "symbol": "U$S",
        ▼ "audit": {
              "createdOn": "2022-09-19T23:53:50.807376",
              "updatedOn": null
          }
      }
  }
```

Figure 4-4. *Result of invoking the country endpoint*

Lazy and Eager Loading

Figure 4-4 shows that when you add the relationship between two or more entities, the endpoint response gives all the information that could not be necessary in all cases. Imagine you want to check if a country exists before sending the information to the database. So, you invoke a method that receives the code and gives the countries this particular code. You don't need to check anything about the relationship with currency, so it's necessary to load the currency information in memory.

JPA offers a mechanism to reduce the number of data in memory until you need it. The way to do it is to add a property **fetch** in the annotation that indicates the relationship between both entities. The property has two potential values.

- **FetchType.LAZY** indicates the implementation of JPA that is not necessary to obtain the information of the relationship until someone invokes the attribute's get method. Behind the scenes, Hibernate, in this case, inserts a proxy in the attribute representing the relationship which knows the query that needs to be executed to obtain the information. This approach spends less memory in the application and gives you a faster load of information; in the other hand, if you need to obtain always information about the relationship, the cost of executing the operation increases and takes more time.

- **FetchType.EAGER** indicates the JPA implementation that must obtain all the other entity's information when executing the query. With this approach, you reduce the time to initialization because when you have one entity in memory, you have all the information; in the other hand, the query execution could take more time and negatively impact the application's performance.

Both approaches have pros and cons related to performance. The standard is to use all the relationships with FetchType.LAZY to increase the application's performance and explicitly obtain the information of the other entities.

Let's modify the Country entity to indicate that the relationship with currency does not need to load all the information when executing the query (see Listing 4-10).

Listing 4-10. Definition of Loading Information

```
import jakarta.persistence.Column;
import jakarta.persistence.Entity;
import jakarta.persistence.FetchType;
import jakarta.persistence.JoinColumn;
import jakarta.persistence.ManyToOne;
import jakarta.persistence.Table;

@Entity
@Table(name= "country")
public class Country implements Serializable {

    @ManyToOne(fetch = FetchType.LAZY)
    @JoinColumn(name = "currency_id", nullable = false)
    private Currency currency;

    // Attributes, constructors, setters, and getters for all the
    attributes
    // Override the hashcode and equals

}
```

Behind the scenes, you see one or two queries, depending on the strategy for fetching from the Country entity, as shown in Table 4-7.

Table 4-7. *Queries Executed to the Database by Strategy*

FetchType.LAZY	FetchType.EAGER
Hibernate: select country0_.id as id1_0_0_, country0_. code as code2_0_0_, country0_.currency_id as currency7_0_0_, country0_.enabled as enabled3_0_0_, country0_.locale as locale4_0_0_, country0_.name as name5_0_0_, country0_.time_zone as time_zon6_0_0_ from country country0_ where country0_.id=? Hibernate: select currency0_.id as id1_1_0_, currency0_. code as code2_1_0_, currency0_.decimal_places as decimal_3_1_0_, currency0_.description as descript4_1_0_, currency0_.enabled as enabled5_1_0_ from currency currency0_ where currency0_.id=?	Hibernate: select country0_.id as id1_0_0_, country0_.code as code2_0_0_, country0_.currency_id as currency7_0_0_, country0_.enabled as enabled3_0_0_, country0_.locale as locale4_0_0_, country0_.name as name5_0_0_, country0_.time_zone as time_zon6_0_0_, currency1_. id as id1_1_1_, currency1_.code as code2_1_1_, currency1_.decimal_ places as decimal_3_1_1_, currency1_. description as descript4_1_1_, currency1_.enabled as enabled5_1_1_ from country country0_ left outer join currency currency1_ on country0_. currency_id=currency1_.id where country0_.id=?

ObjectMapper copies the values from one object to another using the GET method. Hence, JPA thinks someone needs information about the lazy relationship and obtains the information.

For this reason, when you invoke the country endpoint, you obtain all the currency information because MapStruct is not configured to ignore certain attributes during the mapping.

Ordering

When you have two or more connected entities, and one has another's list of elements, JPA or Hibernate executes the query without considering the order. You have two options: order the element in your application or delegate to the database the responsibility to do it.

Let's modify our catalog's application to have a bidirectional relationship between country and state to see the situation in more detail and learn how to solve it (see Listing 4-11). The Country entity adds a List attribute of type State.

Listing 4-11. Add the Bidirectional Relationship

```
@Entity
@Table(name= "country")
public class Country implements Serializable {

    @OneToMany(fetch = FetchType.LAZY)
    @JoinColumn(name = "country_id", nullable = false, updatable = false,
    insertable = false)
    private List<State> states;

    // Attributes, constructors, setters, and getters for all the
    attributes
    // Override the hashcode and equals

}
```

Note   The use of the properties **updatable** and insertable in the **@JoinColumn** annotation with false indicates that it is not the entity's responsibility to modify the connected entities.

The next step implies that you modify the State entity to include the properties **updatable** and **insertable** and do the same with the DTOs (see Listing 4-12).

Listing 4-12. Add the Bidirectional Relationship

```
@Entity
@Table(name= "state")
public class State implements Serializable {

    @ManyToOne(fetch = FetchType.LAZY)
    @JoinColumn(name = "country_id", nullable = false, updatable = false,
    insertable = false)
    private Country country;

    // Attributes, constructors, setters, and getters for all the attributes
    // Override the hashcode and equals

}
```

When you use MapStruct and do it automatically, the mapper from one object to another invokes all the get methods, so Spring Data suppose that you need all the information of the lazy collections. The main problem in this bidirectional relationship is that it produces an infinite loop, so you need to exclude the field country in the State entity. To solve this, you must modify the ApiMapper class and create a custom mapper (see Listing 4-13).

Listing 4-13. Customize the Mapper of the Country Entity

```java
import com.apress.catalog.dto.CountryDTO;
import com.apress.catalog.dto.CurrencyDTO;
import com.apress.catalog.dto.StateDTO;
import com.apress.catalog.model.Country;
import com.apress.catalog.model.Currency;
import com.apress.catalog.model.State;
import org.mapstruct.Mapper;
import org.mapstruct.Mapping;
import org.mapstruct.factory.Mappers;

@Mapper(componentModel = "spring")
public interface ApiMapper {

    ApiMapper INSTANCE = Mappers.getMapper( ApiMapper.class );

    CurrencyDTO entityToDTO(Currency currency);

    Currency DTOToEntity(CurrencyDTO currency);

    CountryDTO entityToDTO(Country country);

    Country DTOToEntity(CountryDTO country);

    @Mapping(target="country", ignore = true) //Exclude the country element
    to prevent a recursive mapping
    StateDTO stateToStateDTO(State state);

    State stateDTOToState(StateDTO state);
}
```

Now let's run the application and request the endpoint to obtain all the information about one country. When you obtain the endpoint's response, all the states are in the same order that appears in the database by ID (see Figure 4-5).

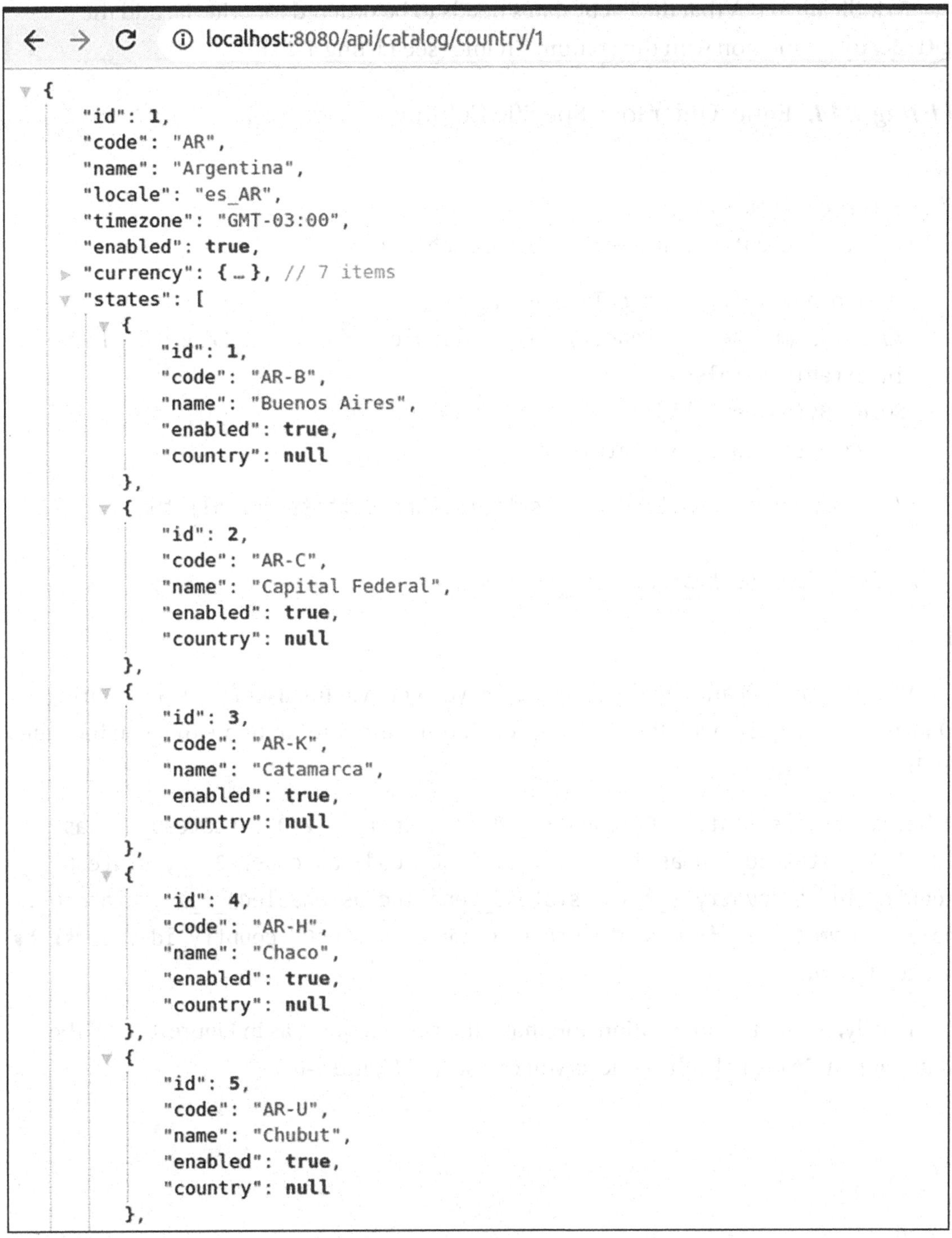

```
←  →  C      ⓘ localhost:8080/api/catalog/country/1

▼ {
      "id": 1,
      "code": "AR",
      "name": "Argentina",
      "locale": "es_AR",
      "timezone": "GMT-03:00",
      "enabled": true,
   ▶  "currency": { … }, // 7 items
   ▼  "states": [
      ▼  {
            "id": 1,
            "code": "AR-B",
            "name": "Buenos Aires",
            "enabled": true,
            "country": null
         },
      ▼  {
            "id": 2,
            "code": "AR-C",
            "name": "Capital Federal",
            "enabled": true,
            "country": null
         },
      ▼  {
            "id": 3,
            "code": "AR-K",
            "name": "Catamarca",
            "enabled": true,
            "country": null
         },
      ▼  {
            "id": 4,
            "code": "AR-H",
            "name": "Chaco",
            "enabled": true,
            "country": null
         },
      ▼  {
            "id": 5,
            "code": "AR-U",
            "name": "Chubut",
            "enabled": true,
            "country": null
         },
```

Figure 4-5. Result of invoking the country endpoint without ordering the states.

117

To indicate to JPA that the list of states needs to be ordered for criteria, add the **@OrderBy** annotation with the column's name (see Listing 4-14).

Listing 4-14. Entity Order for a Specific Column

```
@Entity
@Table(name= "country")
public class Country implements Serializable {

    @OneToMany(fetch = FetchType.LAZY)
    @JoinColumn(name = "country_id", nullable = false, updatable = false,
    insertable = false)
    @OrderBy(value = "id")
    private List<State> states;

    // Attributes, constructors, setters, and getters for all the
    attributes
    // Override the hashcode and equals

}
```

With this modification in the entity, when you get over the list of the states, Spring Data executes a query with the ordering considering the column name that you indicate in the property value.

```
Hibernate: select states0_.country_id as country_5_2_0_, states0_.id as
id1_2_0_, states0_.id as id1_2_1_, states0_.code as code2_2_1_, states0_.
country_id as country_5_2_1_, states0_.enabled as enabled3_2_1_, states0_.
name as name4_2_1_ from state states0_ where states0_.country_id=? order by
states0_.code
```

Finally, re-run the application and make the same request as in Figure 4-5. All the states appear in order by the code as you can see on Figure 4-6.

```
←  →  C    ⓘ localhost:8080/api/catalog/country/1

▼ {
      "id": 1,
      "code": "AR",
      "name": "Argentina",
      "locale": "es_AR",
      "timezone": "GMT-03:00",
      "enabled": true,
   ▶  "currency": { … }, // 7 items
   ▼  "states": [
      ▼  {
            "id": 17,
            "code": "AR-A",
            "name": "Salta",
            "enabled": true,
            "country": null
         },
      ▼  {
            "id": 1,
            "code": "AR-B",
            "name": "Buenos Aires",
            "enabled": true,
            "country": null
         },
      ▼  {
            "id": 2,
            "code": "AR-C",
            "name": "Capital Federal",
            "enabled": true,
            "country": null
         },
      ▼  {
            "id": 19,
            "code": "AR-D",
            "name": "San Luis",
            "enabled": true,
            "country": null
         },
      ▼  {
            "id": 8,
            "code": "AR-E",
            "name": "Entre Ríos",
            "enabled": true,
            "country": null
         },
      ▼  {
            "id": 12,
            "code": "AR-F",
            "name": "La Rioja",
            "enabled": true,
            "country": null
         },
      ▼  {
```

Figure 4-6. *Result of invoking the country endpoint with the order of the states*

119

Finally, this ordering approach always works in the same direction, so if you need different criteria to order the states, the best solution is to define a custom query in the repository that receives the type of ordering as a parameter.

Types of Inherence

Like many object-oriented languages, Java offers the possibility to use inherence to reduce duplicate code and extend the functionality of other classes. JPA is not agnostic of this feature and offers several possibilities to reduce the complexity of your application's domain in Java code. Behind the scenes, in your database, the complexity could be the same as if you don't use the inherence.

Let's go back to our catalog's application to see a common problem. All the entities have an attribute ID with the same strategy of generating the value, so it's not something good to have duplicated in a lot of places this element. To reduce the duplicate code, let's create a Base class that contains the id attribute with the annotation to generate the value (see Listing 4-15).

Listing 4-15. Base Entity To Reduce the Duplicate Code

```
@MappedSuperclass
public abstract class Base implements Serializable {

    @Id
    @GeneratedValue(strategy = GenerationType.SEQUENCE)
    private Long id;

    public Base(){}

    public Base(Long id) {
       this.id = id;
    }

    public Long getId() {
        return id;
    }
```

```
    public void setId(Long id) {
        this.id = id;
    }
}
```

Listing 4-15 shows the **@MappedSuperclass** annotation, which indicates that the class is not a final entity, so it does not exist in the database. Instead, this class is part of another class that inherits it. The next step is to modify the Currency entity, removing the Id attribute and extending it for the new Base class (see Listing 4-16).

Listing 4-16. Currency Entity Extending for the New Base Class

```
@Entity
@Table(name= "currency")
public class Currency extends Base implements Serializable {

    // Attributes, constructors, setters, and getters for all the
    attributes
    // Override the hashcode and equals

}
```

If you run the application after all modifications, everything continues in the same way because you only modify how you represent the database tables in the entities, nothing more.

This is one mechanism of inherence, but there are many others.

Mapped Superclass

The example in the previous section about moving the ID to a superclass is known as a mapped superclass. All the attributes of the abstract class (a requisite of the mapped superclass) are not considered for Spring Data as an entity per se. All attributes of the abstract class are parts of other entities using inherence. But in the database, you see all the columns in the same table, as shown in Figure 4-7.

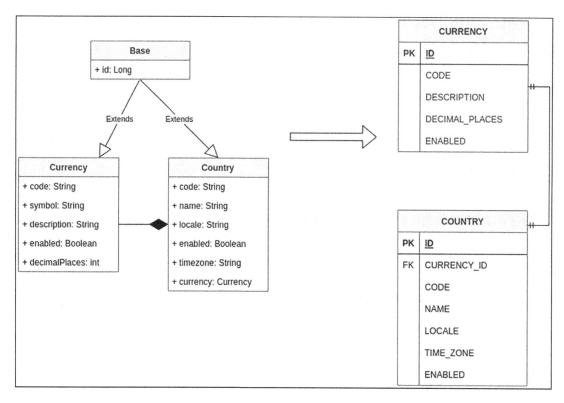

Figure 4-7. *Migrating the entities to a strategy of using a Mapped superclass*

Consider a hypothetical situation where you want to change the name of one attribute of the concrete class without changing anything more. JPA offers the possibility to override certain attributes of the abstract class indicating the new values; for example, let's change the name of the ID in the Currency entity to another value.

```
@Entity
@Table(name= "currency")
@AttributeOverride(
    name = "id",
    column = @Column(name = "currency_id", nullable = false))
 //.This implies that you override the name of the id for another one
public class Currency extends Base implements Serializable {

    // Attributes, constructors, setters, and getters for all the
    attributes
    // Override the hashcode and equals
}
```

This feature is extremely useful when you have multiple classes that have something in common but must include an exception for a certain class.

Table per Class Hierarchy

This approach represents an entire hierarchy of classes inside a single table. An alternative name for this strategy is **single table**. JPA uses this strategy as the default if you don't indicate anything explicitly using the **@Inheritance** annotation.

A table per class hierarchy implies that you need to add an extra column in the tables of the database which not appear in your entities because JPA needs to know to discriminate if the information of one row is from one class to another.

Let's introduce a few modifications to your catalog's applications to represent this specific situation. A new set of entities appear in Figure 4-8, representing that you can have cities and airports that are not directly connected. Both entities extend from the Base class, which no longer has the **@MappedSuperclass** annotation.

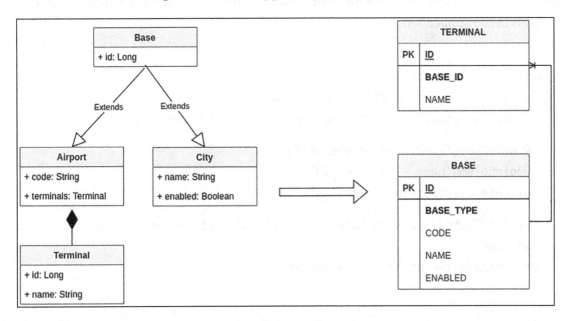

Figure 4-8. *New entities with single table relationship*

There are only two tables because the city and airport are part of one class and the BASE_TYPE column works as a discriminator to know which type of entity represents one row in the database. Remember that the code and name attributes are unique in the different tables.

```
@Entity
@Inheritance(strategy = InheritanceType.SINGLE_TABLE)
@DiscriminatorColumn(name = "BASE_TYPE")
public abstract class Base implements Serializable {

    @Id
    @GeneratedValue(strategy = GenerationType.SEQUENCE)
    private Long id;

    // Attributes, constructors, setters, and getters for all the
    attributes
    // Override the hashcode and equals

}
```

The only things you need to modify now are the City and the Airport entities to have the @DiscriminatorValue annotation with the value used in the database to know what entity is in the application.

```
@Entity
@Table(name= "airport")
@DiscriminatorValue( "AIR")
public class Airport extends Base implements Serializable {

    @OneToMany(fetch = FetchType.LAZY)
    @JoinColumn(name = "AIRPORT_ID")
    private List<Terminal> terminals;

    // Attributes, constructors, setters, and getters for all the
    attributes
    // Override the hashcode and equals

}
```

The city code is about the same but has a different **@DiscriminatorValue** annotation and attributes, but the logic is the same that appears in all the examples of this chapter. The only thing that did not exist previously in the catalog's application is the Terminal class, which has a relationship with the Airport entity.

```
@Entity
@Table(name= "terminal")
public class Terminal implements Serializable {

    @ManyToOne(fetch = FetchType.LAZY, optional = false)
    @JoinColumn(name = "AIRPORT_ID")
    private Airport airport;

    // Attributes, constructors, setters, and getters for all the
    attributes
    // Override the hashcode and equals

}
```

Note These modifications are an example of how the entities look if you want to use this strategy of inherence. This book uses **@MappedSupperclass**.

There are drawbacks to using this strategy; for example, you have several rows that only have columns with the information the other ones have null, so in a way, you lose all the constraints about not null values. Another problem is connected with the normalization of the information, which could impact the performance of the queries because there are many attributes. You decide which are relevant to introduce an index and which are not relevant.

This strategy introduces problems in the long term for stability, performance, and maintainability, so it's not recommended to use, at least in the new system.

Table per Subclass with Joins

This strategy is an alternative to the "table per class" hierarchy to solve the problem of having all the information with many rows with null columns in one table. To solve the problem of the previous strategy, this one produces a table per each concrete class of the hierarchy. You can directly access any of the entities using the repositories that provide Spring Data.

Following the previous example that introduces modifications to your catalog's application to represent a hypothetical situation, let's introduce a little variation in the previous scenario to generate one table per class.

Figure 4-9 shows the relationship between tables and the classes with this type of relationship.

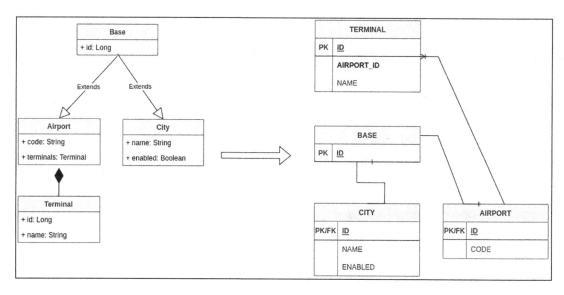

Figure 4-9. *New entities with a table per subclass*

There are the same number of classes that entities exist in the catalog's model where the City and the Airport ID has the same value as the Base table's primary key. To access the information implies a join between two tables. For example, if you want to access the information of a particular city, you create a repository as always, but behind the scenes, make a request to the Base table and join the City table.

Let's modify the Base class to change the strategy of inherence and nothing more. One of the benefits of both strategies, the previous one and this one, have the same representation in the JPA model, so you only need to change the database scripts.

```
@Entity
@Inheritance(strategy = InheritanceType.JOINED)
public abstract class Base implements Serializable {,

    @Id
    @GeneratedValue(strategy = GenerationType.SEQUENCE)
    private Long id;

    // Attributes, constructors, setters, and getters for all the
    attributes
    // Override the hashcode and equals
}
```

The next step is to modify the Airport class to include the attribute to do the joins between tables using the @**PrimaryKeyJoinColumn** annotation. This annotation is not required because JPA infers that both tables use the same ID, but if you want to use the @ **AttributeOverride** annotation, it's necessary to declare the name of the column.

```
@Entity
@Table(name= "airport")
@PrimaryKeyJoinColumn(name = "ID")
public class Airport extends Base implements Serializable {

    @OneToMany(fetch = FetchType.LAZY)
    @JoinColumn(name = "AIRPORT_ID")
    private List<Terminal> terminals;

    // Attributes, constructors, setters, and getters for all the
    attributes
    // Override the hashcode and equals
}
```

The advantage of this approach is that you must normalize the database and reduce the number of columns with null values, allowing the use of NOT NULL validations.

The disadvantage is that you must join between tables to obtain all the information, which could be a big pain if you have many records. Also, this problem appears when you insert or update the rows in this type of table because two sentences are executed per operation. Another problem with this strategy is manually writing the repository queries because they are more complex.

Table per Class

One of the problems of the previous strategy implies that you need to do a join to obtain all the information; in the table per class strategy, you have the information duplicate between the main entity and the inherited classes. You can access the information of both entities, in this case, Base or Airport/City, without doing a join between tables. This is one of the approaches that does not imply many things to do in your entities. Use the @**Inheritance** annotation with the **InheritanceType.TABLE_PER_CLASS** value in the top class. The Inherit classes do not need to include anything; they just extend from the Base class.

Following the previous example, let's do modifications by moving the "enabled" column to the Base class to have a scenario that gives you a better idea of what happens in both worlds, the database, and the catalog's application (see Figure 4-10).

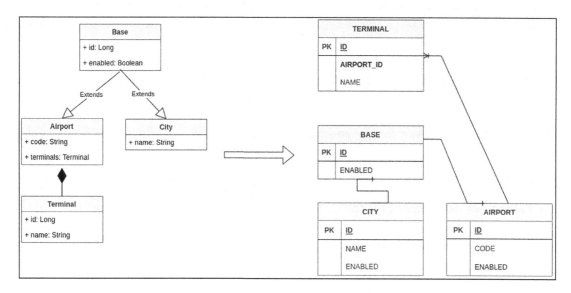

Figure 4-10. *New entities with a table per class*

The City and Airport tables have the same attributes—ID and ENABLED—in all the entities. You save information in the Base table, and one of the tables extends from it. This reduces the complexity. In the classes, the modifications are simple. You need to write the type of inheritance strategy in the Base class and anything else.

```
@Entity
@Inheritance(strategy = InheritanceType.TABLE_PER_CLASS)
public abstract class Base {

    @Id
    @GeneratedValue(strategy = GenerationType.SEQUENCE)
    private Long id;

    // Attributes, constructors, setters, and getters for all the
    attributes
    // Override the hashcode and equals

}
```

In the concrete class, you don't need to include anything. Just remove all the previous annotations that you used in the other strategies.

```
@Entity
@Table(name= "airport")
public class Airport extends Base {

    @OneToMany(fetch = FetchType.LAZY)
    @JoinColumn(name = "AIRPORT_ID")
    private List<Terminal> terminals;

    // Attributes, constructors, setters, and getters for all the
    attributes
    // Override the hashcode and equals

}
```

With this approach, you can create a repository per each table and access the specific information in each entity you want.

One of the cons of this strategy is that you have a lot of information duplicated in different tables. When doing a read operation like a select, you reduce the number of queries or joins necessary to obtain all the information. On the other hand, you need to execute a write operation like INSERT, DELETE, or UPDATE implies that you need to modify two tables to maintain the consistency of the database. All these considerations are valid. You access directly to the entity's repository.

Embeddable Class

All the previous ways of inherence imply that one class inherits from another one to reduce the duplicate code and model the system in a simpler way to understand. The embeddable class changes the paradigm because you can include a class in another, like an attribute but appear as part of the same table in the database.

Let's explore this approach practically by introducing modifications to the catalog's application to obtain something similar to Figure 4-11.

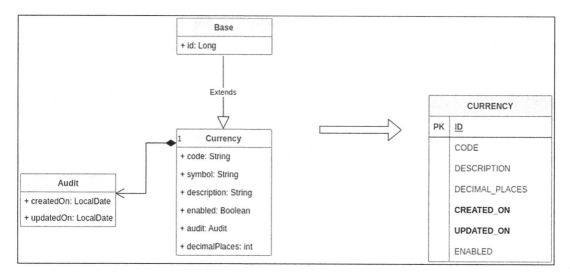

Figure 4-11. *Including an embeddable class in the Currency entity*

The first thing to do is create a new class that contains two attributes to audit when a new row is created in the database and when suffering a modification. The class needs to have the @Embeddable annotation, which means that it is not an entity per se because it lives inside another class using the composition. Listing 4-17 shows the class to audit the different entities, which you can embed on other classes.

Listing 4-17. Embeadeabble Class Which Contains the Attributes To Audit the Changes

```
@Embeddable
public class Audit implements Serializable {

    @Column(name = "created_on", nullable = false)
    private LocalDateTime createdOn;

    @Column(name = "updated_on", nullable = true) //Need to be null
    because the first time this attribute not have a value, only with the
    modifications have a value.
    private LocalDateTime updatedOn;

    // Attributes, constructors, setters, and getters for all the attributes
    // Override the hashcode and equals

}
```

Now that you have a class to include in many other entities, the next step is to modify the Currency entity to embed the Audit class using the @Embedded annotation (see Listing 4-18).

Listing 4-18. Modifications in the Currency Entity to Include the Embeddable Class

```
@Entity
@Table(name = "currency")
public class Currency extends Base implements Serializable {

    @Embedded
    private Audit audit;

    // Attributes, constructors, setters, and getters for all the
    attributes
    // Override the hashcode and equals

}
```

There are two changes that you need to introduce before re-running the application. One is executing the script with the name "**V2.0__audit_tables(run on chapter 4).sql**" that exists in the databases' folder, which includes the modification to the database to consider these new fields. The other changes imply creating a class AuditDTO in the same package containing the DTOs with the same attributes as the Audit class.

Note   The Audit class attributes need to be filled. You need to modify the CurrencyService update and save methods to assign a value. The next section explains how to do it automatically.

After that, if you re-run the application, you see a result similar to Figure 4-12, which invokes `http://localhost:8080/api/catalog/currency/1`.

```
←  →  C      ⓘ localhost:8080/api/catalog/currency/1

▾ {
      "id": 1,
      "code": "ARS",
      "description": "Peso argentino",
      "enable": null,
      "decimalPlaces": 2,
      "symbol": "$",
  ▾  "audit": {
          "createdOn": "2022-09-19T23:53:50.807376",
          "updatedOn": null
      }
  }
```

Figure 4-12. *Result of re-running the application a make a request*

This approach offers a way to reuse a class, including many entities, without using the inherence. Inside the application, you see the classes as a composition, so you can split or show the model differently.

Listening and Auditing Events

In the last section, you added attributes to the entities to audit the rows in the database. But you need to manually set the value of these attributes, which is not the best approach and implies that you repeat the logic in all the services.

JPA offers a set of annotations related to the events to check what happens in the life cycle of an entity and introduce logs or modifications. Let's look at some of the annotations available on the Table 4-8 to use and which is the specific purpose of each of them.

Table 4-8. *Events Available in the Life Cycle*

Events	Description
@jakarta.persistence.PrePersist and @jakarta.persistence.PostPersist	The event calls it after or before the entity has persisted.
@jakarta.persistence.PreUpdate and @jakarta.persistence.PostUpdate	The event calls it after or before the entity has been updated.
@ jakarta.persistence.PreRemove and @jakarta.persistence.PostRemove	The event calls it after or before the entity has been removed.
@ jakarta.persistence.PostLoad	The event calls it after the entity has been loaded successfully.

Note   There is no restriction to using one or more annotations over a method, so you can have the same behavior for **@PrePersist** and **@PreRemove**. Also, you can externalize all the logic of the persistence life cycle in one class and annotate the classes with **@EntityListeners(MyAuditListener.class)**.

In the catalog's application, you need **createdOn** to have a value before sending the insert to the database so let's move the Audit attribute from the Currency entity to the Base class to have the same behavior in all the classes that extend from the Base. Next, create two methods one assigns a value to **createOn** and the second to **updatedOn** using the current date. You can see all these modifications on the Listing 4-19.

Listing 4-19. Modifications in the Base Class to Fill the Fields

```
@MappedSuperclass
public abstract class Base {

    @Embedded
    private Audit audit;

    // Attributes, constructors, setters, and getters for all the
    attributes
    // Override the hashcode and equals
```

```
@PrePersist
public void fillCreatedOn() {
    audit.setCreatedOn(LocalDateTime.now());
}

@PreUpdate
public void fillUpdatedOn() {
    audit.setUpdatedOn(LocalDateTime.now());
}
}
```

In the Base class, there are annotations in each method. Each has a specific purpose and intercepts the persistence life cycle to do something. Let's check if everything works fine, re-run the application, and insert a new row in the Currency entity by making a POST request to `http://localhost:8080/api/catalog/currency`, as you can see on the Figure 4-13.

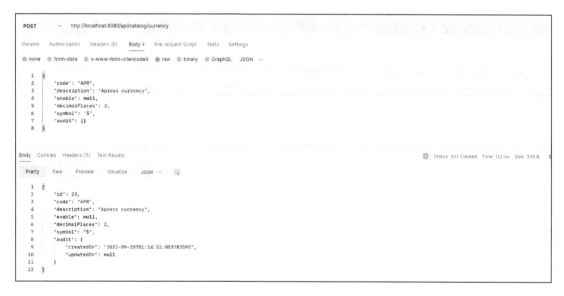

Figure 4-13. *Result of a POST in the Currency entity*

This solution of listening to the events of the JPA life cycle is the standard. In Spring Data, another annotation does about the same but with the idea of auditing when and who does the modifications. You only need to include the **@EnableJpaAuditing** annotation in your main class and add the listener in the classes you need to audit using **@EntityListeners(Aud itingEntityListener.class)** more or less in the same way that if you use the general approach of JPA. Table 4-9 show all the events available that you can use on your application.

Table 4-9. *Events Available in the Spring Data Life Cycle*

Events	Description
@CreatedDate and *@LastModifiedDate*	These annotations are equivalent to *@PreUpdate*, *@PrePersist*
@CreatedBy and *@LastModifiedBy*	These annotations are responsible for doing the modifications in the entity. In most cases, the annotations are used over a String attribute.

The way to obtain who is responsible for the changes is agnostic of which mechanism you use in your application. Spring Data has a good match to use Spring Security to obtain this information.

Validating the Schema

When you try to persist the information of one entity in the database, consider that all fields have valid values. There is no restriction to send a wrong value or an empty attribute, and the database throws an exception because the query is invalid. This situation implies that data travel across the network to produce the same result you can if you validate your application. Cloud providers like AWS and GCP charge for the information that travels the network, so if you can reduce the number of requests that go directly to the database, you reduce your costs.

To solve this problem, Java introduced specification JSR380,[2] which provides a set of annotations that cover the most relevant validations, like checking if something is null, empty, or has a particular size. The specification only declares the interfaces. For many years, the only implementation was Hibernate Validator.[3] But since Spring Boot 2, Spring Validator[4] has been an alternative option.

Note   A good practice is to use the validation in the first layer, a microservice that uses Spring Boot as the controller but is not exclusively. You can use it in another layer, like the service or repositories, if you have an implementation.

---

[2] https://beanvalidation.org/3.0/

[3] https://hibernate.org/validator/

[4] https://docs.spring.io/spring-framework/docs/current/javadoc-api/org/ springframework/validation/Validator.html

Let's modify the catalog's application by adding the dependency to validate the fields in the Currency entity.

Listing 4-20. Dependency to Validate the Fields

```
<dependency>
    <groupId>org.springframework.boot</groupId>
    <artifactId>spring-boot-starter-validation</artifactId>
</dependency>
```

The next step is to introduce the entity validation to cover all potential scenarios that can produce an exception in the database, so let's add it to the Currency entity.

Listing 4-21. Currency's Entity with Validations

```
import jakarta.persistence.*;
import jakarta.validation.constraints.Max;
import jakarta.validation.constraints.Min;
import jakarta.validation.constraints.NotBlank;
import jakarta.validation.constraints.NotNull;
import java.io.Serializable;
import java.util.Objects;

@Entity
@Table(name = "currency")
public class Currency extends Base implements Serializable {

    @Id
    @GeneratedValue(strategy = GenerationType.SEQUENCE)
    private Long id;

    @NotBlank(message = "Code is mandatory")
    @Column(name = "code", nullable = false, length = 4)
    private String code;

    @NotBlank(message = "Symbol is mandatory")
    @Column(name = "symbol", nullable = false, length = 4)
    private String symbol;
```

```
@NotBlank(message = "Description is mandatory")
@Column(name = "description", nullable = false, length = 30)
private String description;

@NotNull(message = "The state of the currency is mandatory")
@Column(name = "enabled", nullable = false)
private Boolean enabled = Boolean.TRUE;

@Min(value = 1, message = "The minimum value is 1")
@Max(value = 5, message = "The maximum value is 5")
@Column(name = "decimal_places")
private int decimalPlaces;

// Attributes, constructors, setters, and getters for all the attributes
// Override the hashcode and equals

}
```

The annotation has a message you see when you check if something is wrong. The message is written in English, but you can customize it. This approach implies a lot of modifications that are beyond the scope of this book. Table 4-10 shows the different annotations that exist to validate the value of the fields.

Table 4-10. *Annotation to Validate the Attributes*

Name	Description
@NotBlank	Validates that the string is not null or with whitespaces
@NotNull	Checks if the property is not null
@Min	Checks if the number is greater or equal to the value
@Max	Checks if the number is smaller or equal to the value
@AssertTrue	Validates if the value of the attribute is true or not
@Past and @PastOrPresent	Validate if the date is in the past or not the present
@Future and @FutureOrPresent	Validate if the date is in the future, including or not the present
@Positive and @PositiveOrZero	Validate if the number is positive, including or not the zero
@Negative and @NegativeOrZero	Validate if the number is negative, including or not the zero

When you define the rules in the entity, the next step is to invoke the validator in the service before persisting the entity and throwing an exception.

Listing 4-22. CurrencyService with Modifications to Validate the Entity

```
@Service
public class CurrrencyService {

    CurrencyRepository repository;     Validator validator;

    @Autowired
    public CurrrencyService(CurrencyRepository repository,  Validator
    validator) {
        this.repository = repository;          this.validator = validator;
    }

    public CurrencyDTO save(CurrencyDTO currency) {
        return saveInformation(currency);
    }

    public CurrencyDTO update(CurrencyDTO currency) {
        return saveInformation(currency);
    }

    private CurrencyDTO saveInformation(CurrencyDTO currency) {
        Currency entity =  ApiMapper.INSTANCE.DTOToEntity(currency);

        Set<ConstraintViolation<Currency>> violations = validator.
        validate(entity);
        if(!violations.isEmpty()) {
            throw new ConstraintViolationException(violations);
        }

        Currency savedEntity = repository.save(entity);
         return ApiMapper.INSTANCE.entityToDTO(savedEntity);
    }
}
```

If you don't do anything else, the stack trace appears when you request the endpoint to persist the information of the currency. Let's create classes to obtain a better response. Let's start creating the DTOs that return the information about the errors.

Listing 4-23. DTO That Contains the Problem Details

```
public class ViolationDTO {

    private String field;
    private String message;

    public ViolationDTO(String field, String message) {
        this.field = field;
        this.message = message;
    }

    // Attributes, constructors, setters, and getters for all the
    attributes
}
```

After that, create a DTO that contains the list of errors because some attributes do not follow the rules.

Listing 4-24. DTO That Contains a List of Problems

```
public class ValidationErrorDTO {
    private List<ViolationDTO> violations;

    public ValidationErrorDTO() {
        violations = new ArrayList<>();
    }

    // Attributes, constructors, setters, and getters for all the
    attributes
}
```

The next step is to create a class that captures all the exceptions that appear in the application and do something depending on which exceptions are thrown. This class listens to all the exceptions that appear in the application. You need to create a specific` behavior for each exception because if not, the application only throws an exception.

Listing 4-25. Declaration of the Handler To Capture the Exceptions in the application

```
@ControllerAdvice
public class ErrorHandlingControllerAdvice {

    @ExceptionHandler(ConstraintViolationException.class)
    @ResponseStatus(HttpStatus.BAD_REQUEST)
    @ResponseBody
    ValidationErrorDTO onConstraintValidationException(
            ConstraintViolationException e) {
        ValidationErrorDTO error = new ValidationErrorDTO();
        for (ConstraintViolation violation : e.getConstraintViolations()) {
            error.getViolations().add(
                    new ViolationDTO(violation.getPropertyPath().toString(),
                    violation.getMessage()));
        }
        return error;
    }
}
```

Lastly, re-run the application and invoke the endpoint to create a new currency with an empty body and see what happens. If everything is okay you will see a result like the Figure 4-14.

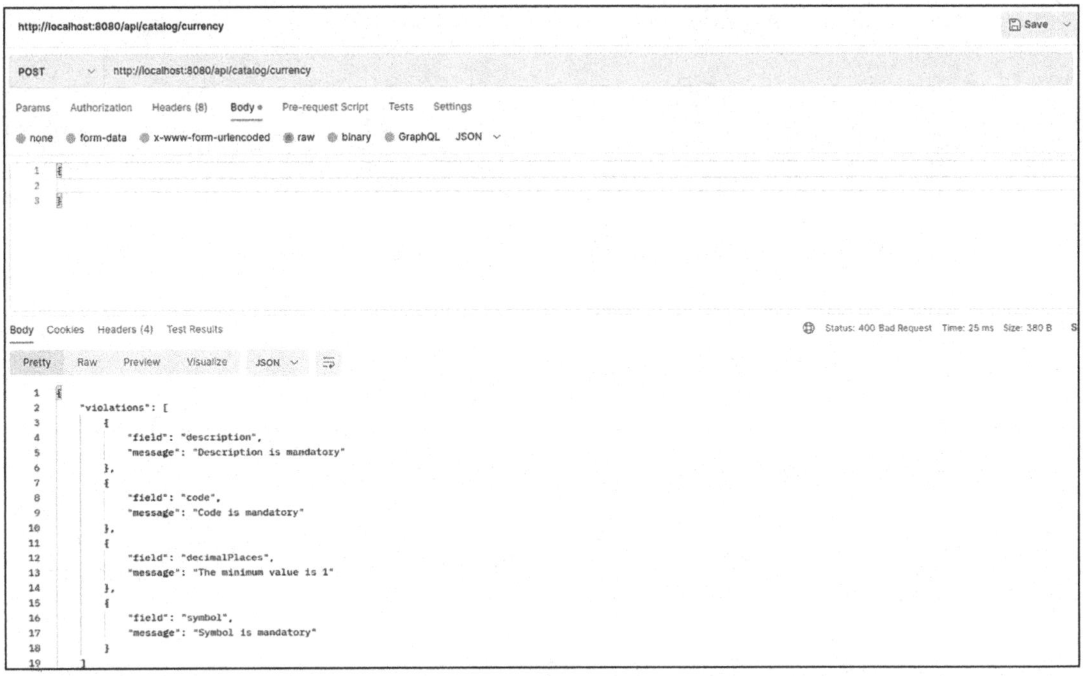

Figure 4-14. *Result of invoking the currency endpoint with the empty body*

Introduce validations to your entity and reduce the risk of sending the information to the database in a bad format that can produce an exception when executing the operation. The exceptions could be related to the size of the attribute, whether it accepts null or not, and other things you can validate.

Summary

This chapter overviewed how to create a structure of the entities that interact to represent a database using strategies to obtain information, like eager or lazy loading, depending on your business. You also learned about hierarchy strategies and their pros and cons.

The chapter included validations in the entities to prevent sending the information to the database to produce an exception. You can do the validations in the first layers that receive the request before going to the layer that accesses the database.

CHAPTER 5

Transaction Management

As you saw in the previous chapters of this book, you can execute simple queries to obtain information. Still, there are other cases when the situation is complex and involves updating/inserting/deleting tables across the same database.

One of the essential features of the relational database is the possibility of having a mechanism that provides security and does not affect the quality of the information if something happens. These terms are known as *consistency* and *integrity*.

You may think this is not extremely important, but imagine you want to transfer money from your bank account to someone. You can lose money if you don't have a mechanism that guarantees an error will not affect your account.

Figure 5-1 shows the problem of not rolling back a bank account status.

© Andres Sacco 2023
A. Sacco, *Beginning Spring Data*, https://doi.org/10.1007/978-1-4842-8764-4_5

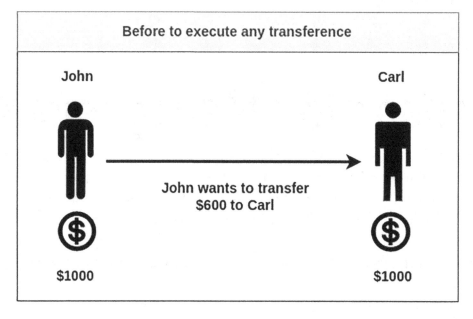

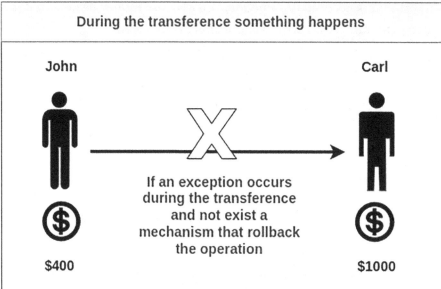

Figure 5-1. *Not rolling back bank account status*

Another problem could be the concurrency of the operations that modify the information in one or more tables. Following the previous example of the bank account, what happens if you share the account with your girlfriend/boyfriend and both simultaneously want to withdraw a certain amount that exceeds the availability of money in the account?

These problems are solved in the database using transactions. This chapter discusses the basic concepts that involve a transaction and how you can transpose the concepts to Spring Data.

What Is a Transaction?

There are multiple definitions of the meaning of one transaction. In this book, a transaction is a set of write and read operations grouped for criteria that need to be executed to ensure that all operations are executed or not one of them.

In 1981, Jim Gray was one of the first to define most of the concepts about transactions in his paper "The transaction concept: virtues and Limitations."[1] This paper inspires some of the SQL standards defined in 1986 and evolved SQL versions. The paper mentioned other concepts connected with transactions, like atomicity, consistency, and durability, which are discussed in the next section.

A transaction in a database starts with the BEGIN_TRANSACTION keyword and needs to indicate that all the operations end successfully using the COMMIT keyword. So, the database takes this instruction and ensures this is the new state for the affected rows. On the other hand, when operations fail, you need to invoke the ROLLBACK keyword to indicate that the database needs to back to the previous state before all the operations are executed. Figure 5-2 shows the transaction process.

---

[1]http://jimgray.azurewebsites.net/papers/thetransactionconcept.pdf

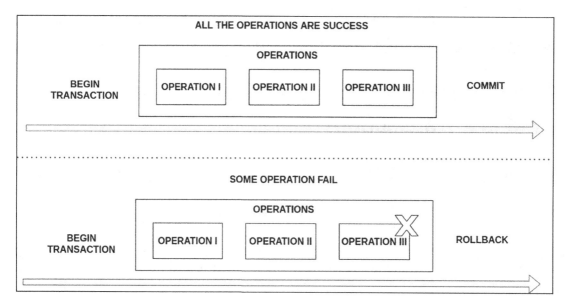

Figure 5-2. *Transaction process*

Let's recap some transaction topics to understand how this concept works before moving it into the Spring Data universe.

What Is ACID?

ACID is an acronym that refers to four concepts: atomicity, consistency, isolation, and durability. These concepts apply to all the transactions in a relational database and must be implemented to preserve the information; let's look at the meaning of each of them.

- **Atomicity** is creating a single work unit that contains one or multiple operations. Each must be finished successfully for the transactions to end okay. If one of the operations fails, all the operations must be rolled back to return the database to the previous state.

- **Consistency** means that you need to move the database from one valid status to another one. Each database has integrity rules to check if everything is okay when insert/update/delete operations are executed; these rules check if the column type, length, and nullability are correct. Also, the rules cover things like the constraint with other tables and if one of the tables needs to have a unique value in a column.

Note   Not all the databases declare the columns or the way to generate the primary key in the same way, so it's important to validate the structure of the tables and the queries.

To reduce the chance of producing errors during any operation (insert/update/delete), you can include the validation annotations you saw in the previous chapter to prevent sending something to the database that produces an exception.

- **Isolation** refers to the possibility that two or more operations try to modify the same information at the same moment. The database needs to guarantee that the information only is visible to other people when all the operations of the transactions finish okay. Each database must provide a mechanism to solve or mitigate this problem. There is a locking mechanism to solve the problems of concurrency in the databases, as discussed later in this chapter.

- **Durability** ensures that all the transactions are completed successfully, and changing the status of the database to a new one needs to be permanent and gives you a chance to obtain the same information that you modified previously. There are cases where the modifications are not impacted into the database, like when you use a copy of the database that is only read-only.

Note   It is not in the scope of this book to explain each concept related to a relational database. These sections overview the concepts connected with a transaction with the idea that you obtain the basic knowledge to understand what happens behind the scenes when you use Spring Data.

Isolation Problems

There are a set of common problems related to the isolation that affect the transactions that are executed simultaneously. Sometimes, you lose updates or read information not confirmed in the database. Let's briefly overview each problem.

- **Lost update**: Imagine that two simultaneous transactions try to modify the same row in a table that contains the code of a particular city in the catalog API. The last commit in the database wins but may not be the correct one. Figure 5-3 shows the problem with having two simultaneous transactions.

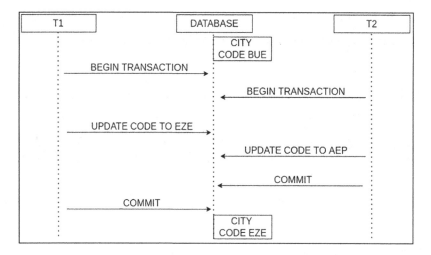

Figure 5-3. *Two transactions at once*

- A **dirty read** occurs when two or more transactions simultaneously obtain or use the information in a database before the changes of another transaction are committed. So the transactions use information that may not exist. For example, imagine that you update an attribute in the countries in your catalog to use a particular currency inserted in another transaction. If the transaction that inserts the new currency fails, you have an inconsistency in your database because most countries will have a currency that does not exist. If someone selects a country before the transaction is committed or rolled back, they could potentially use incorrect information. Figure 5-4 shows the problem connected with a dirty read.

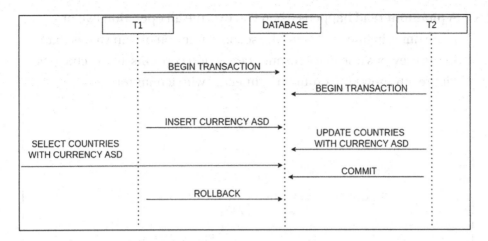

Figure 5-4. *The problem connected with a dirty read*

- An **unrepeatable read** happens when one transaction obtains certain information, but when trying to obtain the same information again, another transaction modifies the information. Figure 5-5 shows the problem connected with an unrepeatable read.

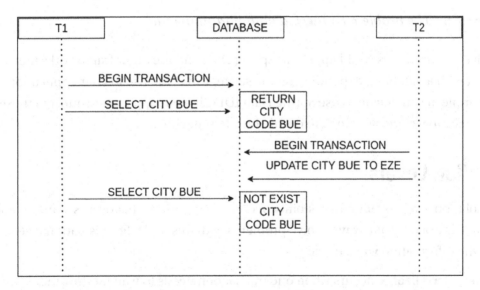

Figure 5-5. *The problem connected with unrepeatable read*

149

- A **phantom read** happens when you execute an operation two or more times in one table, and the second time you obtain values than in the previous one because one transaction commits all the changes. Figure 5-6 shows the problem connected with a phantom read.

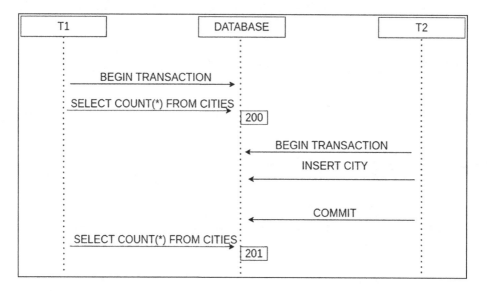

Figure 5-6. *The problem connected with phantom read*

All these problems could appear in Spring Data and the other frameworks that interact with a database, depending on the strategy that you use in your application; for example, if you decide to use Spring Data JDBC in your application, most of these problems appear, and you need to decide how to mitigate it.

Isolation Levels

The isolation levels refer to the visibility of other transactions that occurs simultaneously. But there is not only one way to solve problems with this topic. Four isolation levels affect the information you can see.

- **Serializable** occurs when one transaction needs to wait for the other transaction to finish after starting. The database needs to provide a mechanism to implement this solution, for example, block the entire tables until the transaction is finished. This approach implies that you lost performance in your database.

- **Repeatable reads** allow you to start multiple transactions when one is running, so you can have phantom readings.

- **Read committed** allows you to access the information. But there is a mechanism of locking in the writing transaction that needs to block other transactions that try to access one particular row but do not affect the transactions that only want to read the information.

- **Read uncommitted** is one of the most restricted levels because one transaction may not write a particular row if another transaction is not finished and commit all the changes. This type of restriction does not affect the reading operations.

Table 5-1 represents all the isolations levels with potential issues that can appear, whereas the green arrow represents which problems can appear.

Table 5-1. *Isolation Levels and Associated Issues*

Levels/Issues	Lost update	Dirty read	Unrepeatable read	Phantom reading
Serializable	✔	✔	✔	✔
Repeatable reads	✔	✔	✔	✘
Read committed	✔	✔	✘	✘
Read uncommitted	✔	✘	✘	✘

There is no perfect way to solve the problem with isolation. Each solution has a tradeoff, and you need to sacrifice something to obtain a better performance or improve the quality of the information you use.

The high isolation levels required the database to block other possible transactions that simultaneously affect the same information. The lower levels allow users to find information that could be uncommitted, so you can see something that could produce an exception and rollback.

Locking Types

Locking is a way to solve problems connected with isolation. This is extremely useful when you have an application with many simultaneous operations.

There are two locking mechanisms.

- **Pessimist**: This locking level is the most common because you assume that problems with multiple transactions could happen. You need to create or use a mechanism to indicate into the database to lock the row or the table. This approach guarantees that one transaction has the chance to update the row because you lock the row/table/database, but the main problem with this approach is that a bottleneck in the transactions takes time to be executed.

- **Optimist**: This mechanism does not lock in a database because it uses an alternative way to control the changes. Each row has a numeric column containing the row's version, so when an operation needs to be executed in the row, check which is the version of the column. Each operation that needs to modify the row increments the version number, one transaction has the chance to do it, and you have a mechanism to detect if the information of one row in your application is the latest version or not.

You can use another type of column to represent the version, for example, timestamp, but it's not a good idea because the precision of the type depends on the database.

How Do These Concepts Work in Spring Data?

All the concepts appearing in the previous section are simple to implement using Spring annotations that cover the most relevant scenarios.

@Transactional is an important annotation that you can use in a method, class, or interface which creates a proxy class that has the responsibility to create the transaction and commit/roll back all the operations inside the transaction. This annotation is connected directly with Spring TX (***org.springframework.transaction.annotation. Transactional***), which is not the same as JEE. This annotation only works for the public methods because it's a constraint of the proxy classes of Spring Framework, so if you put the annotation in the private/protected Spring Framework, you ignore them without showing any error on the console or in your IDE.

Figure 5-7 shows how a transaction works with Spring Interceptor, which is part of the Spring Framework.

Controller

```
@DeleteMapping(value = ∘∨"/{id}")
public ResponseEntity<Void> delete(@PathVariable Long id) {
    countryService.delete(id);
    return ResponseEntity.ok().build();
}
```

Spring Interceptor

```
try {

    //Start the transaction

    //Call the service method

    //Commit the transaction
} catch(RuntimeException e) {
    //Rollback the transaction
}
```

Service

```
@Transactional(isolation = Isolation.DEFAULT)
public void delete(Long id) throws InterruptedException {
    Optional<Country> country = countryRepository.findById(id);
    List<State> states = stateRepository.findAllByCountryId(country.get().getId());

    if(country.isPresent()) {
        country.get().setEnabled(Boolean.FALSE);
        countryRepository.save(country.get());

        Thread.sleep( t 2000L);

        for (State state: states) {
            state.setEnabled(Boolean.FALSE);
            stateRepository.save(state);
        }
    }
}
```

Figure 5-7. *A transaction works with Spring Interceptor*

When you use Spring Boot with Spring Data in your application, you don't need to do anything; use the **@Transactional** annotation, but if you don't use Spring Boot, you need to enable the transaction manager creating a bean that follows the hierarchy **PlatformTransactionManager**[2] with the **@EnableTransactionManagement** annotation.

Note   The interceptor only captures RuntimeException and the class hierarchy and executes the rollback. But, you can override the default behavior to do the rollback for certain exceptions using the rollbackFor or rollbackForClassName properties. If you don't want to roll back, there are properties like noRollbackFor and noRollbackForClassName. Another problem can appear if you include a try/catch block in your method that captures RuntimeException and does not throw again. The interceptor does not do anything.

Listing 5-1 modifies the CountryService DELETE method to include the annotation and disables all the states associated with one country.

Listing 5-1. An Example Transaction

```
@Service
public class CountryService {

    @Transactional(readOnly = false)
    public void delete(Long id) throws InterruptedException
{
        Optional<Country> country = countryRepository.findById(id);
        List<State> states = stateRepository.findAllByCountryId(country.
        get().getId());

        if(country.isPresent()) {
            country.get().setEnabled(Boolean.FALSE);
            countryRepository.save(country.get());

            Thread.sleep(2000L); // For the purposes of simulate different
            scenarios
```

---

[2] https://docs.spring.io/spring-framework/docs/current/javadoc-api/org/springframework/transaction/PlatformTransactionManager.html

```
        for (State state: states) {
            state.setEnabled(Boolean.FALSE);
            stateRepository.save(state);
        }
    }
  }
}
```

By default, each method annotated with @Transactional has the chance to only execute one transaction at a time to prevent any of the problems that you read in the previous section. The next section explains how to change this behavior to another.

Now, if you introduce all the changes and try to call more than one at a time to the DELETE method using `http://localhost:8080/api/catalog/country/1`, you see that the first transaction or call executes all the modifications, and the second one wait to start. This happens because the default isolation level only admits one transaction at a time.

Transactional Properties

Listing 5-2 lists things you can indicate with the **@Transactional** annotation.

Listing 5-2. An Example of the Read-Only Attribute

```
@Transactional(readOnly = true)
public CountryDTO getById(Long id) {
    // All the logic of the method
}
```

If the transaction is read-only, the framework and the database introduce optimizations to this type of operation. The main problem with the incorrect use of this property appears when you use it in methods that write modifications in the database. It does not persist, and the modifications are lost.

You can indicate that one transaction must be rollback when particular exceptions happen inside your method or class using the **rollbackFor** or **rollbackForClassName** properties, indicating the name of the exception. Or you can do the opposite using the noRollbackFor or noRrollbackForClassName properties (see Listing 5-3).

Listing 5-3. An Example of Rollback

```
@Transactional(readOnly = true, rollbackFor = { SQLException.class })
public CountryDTO getById(Long id) {
    // All the logic of the method
}
```

You can indicate the level of isolation you want to use in this particular method/class, which could be different from another part of the application (see Listing 5-4). The isolation levels in the annotation are the same as in this chapter's "Isolation Levels" section. The values of the Isolation enum are **ISOLATION_DEFAULT, ISOLATION_ READ_UNCOMMITTED, ISOLATION_READ_COMMITTED, ISOLATION_ REPEATABLE_READ, ISOLATION_SERIALIZABLE**. The default isolation level is **ISOLATION_DEFAULT**, where you obtain the value for your database.

Listing 5-4. An Example of Changing Isolation Level

```
@Transactional(readOnly = true, isolation = Isolation.SERIALIZABLE)
public CountryDTO getById(Long id) {
    // All the logic of the method
}
```

There is no support[3] for isolation levels in versions prior to Spring to 4.1.

One feature that does not have an equivalent in the common transactions is the chance to set a timeout to finish the entire operation (see Listing 5-5). If the transaction does not finish in the timeout, Spring does the rollback automatically. The default value is –1, meaning the transaction could take time to finish.

Listing 5-5. An Example of Setting Timeout

```
@Transactional(readOnly = true, timeout = 1000) // Timeout is expressed in
milliseconds
public CountryDTO getById(Long id) {
    // All the logic of the method
}
```

---

[3] https://github.com/spring-projects/spring-framework/issues/9687

Another property that does not have a direct correlation with the transaction world in a database or it's very frequently seen is when a method/class that is transactional invokes another one, so the second method is executed in which transaction (see Listing 5-6).

Listing 5-6. An Example of Setting Propagation Level

```
@Transactional(readOnly = true, propagation = Propagation.MANDATORY)
public CountryDTO getById(Long id) {
    // All the logic of the method
}
```

There is an enum **Propagation** in the **org.springframework.transaction. annotation** package, which contains the following values.

- **REQUIRED** means that methods or classes use the same transaction and do not create a new one. But if the first method is not transactional, Spring creates a new one. This value is the default that takes Spring Framework.

- **SUPPORTS** means that if there is a transaction in progress, use the same for both methods, but if it does not exist, a transaction does not create one.

- **MANDATORY** is similar to SUPPORTS, but if there is no transaction in progress, **NoTransactionException** occurs.

- **REQUIRES_NEW** means that when a transaction is in progress, it pauses it, and a new one starts; but if there is no transaction in progress, it creates a new one.

- **NOT_SUPPORTED** is a variant of the previous scenario because if a transaction is in progress, it pauses, and all the transactional methods are executed without a transaction.

- **NEVER** means that if a transaction is running when a method with this property, **IllegalTransactionStateException** is thrown.

- **NESTED** is one of the most complex because it implies that it creates a new subtransaction to execute all the code. If an exception occurs, everything returns to the status before calling the method.

You can check to modify the previous example to check each particular property, but there is no magic rule to apply in different situations. In most cases, you must analyze the tradeoff of modifying each property's custom value to use another value.

Transaction Template

There is another way to declare a transaction in Spring without using **@Transactional** with all the properties from the previous section. This alternative allows you to set all the attributes related to one transaction and execute them in a block of code. You can do this using TransactionTemplate like any other template in Spring. Listing 5-7 transforms Listing 5-1 to use TransactionTemplate.

Listing 5-7. Transform Listing 5-1

@Service

```
public class CountryService {

    private final TransactionTemplate transactionTemplate;

    @Autowired
    public CountryService(PlatformTransactionManager transaction manager,
    CountryRepository countryRepository, StateRepository stateRepository,
                Validator validator) {
        this.transactionTemplate = new TransactionTemplate(transactio
        nManager);
        transactionTemplate.setReadOnly(false);
        transactionTemplate.setTimeout(1000);

        //Set other properties of the transaction and other attributes
    }
    public void delete(Long id) throws InterruptedException {

        Optional<Country> country = countryRepository.findById(id);
        List<State> states = stateRepository.findAllByCountryId(country.
        get().getId());

        this.transactionTemplate.execute(new
        TransactionCallbackWithoutResult() {
```

```
public void doInTransactionWithoutResult(TransactionStatus
status) {
    try {
        if(country.isPresent()) {
            country.get().setEnabled(Boolean.FALSE);
            countryRepository.save(country.get());

            Thread.sleep(2000L);

            for (State state: states) {
                state.setEnabled(Boolean.FALSE);
                stateRepository.save(state);
            }
        }
    } catch(NoSuchElementException | InterruptedException ex) {
        status.setRollbackOnly();
    }
}
});
}
}
```

You can sound round only a piece of code in your method with the transaction, not the entire method, so you, as a developer, have control over which sections are relevant to include in a transaction.

The primary problems with this approach are that it is difficult to maintain and multiple blocks of code are duplicated.

Optimistic Locking

In Spring Data, the default locking type is the pessimist type, so you don't need to do anything. You only need to add the mechanism to solve the conflict or problems related to the isolation.

The other approach is to use an optimistic lock that implies including an extra attribute with the @**Version** annotation in each entity that you want to use this type of locking without doing anything else. Let's modify the Base class with the new attribute and the setters/getters (see Listing 5-8).

Listing 5-8. An Example of the Version Attribute

```java
@MappedSuperclass
public abstract class Base {

    //Other properties

    @Version
    private Long version;

    //Other setters and getters
    public Long getVersion() {
        return version;
    }

    public void setVersion(Long version) {
        this.version = version;
    }
}
```

You need to include in the database the alter tables sentences which create the new column responsible for containing the version of the rows (see Listing 5-9).

Listing 5-9. Alter Tables in the Database

```sql
ALTER TABLE currency ADD COLUMN version int NOT NULL DEFAULT 0;

ALTER TABLE country ADD COLUMN version int NOT NULL DEFAULT 0;

ALTER TABLE state ADD COLUMN version int NOT NULL DEFAULT 0;

ALTER TABLE city ADD COLUMN version int NOT NULL DEFAULT 0;
```

Also, you need to include the version attribute in all the DTOs without any type of annotation so that when you do a GET method, you receive the version attribute, which you need to send in all the operations that imply modifications in the database. Another approach is to not expose the version and use the attribute for internal purposes in your microservice.

After that, you can invoke the GET method of the currency to obtain the information in the database before updating it (see Listing 5-10).

Listing 5-10. Request/Response of a GET Endpoint

Request
```
GET localhost:8090/api/catalog/currency/1
```

Response
```
{
    "id": 1,
    "code": "ARS",
    "description": "Peso argentino",
    "enable": null,
    "decimalPlaces": 2,
    "symbol": "$",
    "audit": {
        "createdOn": "2022-05-01T23:19:52.219215",
        "updatedOn": null
    },
    "version": 0
}
```

If you execute the PUT method in the same body multiples times without changing the attribute version, an exception explains that another transaction updated the information in the database. Your last request has an older version of the data (see Listing 5-11).

Listing 5-11. Request/Response of PUT Endpoint

Request
```
PUT localhost:8090/api/catalog/currency/1
```

Response
```
{
    "timestamp": "2022-06-23T03:02:16.390+00:00",
    "status": 500,
    "error": "Internal Server Error",
```

```
"trace": "org.springframework.orm.
ObjectOptimisticLockingFailureException: Object of class [com.apress.
catalog.model.Currency] with identifier [1]: optimistic locking failed;
nested exception is org.hibernate.StaleObjectStateException: Row was
updated or deleted by another transaction (or unsaved-value mapping was
incorrect)"
}
```

Remember, one approach is to expose the "version" attribute in the endpoint, but when an exception occurs, a good practice transforms the message into something more human-readable.

Summary

This chapter discussed the benefits of transactions in your applications. But depending on the propagation approach and isolation level, you may experience associated issues. You must decide the best approach for your application considering your business. In some situations, a dirty read problem is not something so bad, but in other contexts could be an error.

Versioning or Migrating Changes

One of the main problems every developer had at least once in her life was introducing modifications to a database. Changes to a database always have problems like who is in charge of executing the scripts or where you saved it in different environments because some developers use an email or file to send to the database administrator to execute. A common problem is how you are sure that all the changes to the databases are executed before deploying the applications that need those changes, which in most cases implies that someone manually checks if everything is okay or not. Another possible problem could be the rollback of the changes on the database in case that something wrong happens. If you detect that your code is wrong or has problems, you can solve it by doing a rollback manually to revert the changes by executing a new script in the database, but this solution could introduce more failures.

This chapter discusses tools and strategies that reduce the risk of introducing problems with making changes and how you can integrate these tools with Spring Data to execute the changes.

You also learn how to implement a feature flag to reduce the risk of deploying something in production which could fail and need to redeploy the application reverting the changes.

Versioning Changes in a Database

You've had a brief overview of the common problems connected with relational databases that have changes in the structure of the tables or the columns. Most of the problems related to the changes could be mitigated using various methods; for example, if you need to add a new column to a table, you can add accepting null values, check if everything works fine, and then transform it into a not null column. This type of solution could work if the changes are simple and can be executed in the step, but

163

© Andres Sacco 2023
A. Sacco, *Beginning Spring Data*, https://doi.org/10.1007/978-1-4842-8764-4_6

imagine a situation that implies changing the entire table structure or adding new tables with constraints with the existing ones. These scenarios are not simple to introduce the changes because something could fail. Lastly, it's difficult to track the changes during the life of one application that uses a database schema. If you don't have a record of the changes, you don't know which changes affect the application's performance.

Now, versioning the changes into a database try to solve most of the problems of the previous paragraphs sharing all the changes that a database suffers in a way that could be reproducible for anyone in any environment. Other benefits like creating scripts to introduce the changes to load information or modify the structure of the database; this benefit is especially useful when someone wants to run the entire application locally. On the Figure 6-1 you can see the process of versioning the changes of the database.

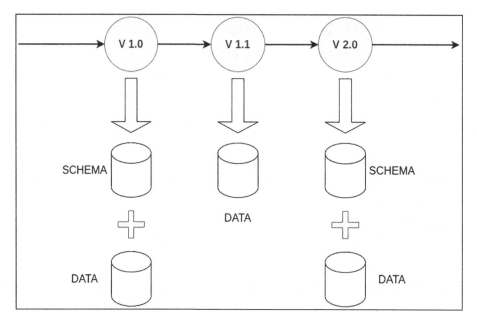

Figure 6-1. *Process of executing changes in a database*

Behind the scenes, most of the tools discussed in the following sections do the same, have a certain number of scripts in folders that have a structure of names that uniquely identify, so when you execute a command to do the migrations of the new changes read each of them and check if the changes are applied in the database. To check if the scripts were executed or not, most of the tools create one or more tables that contain all the information related to the previous executions, which contain the name of the script and other relevant information for the tool. With all this information, the tools could know the actual status of a database and revert to a previously valid status. A valid status is when all the changes in one script are executed. This approach works as a transactional operation because the tools must maintain the database consistently at every moment. An example of how the approach to maintain consistent the changes on the database appears on Figure 6-2.

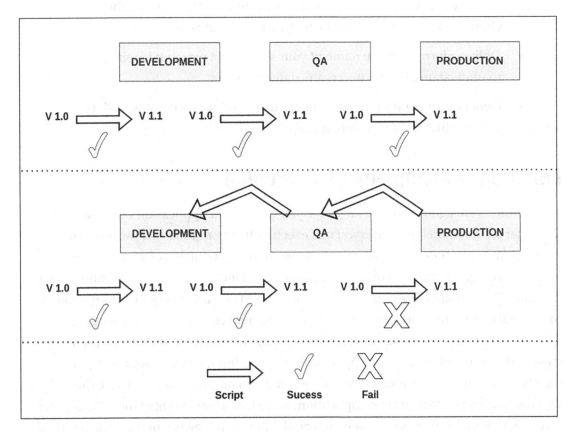

Figure 6-2. *Process of executing changes in different environments*

The following are things to consider in these types of tools.

- All the scripts that represent migrations need to be written in SQL Scripts because the idea is to automatize the process of doing the changes in the database, which in some cases, developers test in their local environment doing the modifications, so it's not a good idea learn a new meta-language to do it.

165

- If you made a mistake with the length or a type of column and executed the changes in your environments, create a new script that solves the problem. You must not change your scripts after they are executed because it could produce an exception depending on which tool you use. Some tools have a checksum to determine if the executed file is the same or suffers changes; others ignore the changes because they do not run the same script again.

- Define a format for the name of your scripts in a way that it's simple to understand, like V1.0__create_database.sql.

- Generate a migration file containing all the relevant changes, and try not to split the changes into multiple files.

Libraries That Implement Versioning

Most libraries are agnostic to the language you use in your application because they offer a command line where you can execute the operations, like introducing the modifications or doing a rollback. If you want to use it outside of a Spring Boot application, a good practice could be running using Docker images with a volume that contains all the changes; this approach is a good decision because you are sure that the tool is well configured and you don't have any problem connected with your machine.

There is not a common approach to versioning the changes, but most of them suggest that you include all the scripts into a git repository, so you have a way to track the changes in the files, not only the changes in the database. When you save the scripts into the same repository of your application, there is the versioning of the changes and give semantics to the scripts about which application is the owner of the information if you follow the principle of the microservices to only one application that accesses one database schema.

In the ecosystem, multiple options like Liquibase,[1] Flyway,[2] and others are not covered in this book because there are few users, and the documentation to integrate with various languages or frameworks is not exhausted.

---

[1] https://www.liquibase.org/
[2] https://flywaydb.org/

Flyway

Flyway[3] is one of the libraries that implement the versioning of the changes offering the possibility to run as a command line in various operating systems, like Windows, macOS, and Linux. Also, you can include it in your Java application using Maven/Gradle.

Note The tool works only with version 8 or up of Java but does not mention that have support for versions 14 or up. But in the official repository, there are bugs associated with version 17, so check the latest version of this library because there is a chance that it solves some reported issues.

This tool offers two alternatives: community and teams edition. The main differences between both alternatives are the number of features they offer; for example, the team's edition provides the following.

- A mechanism to undo the changes in a database (You have a way to indicate the order of the undoing of a certain number of scripts.)
- A way to simulate the changes before doing it in the database to check if everything is okay with your scripts
- A large number of callbacks or hooks
- The possibility of storing the scripts in AWS or GCP

The tool offers a default naming structure to recognize the types of operations, but you can customize the pattern. The file name must have four parts: the first indicates the type of operation, the second states the version, the third briefly describes the file, and the fourth is the suffix, which in most cases is .sql. You can see the structure of the name files of the tool on the Figure 6-3.

[3] https://flywaydb.org/

167

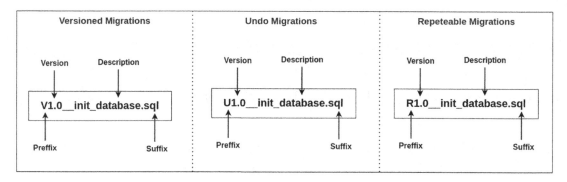

Figure 6-3. *Structure for naming an operation*

The suffix could be .sql, but you can write the sentence in a Java class that extends from **BaseJavaMigration**.[4] In both cases, Flyway generates a table called **flyway_ schema_history**, which contains all the information of the executed scripts. You can imagine this table as the history of a git repository.

Note   In this book's source code, the files related to the database structure follow this name pattern because you include it in the code of the microservice catalog.

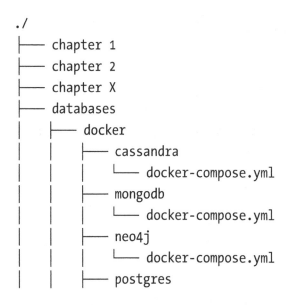

```
./
├── chapter 1
├── chapter 2
├── chapter X
├── databases
│   ├── docker
│   │   ├── cassandra
│   │   │   └── docker-compose.yml
│   │   ├── mongodb
│   │   │   └── docker-compose.yml
│   │   ├── neo4j
│   │   │   └── docker-compose.yml
│   │   ├── postgres
```

---

[4]https://flywaydb.org/documentation/usage/api/javadoc/org/flywaydb/core/api/migration/BaseJavaMigration

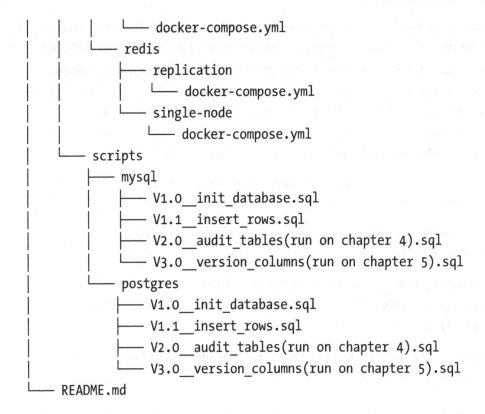

```
|   |   |   └── docker-compose.yml
|   |   └── redis
|   |       ├── replication
|   |       |   └── docker-compose.yml
|   |       └── single-node
|   |           └── docker-compose.yml
|   └── scripts
|       ├── mysql
|       |   ├── V1.0__init_database.sql
|       |   ├── V1.1__insert_rows.sql
|       |   ├── V2.0__audit_tables(run on chapter 4).sql
|       |   └── V3.0__version_columns(run on chapter 5).sql
|       └── postgres
|           ├── V1.0__init_database.sql
|           ├── V1.1__insert_rows.sql
|           ├── V2.0__audit_tables(run on chapter 4).sql
|           └── V3.0__version_columns(run on chapter 5).sql
└── README.md
```

To execute scripts in the database, you need to indicate a user with the password with the right access to execute certain operations. To hide this information from everyone, someone on your DevOps teams could add the user/password in the environments as a variable. Hence, you reduce the risk that something could happen if someone obtains this information.

Lastly, Flyway offers a series of commands that could be helpful, like **validate** to check if all the scripts are executed correctly and clean, which cleans all the information that exists in the schema (only use it in test environments)

Liquibase

Liquibase offers the possibility to use it in separate operating systems and Java projects that use Maven/Gradle. Also, the tool allows you to use it in CI/CD tools, including GitHub Actions[5] and Jenkins.[6]

---

[5] https://docs.liquibase.com/workflows/liquibase-community/setup-github-actions-workflow.html

[6] https://docs.liquibase.com/workflows/liquibase-community/using-the-jenkins-pipeline-stage-with-spinnaker.html

Liquibase has three editions: Open Source, Pro, and Enterprise. It has a UI interface that provides reports and monitoring of the execution of the changes. You can roll back one or a set of changes in your database. It detects malicious scripts in your database and alerts you.

This tool has a lot in common with Flyway, like versioning changes, saving information on the changes in a particular table, and having separate versions.

The following are the main differences between Liquibase and Flyway.

- Liquibase also supports non-relational databases like MongoDB and Cassandra.

- Flyway can write scripts using a variety of formats, such as JSON, YML, SQL, or XML.

- You can add labels or authors of the scripts, which allow you to execute certain scripts; for example, if you want to execute the scripts only in test environments or vice-versa.

- You can take a snapshot of the database in one environment and compare it with another.

Which Library Does the Versioning?

The general answer to this question is "it depends on the context" because there is no answer that covers all the scenarios. Both tools have more or less the same basic features that cover the most relevant scenarios and have support in Spring Boot. The only two libraries in Spring Initializr that can be included in database migration are Flyway and Liquibase. If you want to version the changes in non-relational databases, the only option is Liquibase. Flyway did not have support when this book was written.

The performance of each of these tools is very similar. There is no Internet benchmark that shows the result of which of them uses fewer resources or quick migrations.

Integrating Libraries in Spring Boot

Spring Boot 2.0.0 and higher support Flyway and Liquibase. You can create a new project, find the dependencies in Spring Initializr, or use your preferred IDE plugin, such as IntelliJ. You need to do the following steps to integrate any of these tools.

1. Add a dependency to configuration management tools like Maven or Gradle.

2. Include the scripts in a location, which in most cases is **/src/main/resources**.

3. Include the modifications in **application.yml** to indicate all the basic configurations and define any custom configurations.

Let's examine how to implement these steps on each versioning tool.

Liquibase

You need to add the dependency of Liquibase in your pom file without specifying the version because parent-pom in Spring Boot includes the correct version compatible with Liquibase (see Listing 6-1).

Listing 6-1. Liquibase Dependencies

```
<dependencies>
    <dependency>
        <groupId>org.liquibase</groupId>
        <artifactId>liquibase-core</artifactId>
    </dependency>

    ← Other dependencies ->
</dependencies>
```

The next step is creating the files to populate the database you used in the previous chapters to check concepts. Go to your project and create two folders inside **src/main/resources: db/migrations**, which contains all the scripts, and **db/changelog,** which contains the configuration for the file you want to be executed during the migration. Lastly, create an empty file called **db.changelog-root.xml** inside the changelog folder. Figure 6-4 shows in a graphical way how the structure of the project looks like if you introduce all the modifications.

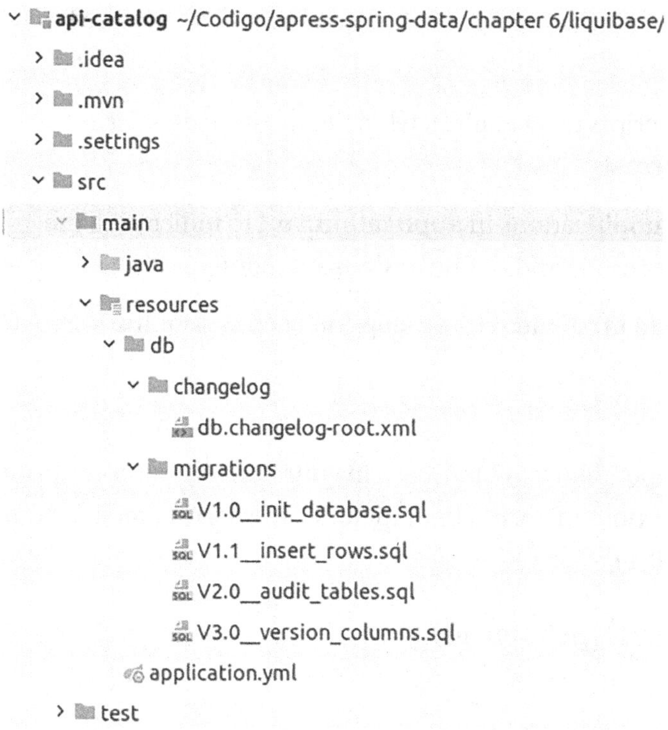

```
∨ 📇 api-catalog ~/Codigo/apress-spring-data/chapter 6/liquibase/
   > 📁 .idea
   > 📁 .mvn
   > 📁 .settings
   ∨ 📁 src
      ∨ 📁 main
         > 📁 java
         ∨ 📇 resources
            ∨ 📁 db
               ∨ 📁 changelog
                     📰 db.changelog-root.xml
               ∨ 📁 migrations
                     🗄 V1.0__init_database.sql
                     🗄 V1.1__insert_rows.sql
                     🗄 V2.0__audit_tables.sql
                     🗄 V3.0__version_columns.sql
            🍃 application.yml
      > 📁 test
```

Figure 6-4. *Project structure after including files*

After that, you include the basic configuration in application.yml. If you allow Liquibase to use the username, password, and the database URL from the data source, the configuration is short. If you do not indicate any of this, take the information from the data source that you defined in Spring Boot. For security purposes, use a different username and password to access the database and try to not include any of these values on any configuration file directly, you can use environment variables (see Listing 6-2).

Listing 6-2. Tool Configurations

```
spring:
  # Other configuration of Spring
  liquibase:
    change-log: classpath:db/changelog/db.changelog-root.xml
```

The last thing before executing the application is completing the **db.changelog-root. xml** with the information about the scripts that need to be executed for Liquibase (see Listing 6-3).

Listing 6-3. Configuration File

```xml
<?xml version="1.0" encoding="UTF-8"?>
<databaseChangeLog
        xmlns="http://www.liquibase.org/xml/ns/dbchangelog"
        xmlns:xsi="http://www.w3.org/2001/XMLSchema-instance"
        xmlns:pro="http://www.liquibase.org/xml/ns/pro"
        xsi:schemaLocation="http://www.liquibase.org/xml/ns/dbchangelog
    http://www.liquibase.org/xml/ns/dbchangelog/dbchangelog-4.1.xsd
    http://www.liquibase.org/xml/ns/pro
    http://www.liquibase.org/xml/ns/pro/liquibase-pro-4.1.xsd">

    <include file="db/migrations/V1.0__init_database.sql"/>
    <include file="db/migrations/V1.1__insert_rows.sql"/>
    <include file="db/migrations/V2.0__audit_tables.sql"/>
    <include file="db/migrations/V3.0__version_columns.sql"/>
</databaseChangeLog>
```

You can indicate each file you want to include in the migrations. Liquibase can indicate all the files in a particular folder that need to be migrated, but a good approach is to indicate the files. Hence, you have granular control of the situation.

When you run the application the first time, you see a large number of logs because the application does all the migrations and takes more time to start (see Listing 6-4).

Listing 6-4. Logs That Appear When Run First Time

```
2022-07-08 01:04:08.405  INFO 352046 --- [ restartedMain] liquibase.
lockservice                   : Successfully acquired change log lock
2022-07-08 01:04:08.563  INFO 352046 --- [ restartedMain] liquibase.
changelog                     : Reading resource: db/migrations/V1.0__
init_database.sql
2022-07-08 01:04:08.574  INFO 352046 --- [ restartedMain] liquibase.
changelog                     : Reading resource: db/migrations/V1.1__
insert_rows.sql
2022-07-08 01:04:08.608  INFO 352046 --- [ restartedMain] liquibase.
changelog                     : Reading resource: db/migrations/V2.0__
audit_tables.sql
```

```
2022-07-08 01:04:08.609  INFO 352046 --- [  restartedMain] liquibase.
changelog                     : Reading resource: db/migrations/V3.0_
version_columns.sql
2022-07-08 01:04:08.610  INFO 352046 --- [  restartedMain] liquibase.
changelog                     : Reading resource: db/migrations/
db.changelog-1.0.sql
2022-07-08 01:04:08.611  INFO 352046 --- [  restartedMain] liquibase.
changelog                     : Reading resource: db/migrations/
db.changelog-1.1.sql
2022-07-08 01:04:08.672  INFO 352046 --- [  restartedMain] liquibase.
changelog                     : Creating database history table with name:
public.databasechangelog
2022-07-08 01:04:08.679  INFO 352046 --- [  restartedMain] liquibase.
changelog                     : Reading from public.databasechangelog
2022-07-08 01:04:08.998  INFO 352046 --- [  restartedMain] liquibase.
lockservice                   : Successfully released change log lock
2022-07-08 01:04:09.003  INFO 352046 --- [  restartedMain] liquibase.
lockservice                   : Successfully acquired change log lock
Skipping auto-registration
2022-07-08 01:04:09.003  WARN 352046 --- [  restartedMain] liquibase.
hub                           : Skipping auto-registration
2022-07-08 01:04:09.048  INFO 352046 --- [  restartedMain] liquibase.
changelog                     : Custom SQL executed
2022-07-08 01:04:09.050  INFO 352046 --- [  restartedMain] liquibase.
changelog                     : ChangeSet db/migrations/V1.0_init_
database.sql::raw::includeAll ran successfully in 42ms
```

The next time you run the application and all the changes are in the database, the number of logs decreases and the time to start up the application too because it locks the database and only executes the validations of the changes (see Listing 6-5).

Listing 6-5. Logs That Appear When You Run the Second Time

```
2022-07-08 01:07:52.089  INFO 354638 --- [  restartedMain] liquibase.
lockservice                   : Successfully released change log lock
```

```
2022-07-08 01:07:52.093   INFO 354638 --- [  restartedMain] liquibase.
lockservice                    : Successfully acquired change log lock
```

Flyway

This tool mostly follows the same steps aș before, but the configuration in Spring Boot may be simpler, depending on the approach that you want to use. Flyway has various ways to execute a migration.

- It includes only the dependency in the pom file so that when the application starts up, it executes all the scripts and validates the consistency of the database.

- It includes a plugin in the pom file and executes a command in the same way you use the CLI interface.

To reduce the complexity, use the first option, which implies that you only include the dependency and delegates the responsibility to execute the command to Spring Boot. Let's add the dependency that appears in Listing 6-6.

Listing 6-6. Flyway Dependencies

```
<dependencies>
    <dependency>
        <groupId>org.flywaydb</groupId>
        <artifactId>flyway-core</artifactId>
    </dependency>

    ← Other dependencies ->
</dependencies>
```

After that, create a new folder in **src/main/resources/db/migration** and paste the SQL files that you used in the previous chapter inside the folder. The structure will have an aspect like Figure 6-5.

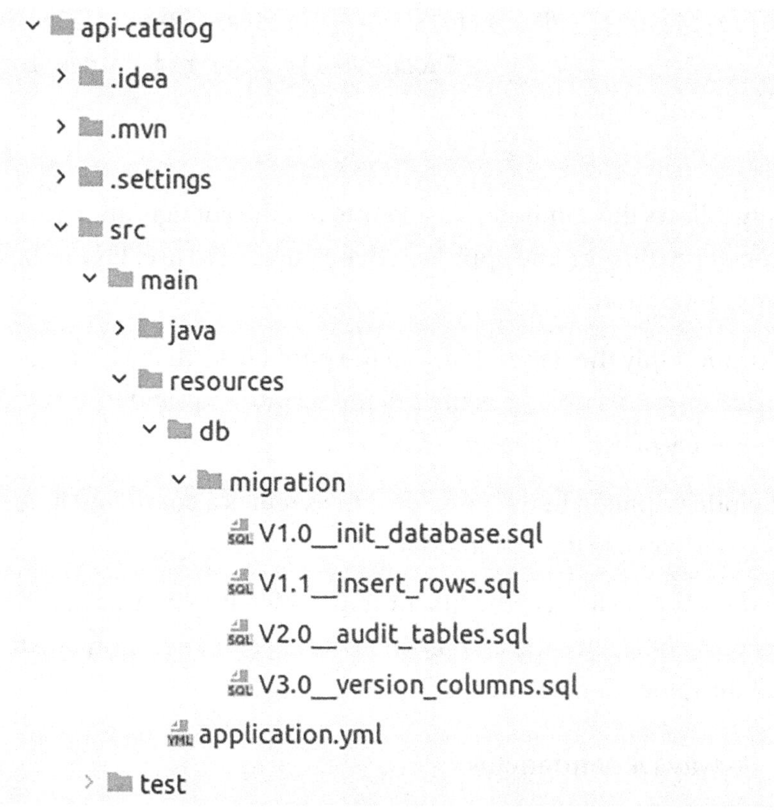

```
∨ ■ api-catalog
  > ■ .idea
  > ■ .mvn
  > ■ .settings
  ∨ ■ src
    ∨ ■ main
      > ■ java
      ∨ ■ resources
        ∨ ■ db
          ∨ ■ migration
            SQL V1.0__init_database.sql
            SQL V1.1__insert_rows.sql
            SQL V2.0__audit_tables.sql
            SQL V3.0__version_columns.sql
      YML application.yml
    > ■ test
```

Figure 6-5. *Project structure after including files*

There are many options to configure. Most of them have default values, like the username/password and the URL, which, if not indicated, takes the information from the data source. Listing 6-7 introduces application.yml, a basic configuration that indicates where the files are located.

Listing 6-7. Tool Configurations

```
spring:
  # Other configuration of Spring
  flyway:
    sql-migration-prefix: V
    sql-migration-separator: __    # The pattern that you use to separate the
    version/description
    sql-migration-suffixes: .sql
```

```
locations: classpath:db/migration # Where the files are located
repeatable-sql-migration-prefix: R
baseline-on-migrate: true
baseline-version: 0 #To indicate which is the first script to use it
```

The last step in using this tool is to run your **api-catalog** application. Before you delete all the tables in the database (not the schema, because the tool cannot create a schema, just tables or indexes), tell Flyway to create and populate the database correctly to check if the scripts were executed or not.

When you execute the application, you see some of the logs from Listing 6-8, which give information about what Flyway did. If something happens during the migration, the console displays all the information related to the error.

Listing 6-8. Logs That Appear When Run the First Time

```
2022-07-08 00:34:06.088  INFO 336864 --- [  restartedMain] o.f.core.
internal.command.DbMigrate      : Migrating schema "public" to version
"2.0 - audit tables"
2022-07-08 00:34:06.099  INFO 336864 --- [  restartedMain] o.f.core.
internal.command.DbMigrate      : Migrating schema "public" to version
"3.0 - version columns"
2022-07-08 00:34:06.101  INFO 336864 --- [  restartedMain] o.f.c.i.s.Defaul
tSqlScriptExecutor      : 0 rows affected
2022-07-08 00:34:06.108  INFO 336864 --- [  restartedMain] o.f.core.
internal.command.DbMigrate      : Successfully applied 4 migrations to
schema "public", now at version v3.0 (execution time 00:30.909s)
2022-07-08 00:34:07.987  INFO 336864 --- [  restartedMain] c.apress.
catalog.ApiCatalogApplication   : Started ApiCatalogApplication in 35.162
seconds (JVM running for 35.588)
```

The first time you execute, all the migrations take a few extra seconds because you initialize the entire database. But the application at startup is shown in Listing 6-9 and takes less because you only validate the checksum and the name of the scripts in the database.

Listing 6-9. Logs That Appear When You Run the Second Time

```
2022-07-08 00:35:42.479  INFO 337966 --- [  restartedMain] o.f.core.
internal.command.DbValidate    : Successfully validated 5 migrations
(execution time 00:00.078s)
2022-07-08 00:35:42.486  INFO 337966 --- [  restartedMain] o.f.core.
internal.command.DbMigrate     : Current version of schema "public": 3.0
2022-07-08 00:35:42.487  INFO 337966 --- [  restartedMain] o.f.core.
internal.command.DbMigrate     : Schema "public" is up to date. No
migration necessary.
```

The second time you run the application, the validations take less than one second, so it's a good way to synchronize your database and version the changes without affecting the application's startup time.

Best Practices

The following are best practices when using these tools.

- Define a pattern with the name of the files to help you identify the sequence of execution and what contains inside. Some tools have a rigid file pattern you need to follow; in others, you can use everything you want.

- Do not include in the configuration the information about the user or the password to do the changes in the database; use external variables or configurations that reduce the risk of problems.

- Each file must contain a certain number of modifications that have meaning. Try creating two files if you need to modify two tables for different reasons.

- Do not modify any file that you previously deployed in an environment. Create a new one with the changes.

- Do not run the scripts manually. Delegate the responsibility to execute the scripts and check if everything is okay with your tool. Remember that most tools create extra tables that verify if the script was executed or not.

- Each developer needs to have a database locally where they can check if the script works fine or not because multiple developers executing changes in a database could produce inconsistencies.

Feature Flags

Most developers need to introduce improvements or fix problems in the code of one microservice that could not work as expected.

Imagine a common situation, you create a new method in the repository which replaces an existing one that is accessed in a way that is not performant, and you discover in production that you have two alternatives to have the previous status of the system: do a rollback of the code to the previous version and another fix problem quickly.

The first two solutions solve the problem but not in the cases that are quick. Imagine a situation where you don't discover the problem with the performance of the query, so your application could affect another part of the platform because taking more time to answer. An alternative to reduce the risk is deploying the changes with a strategy like a canary[7] or blue-green[8] deployment where the old and the new version coexist so you can detect the problem quickly and reduce the risk but not in all situations this solution works. Imagine that you didn't see anything strange in the canary deployment and decided to propagate the change to all the microservice instances weeks after you detected the problem. Hence, you go back again to the first scenario.

Other alternatives allow you to "roll back" the changes without deploying anything again, only changing a value in a database. This solution is called feature flags, a pattern that tries to reduce the risk of deploying changes in production that could affect our application somehow and give developers the responsibility to switch on/off. Also, this pattern helps you introduce A/B testing in your microservices, allowing you to redirect a percentage of the request to the new functionality or do a canary. Only one instance of the microservice has the new feature enabled. A/B testing means there are two different versions of the same application in a production, where some users have access to one version and others have access to another.

---

[7] https://martinfowler.com/bliki/CanaryRelease.html?ref=wellarchitected
[8] https://martinfowler.com/bliki/BlueGreenDeployment.html

> **Note**   This solution is not something new. Martin Fowler's blog features a long article[9] on this topic from 2017.

Another situation could be to change from a relational database to a non-relational database or between non-relational databases. You want to minimize the risk of new problems in the application.

> **Note**   This book covers a variety of databases, so you use this mechanism to migrate from one relational database to a non-relational database and do the tests to check if everything continues working.

There are several types of toggles or feature flags. Some of them are removed from the source code after a while, but others exist for a long time, depending on the feature to test. Let's look at the toggle options.

- **Release** is ideal for a developer who wants to create or modify an existing functionality and minimize the risk of deploying something wrong. In most cases, this toggle is not permanent; after a short time, it is removed from the source code.

- **Experimental** toggles are ideal for doing A/B testing, so you can indicate using criteria like the percentage of the request to one version instead another one. Imagine that you have two ways to do an operation in the database, and you are not sure about the performance and how it can affect each one of the entire applications. The best solution is to send a part of the request to one solution and check the results.

- **Operational** is a common way to enable or disable features; just change the value of one variable. A common use case is for enabling or disabling the connection to external services that can affect your microservices and produce a degradation in the service.

---

[9] https://martinfowler.com/articles/feature-toggles.html

- **Permission** is the most common use of the toggles where you enable or disable access to a part of the platform or microservices for certain users or applications.

Implementing Feature Flags

The first implementation of this type of pattern in Spring Boot used the profiles to enable or disable features, depending on the environment. If you want to enable a feature, you need to redeploy the entire application, which implies time, so this is not a solution that is scalable and performant.

Many tools implement this pattern, but not all have the same number of features or the same level of maturity. In Java and the integration with Spring Boot, there are two options: Togglz[10] and FF4J.[11] Each provides many tutorials and has several developers who report issues and propose new features, but FF4J offers extra features that help you.

- Integration with multiple types of databases to save the information and the metrics about the feature flags

- A good web interface to see all the metrics and enable/disable all the features

- Offers a set of endpoints with good documentation using Swagger

- The possibility of having an audit of which changes happen with the features

Let's create an example to help you understand the mechanisms for multiple implementations, such as using headers or a library.

Including a Header

First, create a new method that queries CountryRepository, which obtains a country by ID (see Listing 6-10).

---

[10] https://www.togglz.org/documentation/spring-boot-starter.html
[11] https://ff4j.org/

Listing 6-10. Repository Modifications

```java
public interface CountryRepository extends CrudRepository<Country, Long> {
        List<Country> findByCode(String code);

        // New query that replaces the old one
        @Query("SELECT c FROM Country c WHERE c.id = ?1")
        Optional<Country> findByIdUsingQuery(Long id);
}
```

Listing 6-11 modifies the CountryService code to receive a parameter that indicates to use a particular implementation.

Listing 6-11. Service Modifications

```java
@Service
public class CountryService {

    CountryRepository countryRepository;

    StateRepository stateRepository;

    Validator validator;

    @Autowired
    public CountryService(CountryRepository countryRepository,
    StateRepository stateRepository, Validator validator) {
        this.countryRepository = countryRepository;
        this.stateRepository = stateRepository;
        this.validator = validator;
    }

    @Transactional(readOnly = true)
    public CountryDTO getById(Long id, Boolean newImplementation) {
        CountryDTO response = null;
        Optional<Country> country = Optional.empty();

        //Receive the parameter and select one strategy to obtain the
        information
```

```
    if(newImplementation) {
        country = countryRepository.findById(id);
    } else {
        country = countryRepository.findByIdUsingQuery(id);
    }

    if(country.isPresent()) {
        response = ApiMapper.INSTANCE.entityToDTO(country.get());
        // This is the mapper to transform the entity in a DTO
    }

    return response;
  }
}
```

Listing 6-12 introduces modifications to CountryController to receive the parameter.

Listing 6-12. Controller Modifications

```
@RestController
@RequestMapping("/country")
public class CountryController {
    private CountryService countryService;

    @Autowired
    public CountryController(CountryService countryService) {
        this.countryService = countryService;
    }

    @GetMapping(value = "/{id}")
    public ResponseEntity<CountryDTO> getById(@PathVariable Long id,
    @RequestParam(value="false") Boolean newImplementation) {
        CountryDTO response = countryService.getById(id,
        newImplementation);
        return new ResponseEntity<>(response, HttpStatus.OK);
    }
  }
```

Now you can use both alternatives and dynamically change the behavior of the API using a header. This is great, but the main problem implies that you must modify the consumer of these microservices and many classes.

Including a Library

One of the best approaches to solve the problem of the possibility of changing the behavior of your application without using headers is using a library like FF4J,[12] which provides a web console to change the values dynamically with restrictions for some users.

The main problem with this library is that they do not have support yet for Spring Boot 3.x.x at the time this booking was written.

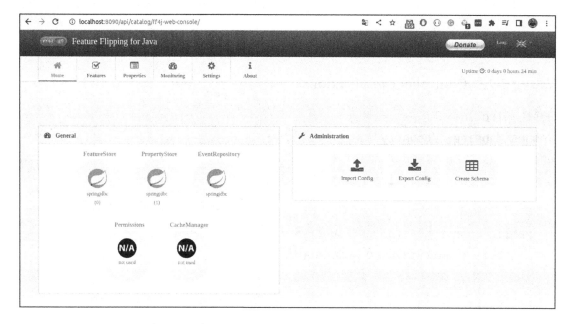

Figure 6-6. *FF4J web console*

---

[12] https://ff4j.org/

Best Practices

The use of the feature flags has recommendations or best practices.

- **Choose the right place to use it**. In Spring Data, determine where the best place is to include it. This situation is not the same and depends on if you use DAOs or repositories.

- **Use descriptive names**. One of the common mistakes is not creating a name that gives me all the information about the feature. Imagine that you have more than one application that saves the information about the toggles in the same database and could appear a conflict of two or more referring to different things.

- **Give a mechanism for technical and non-technical users to have access.** The idea is to provide a mechanism for everyone with a level of responsibility on the microservices or platform to enable or disable the values. The main problem is you need to restrict what can enable features that access the database because not all non-technical users know the performance of the queries.

Summary

Versioning the changes in the database provides a record of all the modifications that happen so you can detect problems and revert them. There are many tools that can solve this situation. Some were covered in this chapter, but others are less popular and do not integrate with multiple frameworks. But Spring Boot includes integrations with new libraries from time to time, so check the official documentation regularly.

PART III

NoSQL Persistence

In Parts I and II, you learned how to interact with Spring Data on relational databases. This makes sense because these databases are long, and most developers use them for different purposes in production environments. Some years ago, however, a new type of database appeared in which the structure to save information was less rigid. You can make changes to this database with minimum risk of producing an exception. Of course, not everything is simple, but there are advantages. These databases are ideal for the high availability of onsite information and large requests.

Spring Data considers the relevance of this new type of database and provides support to most so you can reuse most of the advantages, like the repositories and the configuration to connect with the database.

Part III covers four different databases representing all possible ways to save information. Considering that there are other database options, the idea is largely the same; for example, MongoDB and CouchDB represent documental databases.

Redis: Key/Value Database

Sometimes, you need to persist complex objects in a database and/or for a long period of time. Under these circumstances, the key/value store acts more or less as the Map<K,V> class, wherein you need a key to obtain the values, but the key doesn't need to be a string. It can be another type, and the value can be a simple string or a complex object.

Redis[1] or Memcached[2] are examples of this type of database, which you can use with another module of Spring Boot, such as a cache mechanism.

The main difference between these options is the number of types of information that you can persist. Redis supports the hash, string, list, and set data types, whereas Memcached only supports strings. Another big difference is Redis's ability to persist information in memory or disk if something happens to the database. You don't want to lose all your information.

There are other differences, but this chapter's intent is not to compare the various key/value database options. In light of what I described, let's use Redis.

What Is Redis?

Redis was created in 2009 by Salvatore Sanfilippo. He developed this solution to solve a problem related to the scalability of a web analyzer in the company where he then worked. One of the biggest attributes of this database is its high performance, and it is a lightweight store that can save different types of information.

---

[1] https://redis.io/
[2] https://memcached.org/

Let's delve deeper into the most relevant attributes of this database.

- Redis supports keys/values with a maximum size of 512 MB.

- It supports string, hash, list, set, and sorted set data types. It also supports saving complex data objects such as JSON.

- Redis is single-threaded and can grow horizontally. Additionally, it boasts native support for clustering instances.

Figure 7-1 reflects these benefits.

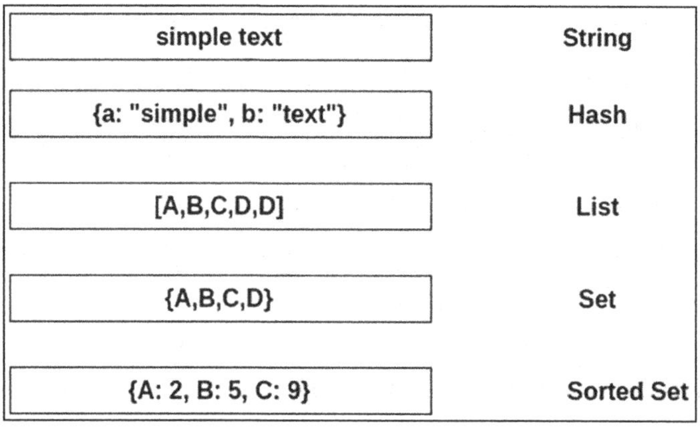

Figure 7-1. *The different data types*

Redis has architectures for persisting and retrieving information; all of them can have the information in memory and save it on disk, depending on your approach. Let's briefly go through the types.

- **Single database**: A unique instance receives all the requests. If something happens, the information is unavailable to access (see Figure 7-2). When the instance is healthy, the information depends on its persistence strategy.

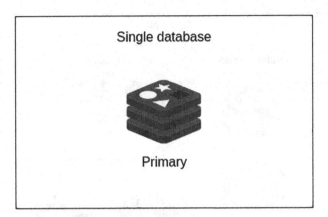

Figure 7-2. *A unique database that contains all the information*

- **High availability**: This type of architecture implies that you have two instances of Redis (see Figure 7-3). The primary receives all the operations and replicates the changes in the secondary, so if the primary database is unhealthy, you can access the information using the other instance. The replication does not instantly take a few milliseconds, so there is little chance you lost information.

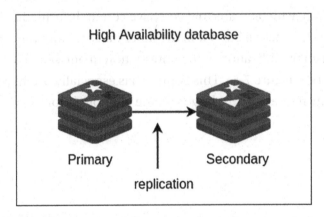

Figure 7-3. *Multiple databases that have a mechanism of replication*

- **Sentinel**: This is a minor modification of the previous approach where some nodes are responsible for detecting if the primary and secondary instances are functional and responding to the request (see Figure 7-4).

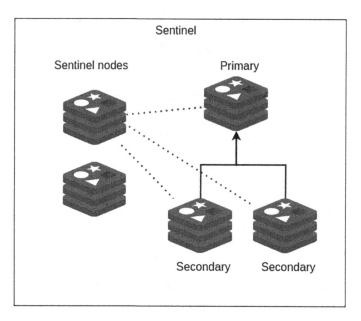

Figure 7-4. *Multiple databases with a Sentinel mechanism*

- **Cluster**: This approach implies the possibility of having multiple primary and secondary instances with the idea of sharing the information, which means that you have certain information in one primary instance but not in the other ones, maintaining the mechanism of replication of the information in one secondary instance (see Figure 7-5). This approach is especially useful when you have many requests and a huge volume of information.

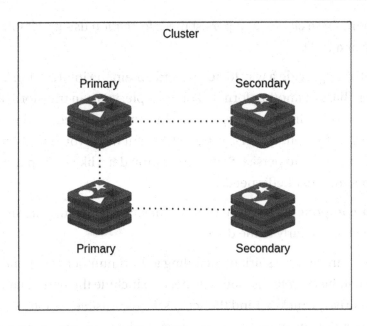

Figure 7-5. *Multiple databases where the master nodes have communication*

Spring Data supports all these alternatives, where you can configure using
application.yml.

Spring Data Structures

Spring Data Redis[3] has the same idea that the JPA version tries to reduce the complexity
of interaction with the database by providing a set of classes or components to interact
simply. They have the following components.

- The **driver** is responsible for interacting with the database to execute
  all the operations.

- **RedisConnection/RedisConnectionFactory** is responsible for
  interacting with the driver and transforming all the operations and
  the exceptions into something similar to the JPA repositories.

- **Entities** represent and contain all the information you persist in
  the database. This is a good way to maintain certain standards for
  implementations of Spring Data (JPA, Redis, Cassandra). Still, you

---

[3] https://spring.io/projects/spring-data-redis

can omit these classes and persist the information using a simple string or a DTO.

- **Serializers** provide a way to persist and obtain the information in the database in another format. For example, you can transform an object into a string and compress the information to reduce the size of the information, which is extremely useful when you have a large number of rows to persist. Some cloud providers, like AWS, pay for the memory that Redis needs.

- **Other components** using Sentinel or master/replica support are connected similarly to the driver.

Spring Data maintains the spirit of including a short number of dependencies to work with each database. In Redis, you only need to include the particular dependency of Redis and the driver, which behind the scenes, is responsible for interacting with the database and executing the operations to save or get the information.

Spring Data Redis supports drivers like Jedis,[4] Lettuce,[5] JRedis,[6] and RJC,[7] but the most popular among developers are the first two options. The main differences between these options are contrasted in Table 7-1.

Table 7-1. *Client Differences*

Jedis	Lettuce
Does not support reactive connections and blocks the connection	A non-blocking Redis client based on Netty
Has a particular instance for each thread	Shares the connection with multiple threads
Does not support master/replica connection	Supports master/replica connection
The default driver in Spring Boot 1.x.x	The default driver in Spring Boot 2.x.x and 3.x.x

---

[4] https://github.com/xetorthio/jedis

[5] https://lettuce.io/

[6] https://github.com/alphazero/jredis

[7] https://github.com/e-mzungu/rjc

Database and Connection Settings

In this section, you will see how to configure your previous api-catalog using Redis but excluding all details about the installation and configuration of the database, which you can see in Appendix E.

Let's add **Redis** dependencies to **api-catalog** as you can see on Listing 7-1. After you finish all the modifications, change the dependency to see the impact of changing the driver. Do not modify the Spring Data Redis versions or the driver because Spring Boot knows which version is compatible. If you change it, there is a risk that something will not work.

Listing 7-1. Dependencies Connected with Redis

```
<dependency>
    <groupId>org.springframework.data</groupId>
    <artifactId>spring-data-redis</artifactId>
</dependency>

<dependency>
    <groupId>redis.clients</groupId>
    <artifactId>jedis</artifactId>
</dependency>
```

The next step is to introduce the configuration to **application.yml** to use your machine's information related to the Redis database (see Listing 7-2). Appendix E explains how to run the database and check the elements inside.

Listing 7-2. Connection Information for Spring Data Redis

```
spring:
  redis:
    host: localhost
    port: 6379
    timeout: 2000        #Connection timed out
    jedis:
      pool:
        max-idle: 6        #Maximum number of idles
        max-active: 10 #Maximum connection
        min-idle: 2        #Minimum number of idles
```

Note   The database configuration using **application.yml** is one alternative. Another creates a @Bean that contains all the host and port information.

```
//Alternative way to configure the Redis connection using Jedis
@Bean
public JedisConnectionFactory connectionFactory() {
    RedisStandaloneConfiguration redisStandaloneConfiguration =
    new RedisStandaloneConfiguration("localhost", 6379);
    return new JedisConnectionFactory(redisStandaloneConfiguration);
}

//Alternative way to configure the Redis connection using Lettuce
@Bean
public LettuceConnectionFactory connectionFactory() {
    RedisStandaloneConfiguration redisStandaloneConfiguration =
    new RedisStandaloneConfiguration("localhost", 6379);
    return new LettuceConnectionFactory(redisStandaloneConfiguration);
}
```

This approach implies that you need to create classes to obtain the information about the hostname and the port because it's not the best approach to have the data of the hostname and port in the source code.

Suppose you run the application with these modifications (if you are unsure how to do this, check Appendix C), and everything continues working fine, but you see messages on the console indicating that you have repositories and entities that are not connected with Redis. Spring Data uses the same approach of repositories for multiple databases, so it makes sense that it indicates that you need to check which type of database you want to use.

```
2022-08-12 00:01:35.547  INFO 160009 --- [ restartedMain] .s.d.r.c.Reposit
oryConfigurationDelegate : Bootstrapping Spring Data Redis repositories in
DEFAULT mode.
```

```
2022-08-12 00:01:35.557  INFO 160009 --- [ restartedMain]
```
.RepositoryConfigurationExtensionSupport : Spring Data Redis - Could not safely identify store assignment for repository candidate interface com. apress.catalog.repository.CountryRepository. If you want this repository to be a Redis repository, consider annotating your entities with one of these annotations: org.springframework.data.redis.core.RedisHash (preferred), or consider extending one of the following types with your repository: org. springframework.data.keyvalue.repository.KeyValueRepository.

The next step consists of defining a template that tells Redis which is the key and the value for a specific row that the database saves. In all the API entities, the key is Long, and you define its value as an object (see Listing 7-3).

Listing 7-3. Definition of Redis Configuration

```
import org.springframework.context.annotation.Bean;
import org.springframework.context.annotation.Configuration;
import org.springframework.data.redis.connection.RedisConnectionFactory;
import org.springframework.data.redis.core.RedisTemplate;
import org.springframework.data.redis.repository.configuration.
EnableRedisRepositories;

@Configuration
@EnableRedisRepositories //This annotation enable the Redis repositories
public class RedisConfiguration {

    @Bean
    public RedisTemplate<Long, Object> redisTemplate(RedisConnectionFactory
    connectionFactory) {
        RedisTemplate<Long, Object> template = new RedisTemplate<>();
        template.setConnectionFactory(connectionFactory);
        // Here you can define custom serialization
        return template;
    }
}
```

To maintain the microservices, remove all the dependencies related to JPA/PostgreSQL and the annotations in the entities related to the relational databases, but do not remove the repositories or the logic to access the information in the services.

After that, you need to modify your previous JPA entities to transform Redis entities using the @RedisHash annotation with the name of the "entity" as you can see on Listing 7-4.

Listing 7-4. Definition of the Redis Entities

```
import org.springframework.data.annotation.Id;
import org.springframework.data.redis.core.RedisHash;

import java.util.List;
import java.io.Serializable;

@RedisHash("country")
public class Country implements Serializable {
    @Id
    private Long id;

    //The previous source code
}
```

Behind the scenes, Spring Data takes the "country" prefix and appends it to the value of the field annotated with @Id, reducing the problem or the risk of having a conflict between multiple entities or objects with the same ID.

If you do all the previous modifications, the application continues working using the same endpoints. But the connection between entities in Redis is impossible because this database works as a key/value store where all the keys do not have any relationship. You can save elements, but you can't refer to other values. You have different elements saved with the same information if your Country entity contains a currency and a list of states. But let's run the application again and create a new country using the **http://localhost:8080/api/catalog/country** POST method in the API (see Figure 7-6).

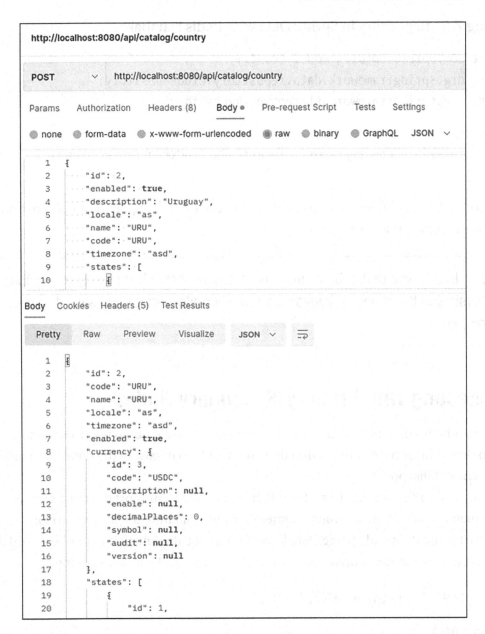

Figure 7-6. *Result of the execution of the POST method*

The changes from one database to another using Spring Data do not imply that you must introduce many changes to all the source code. So you can use all the benefits of the repositories you saw in the previous chapter with minimum changes, as you can check on Listing 7-5. There are classes responsible for mapping or transforming the operations available in the repositories in this database.

Listing 7-5. Repository in Spring Data with Redis Database

```
import com.apress.catalog.model.Country;
import org.springframework.data.repository.CrudRepository;
import org.springframework.stereotype.Repository;

@Repository
public interface CountryRepository extends CrudRepository<Country,
Long> { }
```

To check if everything continues working fine, try doing the other operations you developed in the previous chapters.

Note   In this type of database, there is no tool or library like Flyway or Liquibase for versioning the changes. Instead, you must create a script and save it in the repository.

Connecting with Primary/Secondary Nodes

Let's introduce a little modification in the previous example not to use a single node which depending on the information that you decide to persist in the database, could be critical or not disappear.

You need to change the driver from Jedis to Lettuce to support the most relevant Redis high availability mechanism. Remember not to include the library version because Spring Boot and Spring Data know and define the one that works best. Add the dependency for the Redis driver on the pom file of the application as Listing 7-6.

Listing 7-6. The Lettuce Driver for Redis

```
<dependency>
    <groupId>io.lettuce</groupId>
    <artifactId>lettuce-core</artifactId>
</dependency>
```

The next step is removing all the previous configurations in application.yml related to Redis. You need to manually create the connection and indicate which nodes are primary and which are secondary. After that, create a node named **redis** and define the master/slave nodes on the same way that appears on Listing 7-7.

Listing 7-7. Configuration of the Redis on the application

```
redis:
  master:
    host: localhost
    port: 6379
  slaves:
    - host: localhost
      port: 6380
```

The next step is to define a class (see Listing 7-8) that loads all the configurations from application.yml to be used in the RedisConfiguration class. The new class uses the RedisProperties, which contain the structure of the host/port and other attributes.

Listing 7-8. Configuration File with Modifications

```
package com.apress.catalog.configuration;

import org.springframework.boot.autoconfigure.data.redis.RedisProperties;
import org.springframework.boot.context.properties.ConfigurationProperties;
import org.springframework.context.annotation.Configuration;

import java.util.List;

@ConfigurationProperties(prefix = "redis")
@Configuration
public class RedisSettings {
    private RedisProperties master;
    private List<RedisProperties> slaves;

    //Setters and getters
}
```

The last step introduces the modifications in **RedisConfiguration** to indicate which node is the primary and which others are the secondaries or slaves (see Listing 7-9).

Listing 7-9. Configuration Modifications for Redis

```
import com.apress.catalog.serializer.LongSerializer;
import io.lettuce.core.ReadFrom;
import org.springframework.context.annotation.Bean;
import org.springframework.context.annotation.Configuration;
import org.springframework.data.redis.connection.RedisConnectionFactory;
import org.springframework.data.redis.connection.
RedisStaticMasterReplicaConfiguration;
import org.springframework.data.redis.connection.lettuce.
LettuceClientConfiguration;
import org.springframework.data.redis.connection.lettuce.
LettuceConnectionFactory;
import org.springframework.data.redis.core.RedisTemplate;
import org.springframework.data.redis.repository.configuration.
EnableRedisRepositories;

@Configuration
@EnableRedisRepositories
public class RedisConfiguration {

    final RedisSettings settings;

    public RedisConfiguration(RedisSettings settings) {
        this.settings = settings;
    }

    @Bean
    public RedisTemplate<Long, Object> redisTemplate(RedisConnectionFactory
    connectionFactory) {
        RedisTemplate<Long, Object> template = new RedisTemplate<>();
        template.setConnectionFactory(connectionFactory);
        return template;
    }

    // On this bean you define the connection with the master nodes and
    the slaves or replicas where you can have more than one
    @Bean
```

```
public LettuceConnectionFactory redisConnectionFactory() {
    LettuceClientConfiguration clientConfig =
    LettuceClientConfiguration.builder()
            .readFrom(ReadFrom.REPLICA_PREFERRED)
            .build();
    RedisStaticMasterReplicaConfiguration
    staticMasterReplicaConfiguration = new RedisStaticMasterReplica
    Configuration(settings.getMaster().getHost(),
            settings.getMaster().getPort());
    settings.getSlaves().forEach(slave ->
    staticMasterReplicaConfiguration.addNode(slave.getHost(), slave.
    getPort()));
    return new LettuceConnectionFactory(staticMasterReplica
    Configuration, clientConfig);
    }
}
```

The configuration can support multiple slaves or secondary nodes, so you can reduce the impact on the database of the operations, which only need to obtain the information without making modifications to the information.

Note   It is recommended to always use the configuration available in application. yml. Still, some cases are not covered in that file, like the primary/secondary replica, so this situation could be a good alternative to define the driver's configuration.

In Sentinel, Spring Data can indicate all the nodes in **application.yml**, so it's not necessary for this approach, at least if you want to configure other things.

Object Mapping and Conversion

Spring Data Redis offers a set of templates responsible for executing operations like save/delete/retrieve/update information. In previous sections of this chapter, you defined a custom RedisTemplate that has long as a key and an object as a value, which is necessary because it is not a template for any possible combination. You need to

203

define RedisTemplate for any type of element that you need to persist. You can create something general, such the key is a string as the value is an object. Still, there are other ones like **StringRedisTemplate,** where the key/value is a string, so creating a new RedisTemplate to cover that tuple is unnecessary.

In both cases, you delegate the serialization and deserialization of the information to Spring Data. Still, you do not always want to save the information in a specific format, so you can create your custom serializer by implementing the interface RedisSerializer<T>.[8] To see this with a concrete example, let's create a basic serializer for the key value, a long value as you can see on Listing 7-10.

Listing 7-10. Custom Serializer for Long Values

```
package com.apress.catalog.serializer;

import org.springframework.data.redis.serializer.RedisSerializer;
import org.springframework.data.redis.serializer.SerializationException;
import org.springframework.stereotype.Component;

@Component
public class LongSerializer implements RedisSerializer<Long> {

    @Override
    public byte[] serialize(Long aLong) throws SerializationException {
        if (null != aLong) {
            return aLong.toString().getBytes();
        } else {
            return new byte[0];
        }
    }

    @Override
    public Long deserialize(byte[] bytes) throws SerializationException {
        if (bytes.length > 0) {
            return Long.parseLong(new String(bytes));
        } else {
```

---

[8] https://github.com/spring-projects/spring-data-redis/blob/main/src/main/java/org/springframework/data/redis/serializer/RedisSerializer.java

```
        return null;
    }
  }
}
```

After that, you only need to modify the RedisConfiguration class to indicate which serializer you use for the key values (see Listing 7-11).

Listing 7-11. Add the Key Serializer

```
import org.springframework.data.redis.core.RedisTemplate;
import com.apress.catalog.serializer.LongSerializer;
import org.springframework.context.annotation.Bean;
import org.springframework.context.annotation.Configuration;
import org.springframework.data.redis.connection.RedisConnectionFactory;

@Configuration
@EnableRedisRepositories
public class RedisConfiguration {

    final RedisSettings settings;
    final LongSerializer longSerializer;

    public RedisConfiguration(RedisSettings settings, LongSerializer
    longSerializer) {
        this.settings = settings;
        this.longSerializer = longSerializer;
    }

    @Bean
    public RedisTemplate<Long, Object> redisTemplate(RedisConnectionFactory
    connectionFactory) {
        RedisTemplate<Long, Object> template = new RedisTemplate<>();
        template.setConnectionFactory(connectionFactory);
        template.setKeySerializer(longSerializer);
        return template;
    }

  // Previous source code
}
```

In this case, Redis has a serializer defined to the base data types, but you can change their behavior and create a new one. A possible reason for implementing this type of serializer is to optimize the size of the information you persist in the database, which you learn more about in the final chapter.

Defining Custom Repositories

Until now, you changed the persistence model from a relational database for Redis without changing anything in the repositories. But in Spring Data Redis, you can define a custom repository using the RedisTemplate you defined or the predefined library.

Let's change little your previous repository to do the same but use RedisTemplate instead of delegating everything to the framework. The first thing to do is create an interface containing all the repository's operations on the same way that appears on Listing 7-12.

Listing 7-12. Definition of Custom Repository Interface

```
package com.apress.catalog.repository;

import com.apress.catalog.model.Country;

import java.util.Optional;

public interface CustomCountryRepository {
    Country save(Country entity);

    Optional<Country> findById(Long id);

    void deleteById(Long id);
}
```

The next step is to create a concrete class that implements the previous interface and import **RedisTemplate,** which you defined in the **RedisConfiguration** class. You need to obtain HashOperations from RedisTemplate, which executes all the operations related to the database. You can think of this as EntityManager in JPA (see Listing 7-13).

Listing 7-13. Definition of Custom Repository Concrete Class

```java
package com.apress.catalog.repository;

import com.apress.catalog.model.Country;
import org.springframework.beans.factory.annotation.Autowired;
import org.springframework.data.redis.core.HashOperations;
import org.springframework.data.redis.core.RedisTemplate;
import org.springframework.stereotype.Repository;

import java.util.Optional;

@Repository
public class CustomCountryRepositoryImpl implements
CustomCountryRepository {

    //Use the key to create a unique element in the database like
    country_xxx
    private static final Object COUNTRY_KEY = "country";
    private final RedisTemplate redisTemplate;
    private HashOperations hashOperations;

    @Autowired
    public CustomCountryRepositoryImpl(RedisTemplate redisTemplate) {
        this.redisTemplate = redisTemplate;

        //Obtain the HashOperations to interact directly with the database
        this.hashOperations = redisTemplate.opsForHash();    }

    @Override
    public Country save(Country entity) {
        //Execute a save operation which not return anything so you need to
        do a find operation to return it
        hashOperations.put(COUNTRY_KEY, entity.getId(), (Object) entity);
        return findById(entity.getId()).get();
    }
```

```
@Override
public Optional<Country> findById(Long id) {
    return Optional.of((Country) hashOperations.get(COUNTRY_KEY, id));
}

@Override
public void deleteById(Long id) {
    //This operation only need the "prefix" of the key and the value
    country_xxxx to delete
    hashOperations.delete(COUNTRY_KEY, id);
}
}
```

There are no @Transactional annotations in the methods because this database does not have transactions.

Lastly, change the repository in the **CountryService** to use the new one on the same way that appears on Listing 7-14.

Listing 7-14. Service Modifications

```
@Service
public class CountryService {

    CustomCountryRepositoryImpl countryRepository;

    // Previous source code

    @Autowired
    public CountryService(CustomCountryRepositoryImpl countryRepository,
    StateRepository stateRepository, Validator validator) {
        this.countryRepository = countryRepository;
        this.stateRepository = stateRepository;
                    this.validator = validator;
    }

    // Previous source code
}
```

If you run the applications again and execute the save or retrieve the information using some of the tools mentioned in Appendix B, you have the same behavior used in the previous repository.

Queries by Example

One of the most common problems when you query is writing the entire sentence to be executed, even considering all the advantages that Spring Data offers with creating a method with names of the parameters to filter. To address this problem, Spring Data offers the possibility to create a query using a user-friendly querying technique with a simple interface where it's possible to create a dynamic query.

To use this feature, you only need an object with the values, ExampleMatcher, which contains the logic about which fields filter the results, and Example, which is an interface that is part of the framework and is responsible for passing the information to the matcher.

To do this more simply, let's go back to your previous implementation to access the database using the repositories provided for Spring Data and add the interface QueryByExampleExecutor<T>[9] (see Listing 7-15).

Listing 7-15. Add the interface to use the QueryByExample

```
public interface CountryRepository extends CrudRepository<Country, Long>,
QueryByExampleExecutor<Country> {

}
```

The next step is to create a new method in your service that receives one parameter string with part of the country's name as a parameter. ExampleMatcher needs to indicate the criteria to find on the same way that appears on Listing 7-16.

---

[9] https://github.com/spring-projects/spring-data-commons/blob/main/src/main/java/
org/springframework/data/repository/query/QueryByExampleExecutor.java

Listing 7-16. New Method That Uses ExampleMatcher

```
@Service
public class CountryService {

    CountryRepository countryRepository;
            //Previous source code

    public List<CountryDTO> getAll(String name) {
        List<CountryDTO> response = null;

                        //Here you create the query using a name as an
                        example to do the search, not considering the
                        value that have the "code" attribute
        ExampleMatcher matcher = ExampleMatcher.matching()
                    .withIgnorePaths("code")
                    .withIncludeNullValues()
                    .withMatcher("name", ExampleMatcher.
                    GenericPropertyMatcher.of(ExampleMatcher.
                    StringMatcher.DEFAULT));

        Country entity = new Country();
        entity.setName(name);

        Iterable<Country> country = countryRepository.findAll(Example.
        of(entity, matcher));

        if(country != null) {
            response = mapper.mapAsList(country, CountryDTO.class);
        }

        return response;
    }

    //Previous source code
}
```

This example takes the value of a "name" and generates a query to find the information. The last step is to create a new method in the controller which receives the request and calls to the service (see Listing 7-17).

Listing 7-17. New Method in the Controller

```
@GetMapping(value = "/")
public ResponseEntity<List<CountryDTO>> getAll(@RequestParam String name) {
    List<CountryDTO> response = countryService.getAll(name);
    return new ResponseEntity<>(response, HttpStatus.OK);
}
```

After doing all these modifications, if you make various requests in the new endpoint to filter the results, you may discover that nothing happens and return everything in the database. This happens because you need to add Redis's case that there is a second attribute to filter the information using the @Indexed annotation. Behind the scenes, it creates a new index (see Listing 7-18).

Listing 7-18. Add the Annotation to Create a New Index

```
import org.springframework.data.annotation.Id;
import org.springframework.data.redis.core.RedisHash;
import org.springframework.data.redis.core.index.Indexed;

import java.io.Serializable;
import java.util.List;

@RedisHash("country")
public class Country implements Serializable {
    @Id
    private Long id;
    private String code;
    @Indexed
    private String name;

    //Previous source code

}
```

This solution works fine but is not the best approach for creating multiple indexes in a database.

Summary

This chapter covered the approaches for using Redis. Most of them are supported in Spring Data, like having single or multiple database nodes. You learned how to persist the information using a custom serializer and how to do the configuration in the application.

There is no correct answer about which approach you can use because it depends on your business and the cost associated with having multiple instances of the same database running, for example, on a cloud provider like AWS.

MongoDB: Document Database

When you create an application, you may need to persist information in a specific format that will need modifying in the future. You may think that a relational database could be the best alternative for saving this kind of information. Still, some non-relational databases offer the flexibility to change the structure of the "tables" without problems and save complex objects where you have the chance to create complex queries.

The evolution and the stability of non-relational databases offer excellent performance with large amounts of information. Still, you need to lose something compared with the relational databases, like having duplicate information.

This chapter discusses a new non-relational database that can save all the information like a document and its primary benefits.

What Is a Document Store?

A document store is a non-relational database where you can store the information as a JSON document without having a rigid schema like the relational databases, so you can add, remove, or change the format of the attributes flexibly. Of course, you need to modify your application to not produce exceptions in the source code.

The source offers you a structure that is readable for anyone and, depending on the complexity of your application, could be matched with the response of some endpoints. If you want to transform your **api-catalog** application from multiple tables to only one, it's possible to do it while maintaining the exact structure of the DTO. Still, one of the main problems is the duplicity of the information, which is familiar in non-relational databases. Still, some implementations offer the possibility to create structures and connect them like relational databases.

© Andres Sacco 2023
A. Sacco, *Beginning Spring Data*, https://doi.org/10.1007/978-1-4842-8764-4_8

Figure 8-1 shows the equivalence between the previous relational databases with a document database.

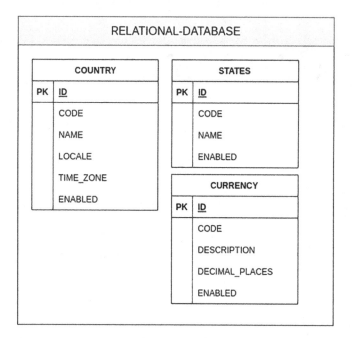
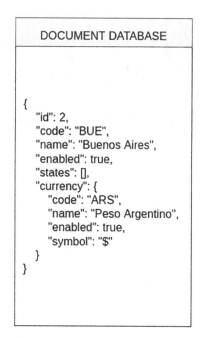

Figure 8-1. *Relational databases vs. document databases*

There is some equivalence between the structures; for example, a table in a relational database is a collection in MongoDB, one of the implementations of document store databases, so it does not remove all the concepts you know. It reconverts to something different.

Possible Uses Cases

There are situations where these databases are good candidates to be used, but there is no restriction about use in other situations. Let's look at some uses.

- **Catalogs**: Some applications store information about the products in e-commerce or places like countries/cities/states or airports relevant to the database's performance. Still, you want to have all the benefits of doing a lot of types of queries. Imagine needing to do a lot of queries to obtain information about a specific country. It could be better to execute one query to a specific structure and obtain the JSON that could be a response of the endpoint.

- **Content management**: If you have applications like blogs or video platforms where the structure could be changed because the platform suffers modifications, but you don't need that, everything with the same structure could be a good choice. Modifying new attributes or removing them only affects some documents, not the entire database. This is one advantage instead the relational databases.

These two examples are among the most relevant. Still, many companies use document store databases as the primary mechanism to save information, replacing relational databases.

Implementations

There are implementations for this type of database. Some of them are stable and used by a lot of developers across the world. Let's look at them.

- **MongoDB**[1] is well-documented and used by many developers worldwide. The last version offers various ways to optimize the queries, indexes, sharing, replication, and load balancing across the cluster's instances. Also, give you the possibility to do map reduction and aggregation during the execution of the queries, reducing the number of codes you need to write in your application. Lastly, this database has support for multiple languages like Java, PHP, Go, Python, and .NET, so there are a lot of possibilities that if something is wrong in one version of the database, many developers report it. The people who maintain the database find a solution. One last thing to mention is that MongoDB uses a particular way to store the information called BSON, similar to JSON but with improvements.

- **Amazon Document DB**[2] is like a fork of MongoDB, which is optimized for AWS, but some of the features available in this database do not work; for example, the BigDecimal precision does not work yet, and you need to persist the numbers as a string. The main

---

[1] https://www.mongodb.com/home

[2] https://aws.amazon.com/documentdb/

benefits of this database are the performance, the ability to have multiple instances in availability zones, and everything related to monitoring.

- **Azure Cosmos DB**[3] works as a combination of other types, not only a document store. You can use it to save information in a relational database, wide-column database, or document store database like MongoDB. This database is optimized to be used in Azure, so have similar features as Amazon DocumentDB and has the same problems. Not all the database features are available, so you need to consider this situation before choosing a database instead of another one.

- **Couchbase**[4] is quite similar to MongoDB. Still, you have the option to indicate to the engine which features are enabled or not, like indexes, search, and analytics, with the idea of optimizing the execution of the operations. The information in this database is stored like a JSON instead of a BSON in MongoDB, reducing some of the operations you can execute.

The available options are document store databases. This book uses MongoDB, which is used by 27% of developers according to a StackOverflow report.[5] It's the most-used non-relational database. Also, Spring Data offers big support to MongoDB since the first versions reduce the complexity of the use.

What Is MongoDB?

MongoDB is one of the most popular non-relational databases, which uses a BJSON-like format to store information. A BJSON is a set of key/values elements, similar to JSON, with representation not related to key/values databases; in the document store, you can save complex documents and create different queries.

---

[3] https://azure.microsoft.com/en-us/services/cosmos-db/
[4] https://www.couchbase.com/
[5] https://insights.stackoverflow.com/survey/2021#technology

Note   This database has grown in popularity because it supports many languages. It has a set of online courses with the idea that anyone can learn most of the concepts related to this database. All the courses are free and give you a certificate.

The database structure has a certain equivalence with relational databases; for example, the concept of a database is the same in both types. Still, a table has the name of the collection. Table 8-1 lists the most relevant equivalence; this helps you to understand many of the annotations that appear in Spring Data Mongo or when you need to find information on the Internet.

Table 8-1. *Equivalence Between Two Types of Databases*

Relational Databases	MongoDB
Database	Database
Table	Collection
Row	Document
Column	Field

The data types that MongoDB supports are similar to what JSON supports but include extras like the possibility to store spatial data, which is relevant if you want to perform certain queries that consider the location/position of something, for example, obtain all the shop near to my current position. Table 8-2 features examples of the different data types that support MongoDB and what it looks like in a JSON structure.

Table 8-2. *Data Types Supported by MongoDB*

Data Type	MongoDB	JSON
Numbers	BSON Number	`{"version": 1}`
String	BSON String	`{"code": "BUE"}`
boolean	BSON Boolean	`{"enabled": true}`
Datetime	Custom Data format	`{ "createdOn": ISODate("2022-12-19T02:15:17.171Z")}`
Spatial data	GeoJSON	`{"geometry": {"type": "Point", "coordinates": [-104.99404, 39.75621]}}`
Null	JSON Null	`{"code": null}`
Objects	Flexible JSON Objects	```{{ "code": "BUE", "currency": { "code": "ARS", "name": "Peso Argentino", "enabled": true, "symbol": "$" }}}```
Arrays	Flexible JSON Arrays	(see below)

For **Objects**:

```
{
    "code": "BUE",
    "currency": {
      "code": "ARS",
      "name": "Peso Argentino",
      "enabled": true,
      "symbol": "$"
    }
}
```

For **Arrays**:

```
{
    "id": 2,
    "code": "BUE",
    "name": "Buenos Aires",
    "enabled": true,
    "states": [
      {
        "code": "BUE",
        "name": "Buenos Aires"
      }
    ]
}
```

Another feature is the relationship between different entities. In Mongo, this is possible. Still, there are restrictions. In a one-to-one relationship, you can include a reference to another collection/document, like a foreign key or embedded object, but there is only one collection. The same occurs in one-to-many or many-to-many relationships. You can embed an array of objects or contain an array of references to other collections.

Introduction Spring Data Mongo

The first chapters of this book covered the modules connected to Spring Data, including Spring Data Mongo,[6] which reduces the complexity of database configuration for aspects like creating queries or configuring the connection, or performance aspects like using indexes.

MongoDB has multiple database instances that replicate all the information. Also, you can share the information, which implies that you have a certain piece of information in multiple instances. In both cases, the impact on the implementation it's just a little change in **application.yml**, and for that reason, it is beyond the scope of this book.

Database and Connection Settings

In this section, you will see how to configure your previous api-catalog using MongoDB but excluding all details about the installation and configuration of the database, which you can see in Appendix E.

Let's add the MongoDB dependencies to api-catalog. You don't need to explicitly include the Mongo driver because the Spring Data dependency includes it. As usual, do not include the version of the dependency related to Spring Data MongoDB, just the dependency, as seen in Listing 8-1. Let Spring Boot choose which version is best.

Listing 8-1. Dependencies Connected with Mongo

```
<dependency>
    <groupId>org.springframework.boot</groupId>
    <artifactId>spring-boot-starter-data-mongodb</artifactId>
</dependency>
```

---

[6]https://spring.io/projects/spring-data-mongodb

The next step is to introduce the configuration to **application.yml** to use the information related to the Mongo database running on your machine as you can see on Listing 8-2.

Listing 8-2. Connection Information for Spring Data Mongo

```
spring:
  data:
    mongodb:
      host: localhost
      port: 27017
      username: root
      password: rootpassword
      database: catalog
```

Some logs refer to the new database when you introduce all the modifications and run the application with the MongoDB. Remember that you can use Spring Data's repositories to access the database, but you don't configure them, so the application continues using the MongoDB repositories. You can see all the output of the application on Listing 8-3 with all the information on the connection with the database.

Listing 8-3. Output after Running the Application with Modifications

```
2022-08-17 00:17:22.608  INFO 223254 --- [ restartedMain] org.
mongodb.driver.cluster                : Cluster created with settings
{hosts=[localhost:27017], mode=SINGLE, requiredClusterType=UNKNOWN,
serverSelectionTimeout='30000 ms'}

2022-08-17 00:17:22.683  INFO 223254 --- [localhost:27017] org.
mongodb.driver.connection             : Opened connection
[connectionId{localValue:1, serverValue:1}] to localhost:27017

2022-08-17 00:17:22.684  INFO 223254 --- [localhost:27017] org.mongodb.
driver.cluster                : Monitor thread successfully connected to
server with description
ServerDescription{address=localhost:27017, type=STANDALONE,
state=CONNECTED, ok=true, minWireVersion=0, maxWireVersion=13,
maxDocumentSize=16777216, logicalSessionTimeoutMinutes=30,
roundTripTimeNanos=20512280}
```

```
2022-08-17 00:17:22.684  INFO 223254 --- [localhost:27017] org.
mongodb.driver.connection              : Opened connection
[connectionId{localValue:2, serverValue:2}] to localhost:27017

2022-08-17 00:17:23.386  INFO 223254 --- [n(13)-127.0.0.1] org.
mongodb.driver.connection              : Opened connection
[connectionId{localValue:3, serverValue:3}] to localhost:27017
```

Remove everything that is not connected with MongoDB. Remove all the dependencies related to JPA/PostgreSQL and the annotations in the entities related to relational databases. But do not remove the repositories or the logic to access the information in the services.

After that, you need to modify your previous JPA entities to transform them into MongoDB entities using the @Document annotation named *entity* as you can see on Listing 8-4.

Listing 8-4. Definition of the Mongo Entities

```
import org.springframework.data.annotation.Id;
import org.springframework.data.mongodb.core.index.Indexed;
import org.springframework.data.mongodb.core.mapping.DBRef;
import org.springframework.data.mongodb.core.mapping.Document;
import org.springframework.data.mongodb.core.mapping.Field;

import java.util.List;
import java.io.Serializable;

@Document("country")
public class Country implements Serializable {
    @Id
    private Long id;

    //The previous source code (setters, getters, and hashcode/equals
    methods)
}
```

If you do all the previous modifications, the application continues working using the same endpoints, but the connection between entities in MongoDB has restrictions. For this example, you store all the information in one collection. To do this, call the POST method to save the country entities in the endpoint at `http://localhost:8080/api/catalog/country` (see Figure 8-2).

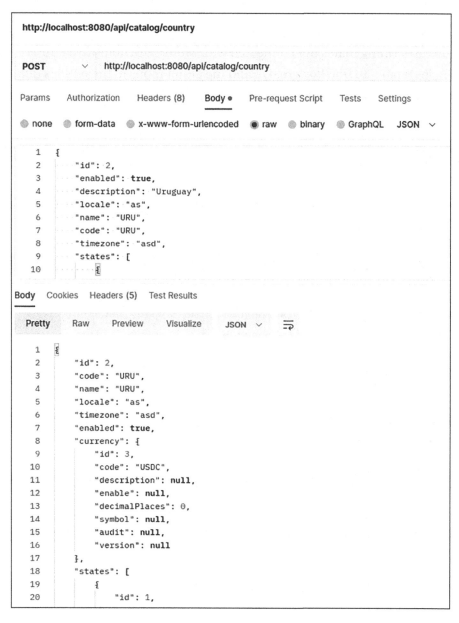

Figure 8-2. *Result of the execution of the POST method*

Annotations for Entities

In Spring Data Mongo, there is a set of annotations that you can apply to the various entities. Table 8-3 describes the most relevant.

Table 8-3. *The Most Common Annotations in Mongo Entities*

Spring Data Mongo Annotation	Meaning
@Document	A domain object that needs to be persisted in MongoDB
@Indexed	A particular field that needs to be indexed to improve the performance of the search operations
@Id	The attribute that contains the identification of the collection
@Transient	Ignores a particular field for the process of persisting the information
@IndexDirection	Indicates which is the direction of the index: DESCENDING or ASCENDING
@Field	Indicates the name of the attribute in the database explicitly, it's like the @Column in JPA
@DBRef	An annotation to connect multiple collections, similar to @OneToMany or @ManyToMany in JPA

If you refer to another entity using **@DBRef**, the changes to that object are not persisted in the database because there is no possibility of having a cascade like in JPA.

With these annotations in mind, I'll introduce minor modifications to the Country entity to not persist the entire currency information. Looks all the modifications on the entity on the Listing 8-5.

Listing 8-5. Definition of the Mongo Entity

```
import org.springframework.data.annotation.Id;
import org.springframework.data.mongodb.core.index.Indexed;
import org.springframework.data.mongodb.core.mapping.DBRef;
import org.springframework.data.mongodb.core.mapping.Document;
import org.springframework.data.mongodb.core.mapping.Field;
```

```
import java.util.List;

@Document(value = "country")
public class Country implements Serializable {
    @Id
    private Long id;

    @Indexed
    @Field(value = "code")
    private String code;

    @DBRef
    private Currency currency;

            // Other fields without changes
}
```

With this simple modification, when you persist the information in the database, you see **DBRef('currency', '2'),** which implies that the field has a reference with another collection. To check if this happens, the best way to do it is using the tools that appear in Appendix E.

Access Using Repositories

Don't change anything from the previous repositories, which use **CrudRepository,** but modify them to extend from **MongoRepository<T, ID>,** which behind the scenes extends for **PaginatingAndSorting<T, ID>** and **QueryByExampleExecutor<T>**[7] but have certain improvements related to Mongo. Listing 8-6 shows the modifications on the repository according MongoDB.

Listing 8-6. Definition of the Mongo Repository

```
public interface CountryRepository extends MongoRepository<Country, Long> {
    List<Country> findByCode(String code);
}
```

---

[7]https://docs.spring.io/spring-data/commons/docs/current/api/org/springframework/data/repository/query/QueryByExampleExecutor.html

MongoDB Keywords for Repositories

Spring Data Mongo offers the possibility of not writing all the queries manually. You can create a method in the repository with all the conditions that the document in the database needs to be satisfied in the same way that you can do with Spring Data JPA.

Table 8-4 lists conditions you can include in the repository.

Table 8-4. *Keyword to Create Queries Without Writing the Entire Sentence*

Keyword	Example	Condition
Equal	fIndByCodeEquals(String code)	{"code": "BUE"}
And	findByCodeAndEnabled(String code, Boolean enabled)	{"code": "BUE", "enabled": true}
Or	findByCodeOrEnabled(String code, Boolean enabled)	{ "$or" : [{ "code" : "BUE"}, { "enabled" : true}]}
Not	fIndByCodeNot(String code)	{"code": {"$ne" :"BUE"}}
StartingWith	fIndByCodeStartingWith(String code)	{ "code" : { "$regularExpression" : { "pattern" : "^BU"}}}
EndingWith	fIndByCodeEndingWith(String code)	{ "code" : { "$regularExpression" : { "pattern" : "UE$"}}}
True	fIndByEnabledTrue()	{"enabled": true}
False	fIndByEnabledFalse()	{"enabled": false}

There are many keywords, but the list covers the most relevant; if you want to learn more about other keywords, check the official documentation.[8]

Note   Remember that you defined custom methods in the chapters connected with JPA, which are functional in MongoDB because, in most databases, Spring Data translates the name of the method in the query to the specific database.

---

[8] https://docs.spring.io/spring-data/mongodb/docs/current/reference/html/#appendix.query.method.subject

```
public interface CurrencyRepository extends
MongoRepository<Currency, Long> {
        // This method is equivalent to use findByCode(String code)
        List<Currency> findByCode(String code);
}
```

Defining Queries

Most of the time, the simple queries that offer Spring Data with the definition of new methods using the keywords are great, but it does not always happen. There are cases when you need to define the query for the complexity that it implies or because you detected performance issues.

If you don't want to use the repositories' default features, Spring Data offers alternatives, like creating the query manually in the repository or using queries by example. Let's discuss this briefly.

Writing the Query Using Annotations

This method is also familiar if you are familiar with MongoDB and writing queries on a UI like Compass. As with JPA, Mongo has the possibility of defining a query using annotations. Listing 8-7 writes the entire query or a part of the query combined with the definition using keywords.

Listing 8-7. Custom Queries

```
public interface CountryRepository extends MongoRepository<Country, Long> {

        //This is a custom query that find just for one field
        @Query(value = "{'code': ?0}")
        List<Country> findCustom(String code);

        //This is a custom query combine the condition on the name of the
        method with the query
        @Query(value = "{'code': ?0}")
        List<Country> findEnabled(String code);
}
```

A good practice to be human-readable is to use one of these methods and not create complex queries that combine conditions using the name of the method. Also, you can use @Param in JPA.

Queries by Example

This is another interesting feature of Spring Data that you implemented in the Redis chapter. Still, there are advantages to using MongoRepository<T,ID>. You don't need to change anything because that interface extends from **QueryByExampleExecutor<T>**. You only need to create the matcher and the object to do the query.

The logic to write a query using an example is the same as in Chapter 7. For simplicity, do not duplicate the code you see at the bottom, just the ExampleMatcher you need to include in CountryService when invoking the repositories.

```
ExampleMatcher matcher = ExampleMatcher.matching()
                 .withIgnorePaths("code")
                 .withIncludeNullValues()
                 .withMatcher("name", ExampleMatcher.GenericProperty
                 Matcher.of(ExampleMatcher.StringMatcher.DEFAULT));
```

Using MongoTemplate with Custom Repositories

As you'll recall, Spring Data offers two alternatives to access the database; one is the most common approach, which implies the creation of an interface as a repository and delegates all the transformation of the information and the creation of the operations to Spring. The second alternative implies that you create a custom repository and use a mechanism to execute the operations, which in Mongo refers to using MongoTemplate.

MongoTemplate improves the performance of certain operations with the database, but you can do many things, like creating queries. Table 8-5 details the main differences between MongoRepository<T, ID> and MongoTemplate, to better help you understand where it is relevant to use one instead the other.

Table 8-5. *Main Differences Between Ways to Access MongoDB*

	Pros	Cons
MongoTemplate	You can indicate which fields need to be updated instead update the entire document. It provides the possibility to do all the operations of Mongo, like updateFirst and upsert.	It has lot of code lines where most operations are simple.
MongoRepository <T, ID>	It follows the same structure of methods as Spring Data JPA, so you have predefined methods or create a new one using the keywords.	It creates the operations and follows a standard, so perhaps the operations could not be performant.

To see this practically, let's create a custom repository, including MongoTemplate. Listing 8-8 shows how to do the same operations as normal repositories.

Listing 8-8. Definition of Custom Repository Interface

```
package com.apress.catalog.repository;

import com.apress.catalog.model.Country;

import java.util.Optional;

public interface CustomCountryRepository {
    Country save(Country entity);

    Optional<Country> findById(Long id);

    void deleteById(Long id);
}
```

After creating the repository's interface, the next step is to create the implementation that interacts with **MongoTemplate**. Listing 8-9 demonstrates this.

Listing 8-9. Implementation of a Custom Repository

```
package com.apress.catalog.repository.impl;

import com.apress.catalog.model.Country;
import com.apress.catalog.repository.CustomCountryRepository;
import org.springframework.beans.factory.annotation.Autowired;
import org.springframework.data.domain.Example;
import org.springframework.data.mongodb.core.MongoTemplate;
import org.springframework.data.mongodb.core.query.Criteria;
import org.springframework.data.mongodb.core.query.Query;
import org.springframework.stereotype.Repository;

import java.util.Optional;

@Repository
public class CustomCountryRepositoryImpl implements
CustomCountryRepository {

    //This class will help you to interact with the database
    private final MongoTemplate mongoTemplate;

    @Autowired
    public CustomCountryRepositoryImpl(MongoTemplate mongoTemplate) {
        this.mongoTemplate = mongoTemplate;
    }

    @Override
    public Country save(Country entity) {
        return mongoTemplate.save(entity);
    }

    @Override
    public Optional<Country> findById(Long id) {
        Country country = mongoTemplate.findById(id, Country.class);
        return Optional.of(country);
    }
```

```
    //On this method you will use the Query class to send into the
    database the criteria to delete the documents
    @Override
    public void deleteById(Long id) {
        Query query = new Query();
        query.addCriteria(Criteria.where("id").is(id));
        mongoTemplate.remove(query, Country.class);
    }
}
```

You can use simple MongoTemplate to find a particular element, persist the information in the database, or write a query using the classes that offer Spring Data Mongo. If you want to write complex queries using the Query class, a good practice is to create a new class with all the definitions of the queries.

To use this repository, you need to modify CountryService in the same way as in the previous chapter. If you rerun the applications and execute the save or retrieve the information, you have the same behavior seen in the previous repository.

One relevant thing to mention that does not appear in these modifications is that MongoDB supports using @Transactional in the same way as in JPA.

Summary

This chapter covered the most relevant aspects of MongoDB, a popular non-relational database supported by Spring Data.

To use this database, you need to analyze the way you want to persist information because you can use @DRef to link or refer to another entity or duplicate information without using it.

Neo4j: Graph Database

Most of the previous databases you've been exposed to throughout this book store information in a similar structure. A diagram or tool is necessary to help you understand how they organize information. But what happens when another type of organizing data is available—one that makes representation and access more easily digested?

This chapter explains how a graph database works and how to perform it with Spring Data. Let's explore a few use cases, implementations, and Neo4j.

What Is a Graph Database?

A graph database is a pictorial representation of directly-connected nodes connected using links that represent the relationship between them, in contrast to using tables or documents like other types of databases. Each node represents an entity and contains all the information connected within one node, and the relationship between nodes is the association.

Let's transform the previous **api-catalog** example into a set of nodes and links to clarify the idea, as shown in Figure 9-1.

© Andres Sacco 2023
A. Sacco, *Beginning Spring Data*, https://doi.org/10.1007/978-1-4842-8764-4_9

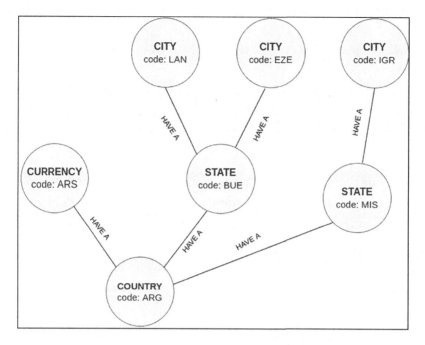

Figure 9-1. *Example of the representation of the nodes and links*

This type of database solves many problems beyond the example shown in Figure 9-1, as shown in the next section.

Possible Uses Cases

There are situations where these databases are good candidates to be used, but there is no restriction about use in other situations. Let's look at a few possible uses.

- **Social networks**: Databases help represent the relationship between people to see the news or publications of each of them.

- **Modeling airline flights**: The nodes could be airports and flights. Using nodes could be simple to represent or find a specific airport and check which flights are available for certain destinations. Also, you could apply this use case to other ground transportation like trains or buses.

- **Detect fraud patterns**: You can modulate the purchases and the IP where each is doing it. If you detect that multiple actions happen in a short period in different locations, you can simplify the detection process.

- **Recommendation engines**: Imagine that you have an e-commerce site where your clients buy various things, so if the products have a certain level of associations, you can offer other options that could be connected to criteria, like the product category. Also, the recommendation engines could apply to suggest a song on Spotify or a new movie on Netflix.

- **Represent the hierarchy**: If you are part of a big company, you usually want to know the partners of a person or the boss. With the use of a graph, you can represent and see the structure of the company without problems.

Implementations

There are implementations for this type of database. Some of them are stable and used by a lot of developers across the world. Let's explore them.

- **Neo4j:**[1] This database is one of the oldest graph databases with support for many languages, including Java, and is used by most of the biggest companies worldwide. It offers the possibility to use the community version where you are responsible for administrating the database, or you can for a cloud service like MongoDB Atlas. It implies that you need to pay for the use of the service, where you can configure the backups, the restore, and the number of instances that are running simply. There are many books, articles, StackOverflow discussions, and videos in this database. Appendix F lists some recommended books.

- **Redis Graph:**[2] This database based on Redis offers the possibility of using graphs. This behind-the-scenes tool implements GraphBLAS, which defines a set of the matrix in a structure of rings to do the representation in a graph. This database model has advantages,

---

[1] https://neo4j.com/v2/
[2] https://redis.io/docs/stack/graph/

like performance, and uses openCypher[3] to write and execute the queries. You can use it as a module that you need to add to your Redis instance, but there are a few articles, books, and videos about the topic, so if something strange happens, perhaps you will not find an answer.

- **Amazon Neptune:**[4] This is a custom implementation of a graph database that works in the AWS environments where you pay for the memory/CPU that your database consumes and a sum of money depending on the traffic inbound/outbound the database receives. The main features of this database are that it is easy to automatically scale because you delegate everything to AWS, load latency between the read instances, and increment the storage size without doing anything.

This book uses Neo4j, a popular graph database. Spring Data offers extensive support to this database since the first versions reduce the complexity of the use.

What Is Neo4j?

Neo4j is a graph database that supports ACID properties like relational databases where you can scale the database without downtime or the risk you lose some information. This database is optimized for queries across the nodes to obtain certain information. It's used in applications that expose an interface with GraphQL.[5]

The following are the most relevant features.

- It is unnecessary to join to obtain the information saved on another node because it obtained the information of the nearby node, which is connected.

- It provides a flexible and simple data model that can be changed without problems.

---

[3] https://opencypher.org/
[4] https://aws.amazon.com/neptune
[5] https://graphql.org/

- Many languages, including Java, Scala, and Node.js, support it.

- It provides a declarative language to write queries that are human-readable.

There is a certain similarity between the relational databases, which could help you to understand how Neo4j is organized, as shown in Table 9-1, which explains some of the annotations that appear in Spring Data Neo4j.[6]

Table 9-1. *Equivalence Between Two Databases*

Relational Databases	Neo4j
Database	Database
Table	Node
Column	Property
Constrain	Relationship

Let's examine these concepts.

- A **node** represents an object which can have one or more properties that are grouped by criteria. The definition of the names needs to be in CamelCase as a suggestion for the official documentation of Neo4j.[7]

- A **property** in Neo4j represents a key-value pair to store the information about one node and the relationships. For example, in api-catalog, a property could be a country's code or a description. Some of the property types supported by Neo4j are string, float, long, date (all the variations), and point.

- A **relationship** connects one or more nodes, which in most cases are unidirectional, but it's possible to do it bidirectional too.

---

[6]https://spring.io/projects/spring-data-neo4j
[7]https://neo4j.com/developer/cypher/style-guide/

> **Note**   There are many tools to draw the graphs without creating the query. The most relevant is Arrows,[8] which Neo4j supports. You can drag and drop nodes, including the link between each of them and include the properties, and when you finish, you can export the result, which could be a Cypher query to run on your Neo4j browser.

Introduction Spring Data Neo4j

Spring Data supports databases by working directly with the drivers. In Neo4j, the Spring Data Neo4j[9] project has been available for many years to help reduce the complexity of the database configuration and the entities.

One thing to consider about the implementation of this project is the support for using clusters of Neo4j; it's possible to do it, but it requires extra configuration in the databases and **application.yml**.

Database and Connection Settings

In this section, you will see how to configure your previous api-catalog using Neo4J but excluding all details about the installation and configuration of the database, which you can see in Appendix E.

Let's add the Neo4j dependencies to api-catalog (see Listing 9-1). You don't need to include the Neo4j driver explicitly because the dependency includes it. Following the same rule, do not include the dependency version of Spring Data Neo4j. Only include the dependency and delegate to Spring Boot which is the best version.

Listing 9-1. Dependencies Connected with Neo4j

```
<dependency>
    <groupId>org.springframework.boot</groupId>
    <artifactId>spring-boot-starter-data-neo4j</artifactId>
</dependency>
```

---

[8] https://arrows.app/
[9] https://spring.io/projects/spring-data-neo4j

The next step is introducing the configuration to **application.yml** to use the information related to the Neo4j database that is running on your machine (see Listing 9-2).

Listing 9-2. Connection Information for Spring Data Neo4j

```
spring:
  neo4j:
    uri: bolt://localhost:7474
    database: catalog
    authentication:
      username: neo4j
      password: changeme
```

Nothing happens if you run the application following the instructions in Appendix C with only this configuration. The application only tries to connect with the database.

```
2022-08-24 17:52:08.996  WARN 1111093 --- [ restartedMain] JpaBaseConfigur
ation$JpaWebConfiguration : spring.jpa.open-in-view is enabled by default.
Therefore, database queries may be performed during view rendering.
Explicitly configure spring.jpa.open-in-view to disable this warning

2022-08-24 17:52:09.353  INFO 1111093 --- [ restartedMain] org.neo4j.
driver.Driver                 : Direct driver instance 1081373891 created
for server address localhost:7474

2022-08-24 17:52:09.705  INFO 1111093 --- [ restartedMain]
o.s.b.w.embedded.tomcat.TomcatWebServer  : Tomcat started on port(s): 8090
(http) with context path '/api/catalog'

2022-08-24 17:52:09.723  INFO 1111093 --- [ restartedMain] c.apress.
catalog.ApiCatalogApplication   : Started ApiCatalogApplication in 4.94
seconds (JVM running for 5.543)
```

To continue with the example, remove everything in the relational database, like the dependencies of JPA, the driver of PostgreSQL, and the configuration in **application. yml**. Also, remove all the annotations in the entities without changing anything about the name of the fields because the next section covers this.

Annotations for Entities

In Spring Data Neo4j, there is a set of annotations that you can apply to the entities to indicate the meaning of each field or class. Let's explore some of the most relevant in Table 9-2.

Table 9-2. *The Most Common Neo4j Entity Annotations*

Spring Data Neo4j annotation	Meaning
@Node	This annotation indicates to Spring Data that the class is a candidate to persist information into the database.
@Id	This annotation indicates that the attribute needs to be unique and works as a primary key in a relational database.
@Relationship	Using this annotation, you indicate that two entities have a certain level of relationship. You can imagine this annotation as a combination of @OneToMany, @OneToOne, and @ManyToMany annotations in JPA.
@GeneratedValue	This annotation indicates that the attribute needs to be generated using a mechanism; it's similar to the same annotation with the same name in JPA.
@Property	Using the property to indicate the name of an attribute that needs to be persisted to only contain certain values. It's like a common column in the JPA.

> **Note**   Some of these annotations changed versions ago, so if you have any problems could not be the same; for example, the annotation **@Node** in previous versions is **@NodeEntity**.

The main difference with other implementations of Spring Data databases is, in this case, when you indicate that one entity has a relationship with others, try to persist all the information like the cascade in JPA and detects when a node exists in the database with the idea to not duplicate information a create the relationship between nodes.

Listing 9-3 modifies the previous Country entity to persist the information using Neo4j annotations in Table 9-1.

Listing 9-3. Definition of the Neo4j Entity

```java
import org.springframework.data.neo4j.core.schema.*;

import java.io.Serializable;
import java.util.List;
import java.util.Objects;

@Node("Country")
public class Country implements Serializable {

    @Id
    @GeneratedValue
    private Long id;

    @Property("code")
    private String code;

    @Property("name")
    private String name;

    @Property("locale")
    private String locale;

    @Property("timezone")
    private String timezone;

    @Property("enabled")
    private Boolean enabled = Boolean.TRUE;

    @Relationship("currency")
    private Currency currency;

    @Relationship("states")
    private List<State> states;

    //Previous setters and getters
    //Override the hashCode and equals methods

}
```

The use of annotations is quite simple to use it. You could indicate the value in the **@Property** or **@Relationship** annotations in the attributes of a class, but it's optionally. If you don't indicate one value, Spring Data Neo4j considers that the property in the database has the same name as in the class. Also, if you don't use the annotation in one attribute, Spring Data Neo4j decides to persist the information in the database with the same name that the attribute has.

The next step is to declare the other entities with a relationship with **Country**, like **State** and **Currency**. Let's take one of them to represent the format to define all of them, as shown in Listing 9-4.

Listing 9-4. Definition of the State Neo4j Entity

```
import org.springframework.data.neo4j.core.schema.Id;
import org.springframework.data.neo4j.core.schema.Node;
import org.springframework.data.neo4j.core.schema.Relationship;

import java.io.Serializable;

@Node("State")
public class State implements Serializable {
        @Id
        private Long id;

        private String code;

        private String name;

        private Boolean enabled = Boolean.TRUE;

        private @Relationship Country country;

        //Previous setters and getters
        //Override the hashCode and equals methods

}
```

There are no differences between the definition of both entities. You need to include attributes in the other class to indicate how to do a bidirectional relationship. If you don't include any attribute to indicate the relationship and run the application, you will see an exception indicating that you need to include the countryId attribute.

Access Using Repositories

In this case, the use of repositories is quite similar to other implementations of other databases. Still, behind the scenes, Spring Data uses Neo4jTemplate[10] to run the operations using a part of the driver.

For example, you can use the general CrudRepository<T, ID> and PagingAndSortingRepository<T, ID> to do the queries in the same way that JPA but take into consideration that just the recent versions can limit and skip the number of node writing a specific query (see Listing 9-5).

Listing 9-5. Definition of the Neo4j Repository

```
public interface CountryRepository extends CrudRepository<Country, Long> {
    List<Country> findByCode(String code);
}
```

The last step to enable the repositories and execute operations into the database implies adding the **@EnableNeo4jRepositories** annotation in the main class or a configuration class (see Listing 9-6). For simplicity, only do it in the main class.

Listing 9-6. Enable the Repositories for Neo4j

```
import org.springframework.boot.SpringApplication;
import org.springframework.boot.autoconfigure.SpringBootApplication;
import org.springframework.data.neo4j.repository.config.
EnableNeo4jRepositories;

@SpringBootApplication
@EnableNeo4jRepositories("com.apress.catalog.repository")
public class ApiCatalogApplication {

    public static void main(String[] args) {
            SpringApplication.run(ApiCatalogApplication.class, args);
    }

}
```

---

[10] https://docs.spring.io/spring-data/neo4j/docs/current/api/org/springframework/data/neo4j/core/Neo4jTemplate.html

The last step is to run the application again and execute POST operations in the country endpoint, which is `http://localhost:8080/api/catalog/country`. This populates the database with information and checks what it looks like using Neo4j Desktop, a recommended tool. If you want more information about how to run this tool or the Neo4j database, check Appendix E.

If you insert different counties with the same currency object or state, you get a graph similar to Figure 9-2. You can also see the information like a table by selecting one of the attributes on the left part of the screen, as shown in Figure 9-3.

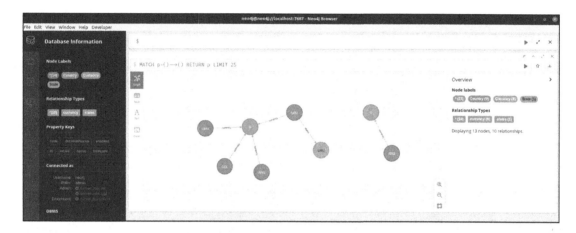

Figure 9-2. *Representation of the entities in the database*

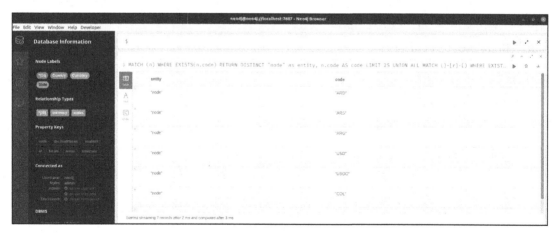

Figure 9-3. *Representation of the entities in the database, like a table*

One last thing to mention about this tool is that you can see the query that was executed to show the results, which is important if you want to write a specific query tested and include it in your repository after that. For example, the following code block includes a query that obtains a list of currencies with the same code.

Writing the Query Using Annotations

There are no significant differences from other databases. Spring Data Neo4j offers the possibility to write the query and include it as part of a method of the repository to simply access the database. Just remember to check the query in a tool previously to verify that everything is okay with the syntax.

```
public interface CurrencyRepository extends
CrudRepository<Currency, Long> {

    //Previous source code
    @Query("MATCH(currency:Currency) WHERE currency.code =~code RETURN
    currency")
    List<Currency> retrieveByCode(String code);
}
```

As a final piece of advice, if the query is so complex and implies many properties, extract the query into a variable inside the interface. Keep the declaration of the methods simple.

Custom Repositories

Most of the projects of Spring Data offer the possibility not to use exclusive repositories; you can create a custom repository that uses the Neo4jTemplate, which provides the same possibility to execute operations like the repository without all the benefits of having all the logic created.

Listing 9-7 creates a custom repository that contains the main operations that use **CountryService** to replace it.

Listing 9-7. Definition of Custom Repository Interface

```
package com.apress.catalog.repository;

import com.apress.catalog.model.Country;

import java.util.Optional;

public interface CustomCountryRepository {
    Country save(Country entity);

    Optional<Country> findById(Long id);

    void deleteById(Long id);
}
```

After creating the repository's interface, the following step is to define the implementation of the repository, which uses Neo4jTemplate (see Listing 9-8). As in previous examples of non-relational databases, this repository does not support @Transactional.

Listing 9-8. The Repository Implementation

```
@Repository
public class CustomCountryRepositoryImpl implements
CustomCountryRepository {
    private final Neo4jTemplate neo4jTemplate;

    @Autowired
    public CustomCountryRepositoryImpl(Neo4jTemplate neo4jTemplate) {
        this.neo4jTemplate = neo4jTemplate;
    }

    @Override
    public Country save(Country entity) {
        return neo4jTemplate.save(entity);
    }

    @Override
    public Optional<Country> findById(Long id) {
        return neo4jTemplate.findById(id, Country.class);
    }
```

```
@Override
public void deleteById(Long id) {
    neo4jTemplate.deleteById(id, Country.class);
}
}
```

The definition of a custom repository using the template is quite similar to the methods in a normal repository when using the find operation to delete. You need to indicate which entity to search for. Also, you can execute the Neo4jTemplate queries using the Cypher language.

Queries by Example

For this database, you can use the same features from the previous database to create a query based on the values of one object. You only need to extend your repository from QueryByExampleExecutor<T> (see Listing 9-9).

Listing 9-9. Add the Interface to Use QueryByExample<Country>

```
public interface CountryRepository extends CrudRepository<Country, Long>,
QueryByExampleExecutor<Country> {

}
```

The next step is to create a new method in your service that receives as a parameter one string with part of the country's name, and the matcher needs to indicate the criteria to find. To not repeat all the logic from the previous chapter, Listing 9-10 shows only the block of code responsible for creating the example and executing the query.

Listing 9-10. Example

```
import com.apress.catalog.dto.CountryDTO;
import com.apress.catalog.mapper.ApiMapper;
import com.apress.catalog.model.Country;
import com.apress.catalog.model.State;
import com.apress.catalog.repository.CountryRepository;
import com.apress.catalog.repository.StateRepository;
import org.springframework.beans.factory.annotation.Autowired;
import org.springframework.data.domain.Example;
```

```java
import org.springframework.data.domain.ExampleMatcher;
import org.springframework.stereotype.Service;
import org.springframework.transaction.annotation.Isolation;
import org.springframework.transaction.annotation.Transactional;

import jakarta.validation.ConstraintViolation;
import jakarta.validation.ConstraintViolationException;
import jakarta.validation.Validator;
import java.util.List;
import java.util.Optional;
import java.util.Set;

@Service
public class CountryService {

    CountryRepository countryRepository;

    StateRepository stateRepository;
    Validator validator;

    @Autowired
    public CountryService(CountryRepository countryRepository,
    StateRepository stateRepository,
                    Validator validator) {
        this.countryRepository = countryRepository;
        this.stateRepository = stateRepository;
        this.validator = validator;
    }

    public List<CountryDTO> getAll(String name) {
        List<CountryDTO> response = null;

        //Declare the example with the name that you want to find in the
        database including the null values
        ExampleMatcher matcher = ExampleMatcher.matching()
                .withIgnorePaths("code")
                .withIncludeNullValues()
                .withMatcher("name", ExampleMatcher.GenericPropertyMatcher.of
                (ExampleMatcher.StringMatcher.DEFAULT));
```

```
Country entity = new Country();
entity.setName(name);

 // Find on the repository using the example
Iterable<Country> country = countryRepository.
findAll(Example.of(entity, matcher));

if(country != null) {
    response = ApiMapper.INSTANCE.entityToDTO(country);
}

return response;
    }
}
```

You can test this logic by invoking the GET method (`http://localhost:8080/api/catalog/country`) that returns the list of countries which is GET `http://localhost:8080/api/catalog/country` passing as a query parameter a name.

Summary

This chapter overviewed Neo4j. This database is not a silver bullet that applies to all cases. In many situations, Neo4j is not the best option; a better idea would be to use a database like Redis or MongoDB. Explore your choices to determine the best database to solve your specific needs.

Cassandra: Wide-Column Database

The non-relational databases you have seen so far can have specific information replicas but imply that you configure a master node indicating the slaves. Another problem is how to replicate the information, which sometimes needs a certain knowledge about configuring it.

This chapter explains how Cassandra offers you the ability to increase the number of nodes without the need to indicate which of them is the master, at least in Spring Data for Apache Cassandra[1] configuration.

What Is Cassandra?

Cassandra[2] is an open-source wide-column database created by Apache. Many developers use this database because it offers high performance for certain operations, the possibility of scaling horizontally, and a flexible schema like non-relational databases.

The idea of Cassandra is to have a certain number of nodes where information is distributed using a partition key, which is like the primary key in a relational database so that you can have one row in one instance and another in a different node. Figure 10-1 illustrates this.

---

[1] https://spring.io/projects/spring-data-cassandra
[2] https://cassandra.apache.org/_/index.html

A. Sacco, *Beginning Spring Data*, https://doi.org/10.1007/978-1-4842-8764-4_10

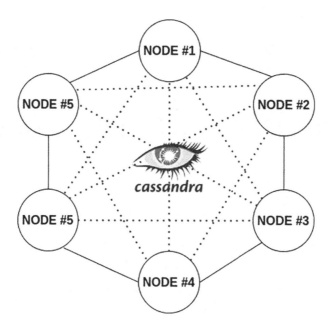

Figure 10-1. *Node architecture in Cassandra*

The following are some of the main benefits of these databases.

- **Highly scalable**: You add or remove nodes without downtime. Each new node report to the other one that exists, so they register to distribute the information.

- **High performance:** No central node or master takes the decision, and the other is replicated. In this database, all the nodes have the same role. Figure 10-2 shows how information is distributed across different nodes.

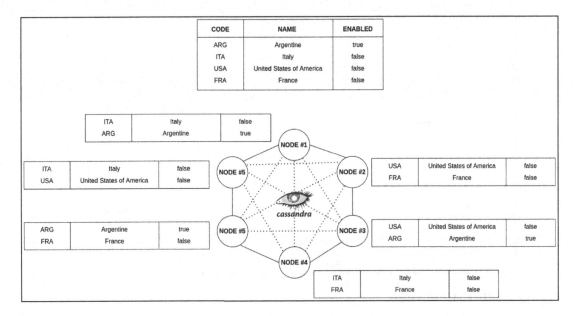

Figure 10-2. *Distribution and replication of information*

- **High availability**: The information stored on one node is replicated on other nodes where you can indicate the factor or replication. Also, you can replicate the information across different regions or cloud providers.

- **Expiration of the information**: The rows can have a TTL in the same way that Redis does; after that, the row disappears.

- **Great for analytics**: This type of database is ideal for doing operations related to big data.

Note   Remember that the non-relational databases do not cover everything in the CAP theorem[3] because it's impossible to guarantee the three attributes at the same time, so you need to sacrifice one of them instead of the other one.

It's not within this book's scope to explain the theorem as a little refresher of the concepts. Figure 10-3 illustrates the main idea.

---

[3] https://www.ibm.com/cloud/learn/cap-theorem

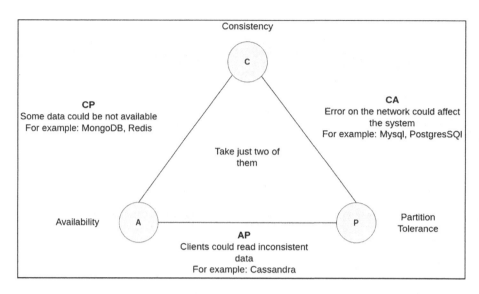

Figure 10-3. *CAP theorem*

Structure

Cassandra provides something similar to SQL, called CQL (Cassandra Query Language), to perform certain operations, such as inserting/updating/reading the information into the database. At some point, there are certain equivalences between relational databases and Cassandra in how they organize information. Table 10-1 illustrates this.

Table 10-1. *Model Equivalence*

Relational Model	Cassandra Model
Database	Keyspace
Table	Column Family (CF)
Primary key	Row key
Column name	Column name/key
Column value	Column value

The equivalence does not mean that all the concepts are the same is a representation to have a mind map. The following describes each of them.

- **Keyspace**: This structure contains tables or column families indicating the database's replication factor. You can indicate how many information replicas exist across data centers or cloud providers.

- **Column family:** It's a type to store rows and columns with a certain number of partitions which means that not all the information in a table exists in the same node. It could be distributed in different replicated nodes.

- **Row key**: This structure contains a partition key or row key, which is mandatory in all the rows to know which node the information is stored.

- **Column name/key**: Works as a secondary key that you can use for certain operations.

- **Column**: A single column that stores certain information.

Configuration

In this section, you will see how to configure your previous api-catalog using Cassandra but excluding all details about the installation and configuration of the database, which you can see in Appendix E.

Before modifying your microservices as suggested, remove all the dependencies and the annotations related to Spring JPA, including the scripts, in the DB folder.

Database and Connection Settings

Let's add the Cassandra dependency to **api-catalog** to use in a non-reactive way, because this database (the other non-relational that Spring Boot provides) supports both alternatives, which is covered in the next chapter. Again, do not include the version in the dependency (see Listing 10-1) because Spring Boot knows the best option.

Listing 10-1. Dependencies Connected with Cassandra

```
<dependency>
  <groupId>org.springframework.boot</groupId>
  <artifactId>spring-boot-starter-data-cassandra</artifactId>
</dependency>
```

This dependency contains a version of the driver, so you don't need to specify any in your pom file. If you have problems with the specific version of the driver that Spring Boot provides, you override it, including the dependency in the pom.

The next step is to introduce the configuration in your **application.yml** to use your machine's information related to the Cassandra database (see Listing 10-2).

Listing 10-2. Spring Data Connection Information for Apache Cassandra

```
spring:
  data:
    cassandra:
      keyspace-name: twa
      schema-action: recreate
      local-datacenter: datacenter1
      contact-points: # The different nodes that Cassandra have
        - 127.0.0.1:9042
        - 127.0.0.1:9043
        - 127.0.0.1:9044
```

The values of the attributes defined in **application.yml** relate to a configuration that appears in **docker-compose.yml**, which you can find in the GitHub repository, related to Cassandra. The contact points in Listing 10-2 are the instances of Cassandra that you are running on your machine. To keep the discussion simple, use the schema action with the **recreate** value, which drops the tables and creates them again.

Let's start with the modifications in the entities, including the annotations to indicate which are the primary keys for each cluster and which are for the partition (see Listing 10-3).

Listing 10-3. Connection Information for Spring Data and Apache Cassandra

```
import com.datastax.oss.driver.api.core.uuid.Uuids;
import org.springframework.data.cassandra.core.cql.Ordering;
import org.springframework.data.cassandra.core.cql.PrimaryKeyType;
import org.springframework.data.cassandra.core.mapping.Column;
import org.springframework.data.cassandra.core.mapping.PrimaryKeyColumn;
import org.springframework.data.cassandra.core.mapping.Table;

import java.io.Serializable;
import java.util.List;
import java.util.UUID;

@Table("country")//It's not the same package like JPA
public class Country implements Serializable {

    @PrimaryKeyColumn(
            name = "id",
            type = PrimaryKeyType.CLUSTERED,
            ordering = Ordering.DESCENDING)
    private UUID id = Uuids.timeBased();

    @PrimaryKeyColumn(
            name = "code",
            type = PrimaryKeyType.PARTITIONED,
            ordering = Ordering.DESCENDING)
    private String code;

    @Column
    private String name;

        //Other columns

    @Column("currency")
    private Currency currency;

    @Column("states")
    private List<State> states;

        //Previous setters and getters
}
```

There are differences in the ways that JPA defines things. Cassandra lets you indicate the order of the information, as shown in Listing 10-3, but only in **@PrimaryKeyColumn** because the other columns can't be filtered. The normal queries need to be indicated using the **@Column** annotation, where you can indicate the real name if it differs from what's in the database.

In the previous example, some columns are objects which is one of the main differences with JPA because you can save complex objects in a column like a JSON. Now, if you run your application only modifying the Country entity, an exception appears on the console indicating that something is wrong with the columns that are complex objects. This happens because you need to indicate the other objects that are not entities. To do this, you only need to include the **@UserDefinedType("currency")** annotation in the Currency class (see Listing 10-4).

Listing 10-4. Connection Information for Spring Data and Apache Cassandra

```
import org.springframework.data.cassandra.core.mapping.UserDefinedType;
import java.io.Serializable;

@UserDefinedType("currency")
public class Currency implements Serializable {
    //Previous attributes without any annotation
}
```

The next step is to define the repositories that do not suffer major changes between databases (see Listing 10-5). After writing custom methods to do the queries, there are things to consider.

Listing 10-5. Cassandra Repository

```
public interface CountryRepository extends CrudRepository<Country, Long> {
    List<Country> findByCode(String code);
}
```

Note   One of the big differences with other non-relational databases is that you don't need to enable the repositories for Cassandra with a specific annotation.

This repository works fine because the method's name involves a partition key, so Spring Data for Apache Cassandra can create and execute the query. If you try to filter for another attribute like time zone, an exception indicates that the operation is not valid.

Note   Caused by com.datastax.driver.core.exceptions.InvalidQueryException: Cannot execute this query as it might involve data filtering and thus may have unpredictable performance. If you want to execute this query despite the performance unpredictability, use ALLOW FILTERING.

The driver suggests you use the **@Query(allowFiltering = true)** annotation in the method to execute the operation. This annotation could generate problems related to the performance because you can try to do an operation where it's not supported by default for the driver. If you need to filter for another attribute that is not a partition key, perhaps it could be a good idea to change the definition of the columns in the database using a tool like Cassandra Web.

Note   This database offers a similar way to write the entire query and declare it in repositories like JPA.

```
public interface CountryRepository extends CrudRepository<Country, Long> {
    // Manual query
    @Query("SELECT c FROM country c where c.code = :code")
    Currency retrieveByCode(@Param("code") String code);
}
```

Now, if you run the application, behind the scenes Spring Data for Apache Cassandra generates the table structure with the relationships, which you can check in Cassandra Web on localhost:3000. If you want more information about how to run this tool and the database, check the Appendix E.

If you access the visual tool to check what happens with the database you will see something more or less like Figure 10-4.

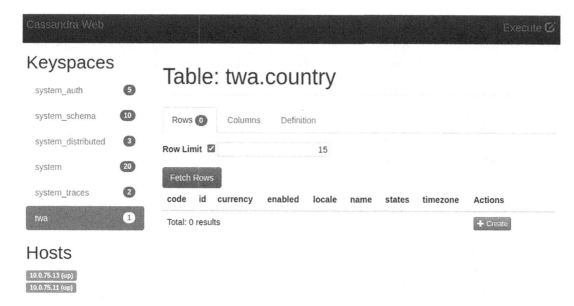

Figure 10-4. *The table generated after the start of the microservice*

If you inspect the definition of the table doing click the Definition link, you see
something like the following structure, which you delegate to Spring Data for Apache
Cassandra, the creation of the queries, and the execution.

```
CREATE TABLE twa.country (
  code text,
  id uuid,
  currency frozen <currency>,
  enabled boolean,
  locale text,
  name text,
  states list<frozen<twa.state {code text, countryid text, enabled boolean,
  id bigint, name text}>>,
  timezone text,
  PRIMARY KEY ((code, id))
)
WITH bloom_filter_fp_chance = 0.01
 AND caching = {'keys': 'ALL', 'rows_per_partition': 'NONE'}
 AND comment = ''
```

```
AND compaction = {'class': 'SizeTieredCompactionStrategy', 'max_
threshold': '32', 'min_threshold': '4'}
AND compression = {'chunk_length_in_kb': '16', 'class': 'LZ4Compressor'}
AND crc_check_chance = 1.0
AND dclocal_read_repair_chance = 0.0
AND default_time_to_live = 0
AND gc_grace_seconds = 864000
AND max_index_interval = 2048
AND memtable_flush_period_in_ms = 0
AND min_index_interval = 128
AND read_repair_chance = 0.0
AND speculative_retry = '99p';
```

The next step is to check if the methods in the repositories work. Execute operations to insert countries in the database by making requests to the http://localhost:8080/ api/catalog/country POST method. If everything works fine, you can ingress to Cassandra Web and check how the rows are stored in the database (see Figure 10-5).

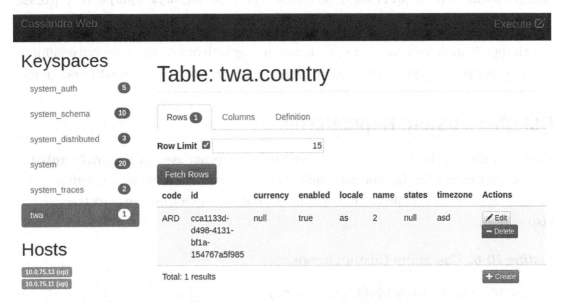

Figure 10-5. *How the information is stored in the table*

One last thing you can do is stop one of the nodes to check what happens with the information and how to react to Spring Data for Apache Cassandra. Let's stop the first node of Cassandra and run the application again to check. You only need to execute the **docker-compose stop** command to stop the nodes when you use the docker-compose file.

```
2022-08-23 23:07:54.364  WARN 904342 --- [      s0-admin-1]
c.d.o.d.i.c.control.ControlConnection    : [s0] Error connecting to
Node(endPoint=/127.0.0.1:9043, hostId=null, hashCode=434203ad), trying
next node (ConnectionInitException: [s0|control|connecting...] Protocol
initialization request, step 1 (OPTIONS): failed to send request (io.netty.
channel.StacklessClosedChannelException))

2022-08-23 23:07:54.564  WARN 904342 --- [      s0-admin-0] c.d.o.d.i.c
.l.h.OptionalLocalDcHelper    : [s0|default] You specified datacenter1
as the local DC, but some contact points are from a different DC:
Node(endPoint=/127.0.0.1:9042, hostId=null, hashCode=1a8bfdf6)=null,
Node(endPoint=/127.0.0.1:9043, hostId=null, hashCode=434203ad)=null; please
provide the correct local DC, or check your contact points
```

The application indicates that something is wrong with one of the nodes but continues working, and you can check if the information is available by invoking the GET endpoints.

Defining Custom Repositories

The Cassandra database can create a custom repository that uses **CassandraTemplate** scenes, but this implies that you must define all the operations. Let's start creating the interface, which contains all the operations that api-catalog uses to work (see Listing 10-6).

Listing 10-6. Cassandra Custom Repository

```
public interface CustomCountryRepository {
    Country save(Country entity);

    Optional<Country> findById(Long id);

    void deleteById(Long id);
}
```

The next step is to create a concrete class that implements the methods and does the operations using CassandraTemplate (see Listing 10-7). The main advantage of this template is that you have a certain equivalence with the methods that exist in common repositories like findById or deleteById.

Listing 10-7. Implementation of the Custom Repository

```
import com.apress.catalog.model.Country;
import com.apress.catalog.repository.CustomCountryRepository;
import com.datastax.oss.driver.api.querybuilder.QueryBuilder;
import org.springframework.data.cassandra.core.CassandraOperations;
import org.springframework.data.cassandra.core.mapping.Table;
import org.springframework.stereotype.Repository;
import org.springframework.util.StringUtils;

import java.time.Duration;
import java.util.Optional;
import java.util.UUID;

@Repository
public class CustomCountryRepositoryImpl implements
CustomCountryRepository {

    //Help you to execute the operations on the database in a simple way
    private CassandraOperations cassandraTemplate;

    public CustomCountryRepositoryImpl(CassandraOperations cassandra
    Template) {
        this.cassandraTemplate = cassandraTemplate;
    }

    @Override
    public Country save(Country entity) {
        return cassandraTemplate.insert(entity);
    }

    @Override
    public Optional<Country> findById(UUID id) {
```

```
        return Optional.of(cassandraTemplate.selectOneById(id, Country.
        class));
    }

    @Override
    public void deleteById(UUID id) {
        cassandraTemplate.deleteById(id, Country.class);
    }
}
```

There are other ways to execute queries into the database that do not directly imply using CassandraTemplate. One alternative is to use the QueryBuilder class to declare the operation you want to execute. For example, let's transform the insertion of CassandraTemplate using QueryBuilder from the database driver.

```
import com.apress.catalog.model.Country;
import com.apress.catalog.repository.CustomCountryRepository;
import com.datastax.oss.driver.api.core.cql.Statement;
import com.datastax.oss.driver.api.querybuilder.QueryBuilder;
import org.springframework.data.cassandra.core.CassandraOperations;
import org.springframework.data.cassandra.core.mapping.Table;
import org.springframework.stereotype.Repository;
import org.springframework.util.StringUtils;

@Repository
public class CustomCountryRepositoryImpl implements
CustomCountryRepository {
    //Previous source code

    //This is another alternative to do an insert into the database
    private void insertByDriver(Country entity) {
        //Equivalence using the driver
        Statement query = QueryBuilder
            .insertInto(toTableName(Country.class))
            .value("id", QueryBuilder.literal(entity.getId()))
            .value("code", QueryBuilder.literal(entity.getCode()))
            .value("name", QueryBuilder.literal(entity.getName()))
            .value("enabled", QueryBuilder.literal(entity.getEnabled()))
```

```
        .build();

    cassandraTemplate.execute(query);
}

 //These methods obtain the name of the table into the database from
the entity
@SuppressWarnings("unused")
private String toTableName(Object obj) {
    return toTableName(obj.getClass());
}

private String toTableName(Class<?> type) {

    Table tableAnnotation = type.getAnnotation(Table.class);

    return tableAnnotation != null && StringUtils.hasText(
    tableAnnotation.value())
        ? tableAnnotation.value()
        : type.getSimpleName();
    }
}
```

Defining a TTL

This feature implies that the information is only available for some time. After that disappears, it is not recommended to indicate in the application because there are bugs related to how it works depending on the version of the driver and Spring Data for Apache Cassandra. Hence, as a recommendation, try to define the structure of the ability using the CQL and indicate the TTL for all the rows in that sentence.

By the way, you can do it but using QueryBuilder and writing the entire sentence.

```
Statement query = QueryBuilder
                .insertInto("country")
                .value("id", QueryBuilder.literal(entity.getId()))
                .value("code", QueryBuilder.literal(entity.getCode()))
                .value("name", QueryBuilder.literal(entity.getName()))
```

```
        .value("enabled", QueryBuilder.literal(entity.getEnabled()))
        //Declare all the attributes to insert
        .build();
```

```
query.setTimeout(Duration.ofMillis(100L));
```

Summary

Spring Data for Apache Cassandra offers many features to interact with the database without problems. If the common repositories offered for the framework do not cover your requirements, you can create a custom and add all the logic.

Apache Cassandra offers a few benefits over other non-relational databases, such as no master, so you can add new nodes without problems. There is a problem related to the declaration of the nodes in your application because you need to specify the host of each node, so at some point, you need to redeploy the application.

PART IV

Advanced testing and best practices

The last part of this book does not cover interacting with new databases. Instead, you learn advanced concepts relevant to improving the performance or reducing the risk of not testing your queries until deploying the source code in some environment.

One of the most relevant topics is related to testing, which in most cases is not considered appropriate, at least on the repositories or the layer that accesses the database, because it implies problems with using a fake database.

Finally, you see some improvements to potentially increase the performance or the latency to transfer information across the network from your microservice to the database.

CHAPTER 11

Reactive Access

Most of the communication that an application establishes using HTTP connections implies a request, a specific process to obtain the response, and the response, which could be an exception or a type of information.

This approach comes with issues. For instance, you need to wait until the services that your API consumes answer before you can start processing the information. But what if there were a mechanism that could return the information in a streaming fashion so that your API can start performing its operation before having all the information? Figure 11-1 visualizes the standard way the database is accessed.

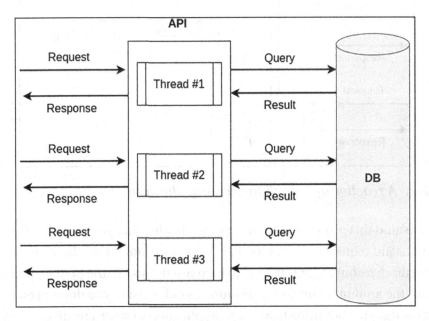

Figure 11-1. *The standard way to access the database*

This chapter explains how reactive programming offers solutions to these problems.

© Andres Sacco 2023
A. Sacco, *Beginning Spring Data*, https://doi.org/10.1007/978-1-4842-8764-4_11

What Is Reactive Access?

In a traditional application, each request allocates a thread for a period of time to execute certain operations; this approach is known as the thread-per-request model. During this time, the process consumes memory and CPU exclusively. Figure 11-2 shows how a certain number of requests access the database simultaneously, wasting resources such as memory/CPU until each operation returns a result. Reactive programming is an alternative that addresses problems like the proper use of resources, which in turn provides the ability to improve scalability.

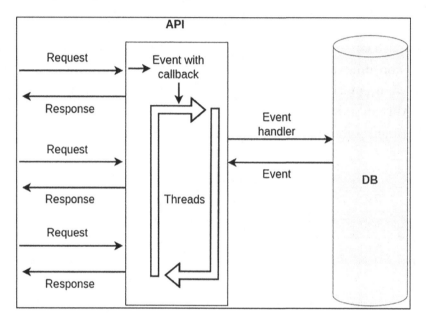

Figure 11-2. *A reactive approach to accessing the database*

To understand this problem in another way, imagine that you have the chance to receive a thousand requests simultaneously. Your application can't be scaled for factors like needing more resources or the need to increase the size of the pool of connections. If you reduce the amount of time each resource is being used, you don't need to make significant changes to your infrastructure or application to return results.

The idea behind reactive programming is not to block a thread. Instead, the application receives the request like an event with a callback. This concept was popular many years ago in other languages like JavaScript. It implied waiting until to have something returned and using the callback to send a notification to the owner of the request and the result of the operation.

During this process, the application's thread can be used for another request. The information could be returned as a stream of information so you can execute different things when you receive the response instead of waiting until you have all the information. If an error occurs during the streaming process, the operation finishes, which makes sense because the same can happen when you try to do the same in the blocking method.

In Spring Boot, the framework has a project for general reactive programming, called Spring WebFlux, which appears with the use of two publishers of events in the stream of information.

- **Mono<T>** can emit zero or one element. For example, an endpoint that receives an id with the idea of returning all the information of one entity could return only one element.

- **Flux<T>** implies that you will return zero to N elements until receiving the notification that there are no more elements to send. For example, an endpoint returns all the existing countries into the database.

Spring WebFlux is the application layer that returns the results or interacts with other applications that do not directly access the database. For this operation, there are Spring projects[1] that offer these abilities.

Modifying Queries to Be Reactive

Reactive in Spring Data appeared in 2016 when the first versions of the modules that access non-relational databases like MongoDB, Redis, Cassandra, and Neo4j offered the possibility of obtaining the results of the queries as a stream of information.

Another situation happens with relational databases. Not all of them have support to use the reactive paradigm. R2DBC[2] is one of the most used libraries to work reactively with databases like MySQL, PostgreSQL, and SQL Server and has plans to incorporate support for other databases.

---

[1] https://spring.io/projects/spring-data-r2dbc
[2] https://r2dbc.io/

Non-Relational Databases

This section shows how implemented reactive programming in MongoDB. Still, all the databases have the same support and could be redundant to do the same four different times.

In MongoDB and other databases, the complexity of transforming your blocking application into a reactive one implies little changes. The first is to include a dependency that provides all the interfaces you need to use in the repositories, like in Listing 11-1.

Listing 11-1. Mongo Reactive Dependencies

```
<dependency>
    <groupId>org.springframework.boot</groupId>
    <artifactId>spring-boot-starter-data-mongodb-reactive</artifactId>
</dependency>
```

The second step implies enabling the configuration to use the reactive repositories using the @EnableReactiveMongoRepositories annotation and creating a specific class with the configuration, shown in Listing 11-2.

Listing 11-2. Enable the Support to the Reactive Access

```
import com.mongodb.reactivestreams.client.MongoClient;
import com.mongodb.reactivestreams.client.MongoClients;
import org.springframework.context.annotation.Bean;
import org.springframework.data.mongodb.config.
AbstractReactiveMongoConfiguration;
import org.springframework.data.mongodb.core.ReactiveMongoTemplate;
import org.springframework.data.mongodb.repository.config.
EnableReactiveMongoRepositories;

//Enable the support for reactive repositories
@EnableReactiveMongoRepositories
public class MongoReactiveConfiguration
        extends AbstractReactiveMongoConfiguration {

    //Declare the client to use with the database
    @Bean
    public MongoClient mongoClient() {
```

```
        return MongoClients.create();
    }

    @Override
    protected String getDatabaseName() {
        return "catalog";
    }

    //Declare the reactive MongoTemplate which use the MongoClient
    @Bean
    public ReactiveMongoTemplate reactiveMongoTemplate() {
        return new ReactiveMongoTemplate(mongoClient(), getDatabaseName());
    }
}
}
```

Now your application has repositories that extend from **MongoRepository<T, ID>.**; the idea is to replace it with **ReactiveMongoRepository<T, ID>**. If your repositories extend from **CrudRepository<T, ID>**, you need to replace them with **ReactiveCrudRepository<T, ID>**.

If you don't change anything in the custom methods you defined in your repositories, everything continues working in a blocking way, so you need to change the return of each method (see Listing 11-3).

Listing 11-3. Reactive Repository

```
import com.apress.catalog.model.Country;
import org.springframework.data.mongodb.repository.Query;
import org.springframework.data.mongodb.repository.ReactiveMongoRepository;
import reactor.core.publisher.Flux;

public interface CountryRepository extends ReactiveMongoRepository<Count
ry, Long> {
    Flux<Country> findByCode(String code);

    //This is a custom query that find just for one field
    @Query(value = "{'code': ?0}")
    Flux<Country> findCustom(String code);
```

```
    //This is a custom query combine the condition on the name of the
    method with the query
    @Query(value = "{'code': ?0}")
    Flux<Country> findEnabled(String code);
}
```

These modifications affect the Service class that expects to receive an object instead of something reactive, so you have two options: one is to transform all the applications into a reactive, which implies that you need to modify all the services and the controllers, and the other one is called to the block() method, which transforms the reactive operation into a blocking operation. The second approach is not the best because you have support for reactive operations, but you use it in a standard way. This approach could be the first step to transforming the API reactively.

This book does not modify all the source code because it implies a lot of effort to do it, but the modification in the source code is just a few lines.

Relational Databases

Relational databases differ greatly from non-relational ones because Spring is not offered by default support to the reactive approach. In this case, you need to use a library called R2DBC (Reactive Relational Database Connectivity), which brings support to databases to the reactive paradigm.

This library has extensive support for the community by having many articles and talks at conferences. Spring Data includes support for this library, reducing the complexity to use in Spring Boot applications. Still, there is no support for all the vendors of relational databases. Each year, a new database with support appears, but the most relevant ones used for the community have support like MySQL, PostgreSQL, MariaDB, and SQL Server.

The following are restrictions in using this library when this book was written.

- You can't use embedded IDs, so you can generate composite primary keys.

- The @Version annotation is supported, so you can continue using the optimistic locking.

- There is no automatic generation of IDs, so you need to indicate which strategy of generation of Id you want to use.

- If you have an application that uses the @CreatedDate or @LastModifiedDate annotations, it's possible to continue using but enabling the auditing logic of R2DBC with the @EnableR2dbcAuditing annotation.

- You can automatically create the database using this approach, so you need a mechanism to generate the entire database structure. One solution is to connect to the database and run a script.

The first step to using reactive in the application is adding the dependencies in the pom.xml file (see Listing 11-4).

Listing 11-4. Add the Dependencies to Use Reactive in the Application

```xml
<dependency>
    <groupId>org.springframework.boot</groupId>
    <artifactId>spring-boot-starter-data-r2dbc</artifactId>
</dependency>

<dependency>
    <groupId>io.r2dbc</groupId>
    <artifactId>r2dbc-postgresql</artifactId>
    <version>0.8.12.RELEASE</version>
</dependency>
```

The next step is to replace the previous CrudRepository<T, ID> from Spring Data with the new repositories, which provide the same method but in a reactive way (see Listing 11-5).

Listing 11-5. Reactive Repository

```java
import com.apress.catalog.model.State;
import org.springframework.data.r2dbc.repository.R2dbcRepository;
import reactor.core.publisher.Flux;

public interface StateRepository extends R2dbcRepository<State, Long> {
    Flux<State> findByCode(String code);

    Flux<State> findAllByCountryId(Long id);
}
```

The configuration you declared to use in your application is not valid. You need to change the way that R2DBC understands it (see Listing 11-6).

Listing 11-6. Add the Configuration to Use Reactive

```
spring:
  r2dbc:
    username: postgres
    password: postgres
    url: r2dbc:postgresql://localhost:5432/catalog?autoReconnect=true
    pool:
      max-create-connection-time: 2s
      initial-size: 5
      max-size: 10
```

All these changes look great, but you need to explicitly enable the support to the reactive repositories using the @EnableR2dbcRepositories annotation. If you don't enable it, the application shows you an exception indicating that you have not found any repositories (see Listing 11-7).

Listing 11-7. Enable Support to the Reactive Repositories

```
import org.springframework.boot.SpringApplication;
import org.springframework.boot.autoconfigure.SpringBootApplication;
import org.springframework.data.r2dbc.repository.config.
EnableR2dbcRepositories;

@SpringBootApplication
@EnableR2dbcRepositories(basePackages = "com.apress.catalog")
public class ApiCatalogApplication {
    //Previous source code
}
```

There are embedded entities in your application to save the information about the audit, so for this example, let's remove them for all your entities. Everything continues working if you run the application and start operations with the endpoints.

Considerations

This approach takes several advantages. The main problem is that not all the databases have all the features to support a migration to a reactive approach without suffering problems.

There are exceptions, like MongoDB, where all the features are available for both approaches. Still, there are others where the migration implies changes in the database, like the embedded object in **api-catalog**. These changes have certain risks, so it's not so trivial.

Summary

This chapter discussed how the reactive approach helps reduce the time you spend and the number of resources your application needs because each request does not imply that you wait until to have all the responses to return the result. Non-relational databases supported this approach many years ago. Relational databases do not have support for all vendors, so if you want to use this approach, first check if your database has support or not.

The next chapter discusses how to test the repositories that access the database in a way that does not imply that you deploy the entire application in an environment.

CHAPTER 12

Unit and Integration Testing

Testing is one of the topics you never stop learning about because new techniques and tools are always emerging, whether to write tests or simplify the way to perform tasks like creating mocks to check if a part of your source code works properly. The reasons for testing your applications are many and are explained in countless resources. You want to be assured that your logic does what you expect it to, to discover potential bugs, and to know whether you need to modify your source code to ensure everything works as planned.

Note   One of the best resources to learn more about testing is Martin Fowler's[1] blog, which tackles topics like BDD, different types of testing, and good practices.

To be honest, many developers don't like to write tests to cover basic scenarios. In this context, it doesn't make a ton of sense to spend a lot of time testing the layer that accesses a database, which in most cases in Spring Data, is an interface with methods to represent custom queries. The main problem with this approach is you may detect problems with your queries in an environment or integration test that do not cover only the access to the database because, for example, the endpoint of our catalog's application before and after saving information causes changes, so you can check if the logic of the service layer works fine. Still, you can't check if everything works fine in the repository.

---

[1] https://martinfowler.com/tags/testing.html

© Andres Sacco 2023
A. Sacco, *Beginning Spring Data*, https://doi.org/10.1007/978-1-4842-8764-4_12

Another problem with not doing correct application testing is the database versions. Some developers use in-memory databases like H2 to perform specific tests. This approach works fine for certain conditions, but not all the databases have the same features, so you need to perform the test with the same database that your application uses in all environments.

To summarize, one of the main problems with testing data access layers is how to perform a test *only* in a repository. The second one is how to test database access to allow you to execute your test multiple times without a problem. Throughout this chapter, you learn the solution to both problems. This book does not cover unit and integration testing in detail. For that, I encourage you to check out Martin Fowler's website.[2]

Unit Testing with Mocks

One of the most used libraries to test a Java/Kotlin application is Junit,[3] which has many other libraries that add extra features, including Spring Boot Test,[4] which uses the latest version of JUnit to do certain operations.

Note   There are other Java testing alternatives, such as Spock[5] or TestNG.[6]

Let's start creating a common unit test using JUnit to check the logic of your **save** method in **CountryService** if it works fine or not. The first thing to do is add all the dependencies necessary to create and use the unit test using JUnit; these dependencies you reuse in the final solution too. Listing 12-1 show the dependencies that you need to add on the pom file to create unit test.

---

[2] https://martinfowler.com/articles/practical-test-pyramid.html
[3] https://junit.org/junit5/
[4] https://docs.spring.io/spring-boot/docs/current/reference/html/features.html#features.testing
[5] https://spockframework.org/
[6] https://testng.org/doc/

Listing 12-1. Junit/Mockito Dependency

```
<dependencies>
    <dependency>
        <groupId>org.mockito</groupId>
        <artifactId>mockito-junit-jupiter</artifactId>
        <version>4.6.1</version>
        <scope>test</scope>
    </dependency>

    ← Other dependencies ->
</dependencies>

<build>
    <plugins>
        ← Other Plugins →

        <plugin>
            <groupId>org.apache.maven.plugins</groupId>
            <artifactId>maven-surefire-plugin</artifactId>
            <version>${maven-surefire-plugin.version}</version>
        </plugin>
    </plugins>
</build>
```

After that, you only need to create a test that checks if the service that uses the repository to persist the information works fine or not (see Listing 12-2).

Listing 12-2. Service Unit Test

```
import com.apress.catalog.dto.CountryDTO;
import com.apress.catalog.model.Country;
import com.apress.catalog.repository.CountryRepository;
import com.apress.catalog.repository.StateRepository;
import jakarta.validation.Validator;
import org.junit.jupiter.api.BeforeEach;
import org.junit.jupiter.api.Test;
```

```java
import static org.junit.jupiter.api.Assertions.assertNotNull;
import static org.mockito.ArgumentMatchers.any;
import static org.mockito.Mockito.mock;
import static org.mockito.Mockito.when;

public class CountryServiceTest {

    private CountryService service;
    private CountryRepository countryRepository;
    private StateRepository stateRepository;
    private MapperFacade mapper;
    private Validator validator;

    @BeforeEach
    public void setUp() {
        countryRepository = mock(CountryRepository.class);
        stateRepository = mock(StateRepository.class);
        mapper = mock(MapperFacade.class);
        validator = mock(Validator.class);

        service = new CountryService(countryRepository, stateRepository,
        mapper, validator);
    }

    //This test only check that the service works fine mocking all the
    interaction with the database
    @Test
    public void should_save_a_country() {
        CountryDTO countryDTO = new CountryDTO();
        countryDTO.setEnabled(Boolean.TRUE);
        countryDTO.setCode("ARG");
        countryDTO.setName("Argentina");

        Country country = new Country();
        when(countryRepository.save(any())).thenReturn(country);
        assertNotNull(service.save(countryDTO));
    }
}
```

The unit test does not check anything about **CountryRepository,** which makes sense because it is not part of the class's code, but it's an interface which implies that it is not simple to test this type of object. Some approaches imply that you create a concrete class that extends from the repository and uses DataSource to access the database. Still, this solution is not the best because you need to create extra objects and modify the logic of your application to do a test.

Integration Testing with a Database

To do testing of your database, you need to go to the next level of testing because you need to run the entire application to test the interaction between the persistence layer and the database. Behind the scenes, Spring Data generates the concrete classes to access the database, so for you, the only object you can use is the repositories with the queries you defined. Of course, you can use Spring Boot Test without anything else to check a part of the logic that accesses the database, but you need to access a database. Hence, if you insert a row with an attribute that needs to be unique in a table, it is impossible to run the same test multiple times in the same database, so you need to find another way; for example, using a tool like DbUnit.[7] An alternative to solving the problem of testing database access is a library called Testcontainers.

Testcontainers

Testcontainers[8] is a lightweight and open-source library that allows you to run containers in your application and reuse test cases. This library has support for multiple testing frameworks like different versions of Junit and Spock. And you can use it in Java or Kotlin projects.

---

[7] http://www.dbunit.org/
[8] https://www.testcontainers.org/

The containers could be databases or other services that your application requires; for example, if your application needs to use a specific service of AWS, you can use the image of LocalStack.[9] Testcontainers develops a set of modules to reduce the complexity of running a container and configure this image. These modules include all the common relational databases and some of the most relevant non-relational databases like MongoDB, Cassandra, Neo4j, and ElasticSearch. If you need to use a database not included in the list of modules, you can run any container, but you need to define all the logic related to the configuration. Figure 12-1 shows the different connections that an API could have, like databases, queues, and cloud provider services.

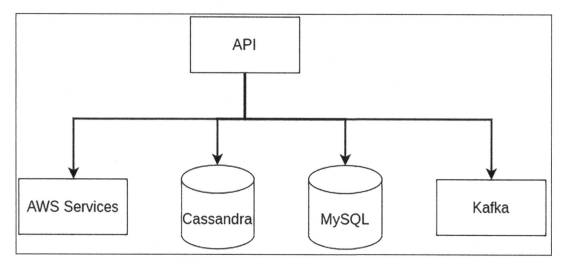

Figure 12-1. *An example that all the external connections that can have an API*

Behind the scenes, this library uses Docker[10] to download and run the containers, so before using your project, check the general requirements[11] related to the versions of Docker that the library needs to satisfy. In November 2020, DockerHub introduced restrictions in using the various images in the repository, like the number of times you downloaded. If you use this library in a pipeline, the machine that runs it must satisfy the same requirements.

---

[9] https://github.com/localstack/localstack

[10] https://www.docker.com/

[11] https://www.testcontainers.org/supported_docker_environment/

Listing 12-3 is a simple example of how you can define a container and start it without any special instructions about Docker or the database.

Listing 12-3. An Example of How to Configure and Run a Container

```
PostgreSQLContainer postgreSQL = new PostgreSQLContainer("postgres:145")
        .withDatabaseName("integration-tests-database")
        .withUsername("test")
        .withPassword("test");

postgreSQL.start();
```

One last thing to consider about this library is having sponsor companies like Elastic and Red Hat, which are used by many recognized companies like Wise, Zalando, Instana, and Skyscanner, so you can be sure it is not new library without support.

Testcontainers vs. Embedded

Databases like MongoDB allow you to run an embedded database using another library that you need to include in your pom file. There are problems with this approach, however.

- Not all databases can support using an embedded database, so it's a solution that works with a reduced number.

- You don't know which version of the database is used, so you can have one of the problems that appear in previous sections: the repositories and queries work fine in your test but in a real environment fail. Also, a new database version could appear and not be supported, so you have certain restrictions on its use.

- If you use a migration tool like Flyway or Liquibase, the scripts could fail if you use an H2 database because you use specific structures or keywords that only work in PostgreSQL or MySQL.

Using Testcontainers, all these problems disappear because you can use containers to represent the real version of the database. Also, you can initialize the database with specific information using the configuration of Docker.

Using Testcontainers

To start using it is simple; you only need to add the basic dependency about Testcontainers and the module you need; in **api-catalog,** you use the **PostgreSQL** module (see Listing 12-4).

Listing 12-4. Dependencies to Include in Your Application

```
<dependency>
    <groupId>org.testcontainers</groupId>
    <artifactId>junit-jupiter</artifactId>
    <version>1.17.3</version>
    <scope>test</scope>
</dependency>

<dependency>
    <groupId>org.testcontainers</groupId>
    <artifactId>postgresql</artifactId>
    <version>1.17.3</version>
    <scope>test</scope>
</dependency>
```

The **jupiter** dependency is connected directly with Junit5, which includes the core dependency of Testcontainers behind the scenes. If you want to use this library without a specific implementation—for example, you want to use a MySQL or MariaDB implementation, only include the core and add the name of the image you want to run without Testcontainers' support.

Running a container that only starts and stops a PostgreSQL image creates a class like Listing 12-5 but adds at least one test.

Listing 12-5. A Basic Unit Test That Runs a Database

```
import org.junit.jupiter.api.AfterAll;
import org.junit.jupiter.api.BeforeAll;
import org.junit.jupiter.api.Test;
import org.springframework.beans.factory.annotation.Autowired;
import org.springframework.boot.test.context.SpringBootTest;
import org.springframework.test.context.DynamicPropertyRegistry;
```

```java
import org.springframework.test.context.DynamicPropertySource;
import org.testcontainers.containers.PostgreSQLContainer;
import org.testcontainers.junit.jupiter.Testcontainers;

import static org.junit.jupiter.api.Assertions.*;

//This annotation enable the support of Testcontainers
@Testcontainers
@SpringBootTest(webEnvironment = SpringBootTest.WebEnvironment.RANDOM_PORT)
public class CountryRepositoryIntegrationTest {

    //Define the container thar you will use
    public static PostgreSQLContainer postgreSQL =
            new PostgreSQLContainer("postgres:14")
                    .withUsername("postgres")
                    .withPassword("postgres")
                    .withDatabaseName("catalog");

    //Start the container
    static {
        postgreSQL.start();
    }

    //Override the configuration of Spring Boot to use the container
    @DynamicPropertySource
    static void postgresqlProperties(DynamicPropertyRegistry registry) {
        registry.add("spring.datasource.url", postgreSQL::getJdbcUrl);
        registry.add("spring.datasource.username",
        postgreSQL::getUsername);
        registry.add("spring.datasource.password",
        postgreSQL::getPassword);
    }

    @Test
    public void should_save_a_country() {
        //Just for the propose to check TestContainers
        assertTrue(Boolean.TRUE);
    }
}
```

Now, if you run the **mvn test** command in your terminal, you see something like the following in the logs.

```
11:10:21.531 [main] INFO org.testcontainers.DockerClientFactory - Connected
to docker:
  Server Version: 20.10.12
  API Version: 1.41
  Operating System: Ubuntu 20.04.4 LTS
  Total Memory: 32032 MB
11:10:21.539 [main] DEBUG org.testcontainers.utility.RyukResourceReaper -
Ryuk is enabled
11:10:21.541 [main] DEBUG org.testcontainers.utility.
PrefixingImageNameSubstitutor - No prefix is configured
11:10:21.541 [main] DEBUG org.testcontainers.utility.
ImageNameSubstitutor - Did not find a substitute image for testcontainers/
ryuk:0.3.3 (using image substitutor: DefaultImageNameSubstitutor
(composite of 'ConfigurationFileImageNameSubstitutor' and
'PrefixingImageNameSubstitutor'))
```

The logs indicate that Testcontainers connects with Docker to use the image **testcontainers/ryuk** that contain all the containers you use in tests. With this library running in Docker, you can share the same database container between tests. Figure 12-2 shows how is the process of running the integration tests using TestContainers.

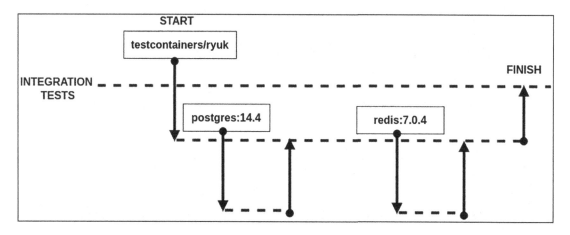

Figure 12-2. *The flow of execution of the containers*

To create a test that checks whether your repository works fine, you only need to introduce modifications to the previous test classes. The first thing to do is add the repository and invoke any method to simplify the example (see Listing 12-6). The **findById** method is used because Flyway populates the database when the application starts.

Listing 12-6. A Basic Unit Test That Checks if the Select Operation Works Fine

```java
import com.apress.catalog.model.Country;
import org.junit.jupiter.api.AfterAll;
import org.junit.jupiter.api.BeforeAll;
import org.junit.jupiter.api.Test;
import org.springframework.beans.factory.annotation.Autowired;
import org.springframework.boot.test.context.SpringBootTest;
import org.springframework.test.context.DynamicPropertyRegistry;
import org.springframework.test.context.DynamicPropertySource;
import org.testcontainers.containers.PostgreSQLContainer;
import org.testcontainers.junit.jupiter.Testcontainers;

import java.util.Optional;
import static org.junit.jupiter.api.Assertions.*;

@Testcontainers
@SpringBootTest(webEnvironment = SpringBootTest.WebEnvironment.RANDOM_PORT)
public class CountryRepositoryIntegrationTest {

    @Autowired
    CountryRepository countryRepository;

     //Previous code without modifications

    @Test
    public void should_get_a_country() {
        Optional<Country> country = countryRepository.findById(1L);

        assertAll(
                ()-> assertTrue(country.isPresent()),
                ()-> assertEquals("AR", country.get().getCode())
        );
    }
}
```

If everything works fine when you run the test in your console or IDE, the test finishes successfully. But, as you can see on the console, other tests are running with the same command, so a good practice is to separate this type of test into another profile to reduce the execution of the unit test. Listing 12-7 introduces a few modifications to the pom.xml file to run with a specific profile integration test. But you can do the same by passing the name of the test that you want to execute in one goal in Maven.

Listing 12-7. Modifications to the pom File to Run the Integration Tests in a Separate Profile

```xml
<?xml version="1.0" encoding="UTF-8"?>
<project xmlns="http://maven.apache.org/POM/4.0.0"
      xmlns:xsi="http://www.w3.org/2001/XMLSchema-instance"
      xsi:schemaLocation="http://maven.apache.org/POM/4.0.0
      https://maven.apache.org/xsd/maven-4.0.0.xsd">

      <!-- Not changes on the rest of the POM file -->
      <build>
          <plugins>
              <plugin>
                  <groupId>org.springframework.boot</groupId>
                  <artifactId>spring-boot-maven-plugin</artifactId>
              </plugin>

              <plugin>
                  <groupId>org.apache.maven.plugins</groupId>
                  <artifactId>maven-surefire-plugin</artifactId>
                  <version>${maven-surefire-plugin.version}</version>
                  <configuration>
                      <excludes>
                          <exclude>**/*IntegrationTest.java</exclude>
                      </excludes>
                  </configuration>
              </plugin>
          </plugins>
      </build>

      <profiles>
```

```xml
<profile>
    <id>IT</id>
    <build>
        <plugins>
            <plugin>
                <groupId>org.apache.maven.plugins
                </groupId>
                <artifactId>maven-failsafe-plugin
                </artifactId>
                <version>${maven-failsafe-plugin
                .version}</version>
                <configuration>
                    <includes>
                        <include>**/*Integration
                        Test.java</include>
                    </includes>
                </configuration>
                <executions>
                    <execution>
                        <id>integration-test</id>
                        <goals>
                            <goal>integration-
                            test</goal>
                        </goals>
                    </execution>
                    <execution>
                        <id>verify</id>
                        <goals>
                            <goal>verify</goal>
                        </goals>
                    </execution>
                </executions>
            </plugin>
        </plugins>
    </build>
```

```
        </profile>
    </profiles>
</project>
```

With this modification in the pom file, you only need to use the **mvn test** command to run the unit test, and the **mvn verify -P IT** command to run the integration tests. The definition of the profile appears in Listing 12-7 with the idea to execute a group of tests to check that everything in the database works fine.

One thing that could be helpful for you if a problem occurs with your container is the logs which, by default, do not appear on the test console. Testcontainers exports the logs of the containers. It's simple to do it. You only need to indicate where the logs need to be exported and attach a consumer to stdout (see Listing 12-8).

Listing 12-8. Export the Containers Logs in a File

```
import com.apress.catalog.model.Country;
import org.junit.jupiter.api.AfterAll;
import org.junit.jupiter.api.BeforeAll;
import org.junit.jupiter.api.Test;
import org.springframework.beans.factory.annotation.Autowired;
import org.springframework.boot.test.context.SpringBootTest;
import org.springframework.test.context.DynamicPropertyRegistry;
import org.springframework.test.context.DynamicPropertySource;
import org.testcontainers.containers.PostgreSQLContainer;
import org.testcontainers.containers.output.OutputFrame;
import org.testcontainers.containers.output.ToStringConsumer;
import org.testcontainers.junit.jupiter.Testcontainers;

import java.io.IOException;
import java.nio.file.Files;
import java.nio.file.Path;
import java.nio.file.StandardOpenOption;
import java.util.Optional;

import static org.junit.jupiter.api.Assertions.*;

@Testcontainers
@SpringBootTest(webEnvironment = SpringBootTest.WebEnvironment.RANDOM_PORT)
```

```
public class CountryRepositoryIntegrationTest {

    //Previous source code without changes

    //This class have the responsibility to obtain all the logs from the
    container
    public static ToStringConsumer consumer = new ToStringConsumer();

     //Contain all the definition to send the logs from the container to
     the consumer
    @BeforeAll
    public static void setUp() {
        postgreSQL.start();

        postgreSQL.followOutput(consumer,
                OutputFrame.OutputType.STDOUT,
                OutputFrame.OutputType.STDERR);
    }

     //Take the logs that have the consumer and write a file
    @AfterAll
    public static void tearDown() throws IOException {
        Path log = Path.of("./logs.log");
        byte[] bytes = consumer.toUtf8String().getBytes();
        Files.write(log, bytes, StandardOpenOption.CREATE);
    }

    //Previous source code without changes
}
```

When you run the test using the commands, you see a file that only contains all the information about the PostgreSQL database, which has the same information that appears in Listing 12-9.

Listing 12-9. File Output After Running the Test

```
The files belonging to this database system will be owned by user
"postgres".
This user must also own the server process.
```

The database cluster will be initialized with locale "en_US.utf8".
The default database encoding has accordingly been set to "UTF8".
The default text search configuration will be set to "english".

Data page checksums are disabled.

fixing permissions on existing directory /var/lib/postgresql/data ... ok
creating subdirectories ... ok
selecting dynamic shared memory implementation ... posix
selecting default max_connections ... 100
selecting default shared_buffers ... 128MB
selecting default time zone ... Etc/UTC
creating configuration files ... ok
running bootstrap script ... ok
performing post-bootstrap initialization ... ok
syncing data to disk ... ok

Success. You can now start the database server using

    pg_ctl -D /var/lib/postgresql/data -l logfile start

initdb: warning: enabling "trust" authentication for local connections
You can change this by editing pg_hba.conf or using the option -A, or
--auth-local and --auth-host, the next time you run initdb.
waiting for server to start....2022-09-23 15:51:13.348 UTC [47]
LOG: starting PostgreSQL 13.1 (Debian 13.1-1.pgdg100+1) on x86_64-pc-
linux-gnu, compiled by gcc (Debian 8.3.0-6) 8.3.0, 64-bit
2022-09-23 15:51:13.348 UTC [47] LOG: listening on Unix socket "/var/run/
postgresql/.s.PGSQL.5432"
2022-09-23 15:51:13.350 UTC [48] LOG: database system was shut down at
2022-09-23 15:51:13 UTC
2022-09-23 15:51:13.354 UTC [47] LOG: database system is ready to accept
connections
done
server started
CREATE DATABASE

/usr/local/bin/docker-entrypoint.sh: ignoring /docker-entrypoint-initdb.d/*

```
2022-09-23 15:51:13.579 UTC [47] LOG:  received fast shutdown request
waiting for server to shut down...2022-09-23 15:51:13.579 UTC [47]
LOG:  aborting any active transactions
.2022-09-23 15:51:13.581 UTC [47] LOG:  background worker "logical
replication launcher" (PID 54) exited with exit code 1
2022-09-23 15:51:13.581 UTC [49] LOG:  shutting down
2022-09-23 15:51:13.590 UTC [47] LOG:  database system is shut down
done
server stopped

PostgreSQL init process complete; ready for start up.

2022-09-23 15:51:13.700 UTC [1] LOG:  starting PostgreSQL 13.1 (Debian
13.1-1.pgdg100+1) on x86_64-pc-linux-gnu, compiled by gcc (Debian 8.3.0-6)
8.3.0, 64-bit
2022-09-23 15:51:13.700 UTC [1] LOG:  listening on IPv4 address "0.0.0.0",
port 5432
2022-09-23 15:51:13.700 UTC [1] LOG:  listening on IPv6 address "::",
port 5432
2022-09-23 15:51:13.700 UTC [1] LOG:  listening on Unix socket "/var/run/
postgresql/.s.PGSQL.5432"
2022-09-23 15:51:13.702 UTC [75] LOG:  database system was shut down at
2022-09-23 15:51:13 UTC
2022-09-23 15:51:13.706 UTC [1] LOG:  database system is ready to accept
connections
```

Multiple Integration Tests

There is no problem when you need to test the repository and put all the logic to run the containers inside that class, but what happens if you have a lot of repositories that you want to check? Testcontainers offers alternatives for reuse: one container to be used in all the tests of the one class or one container to be used in the execution of all the tests.

In the previous sections, you saw the strategy to use the database or container for each test in this library. Still, you can explicitly indicate that each test needs a fresh container or mix tests that can reuse the database. To do this, use the **withReuse** method to indicate to Testcontainers to keep this container live for the next run.

```
public static PostgreSQLContainer postgreSQL =
        new PostgreSQLContainer<>("postgres:14")
                .withUsername("postgres")
                .withPassword("postgres")
                .withDatabaseName("catalog")
                .withReuse(true); //This indicates that you want to
                keep alive the container
```

You need to remove the sentence that stops the container explicitly because the instruction does not work in this case. The next integration test starts with a fresh container.

Initialization Strategies

When you use a database, you need to initialize it with information before running all the tests to solve this problem. The following are strategies.

- Use database migration tools like Flyway or Liquibase, but not in all cases. These tools are used to populate information in a database. If you use them to create the structure of tables, you need to find another tool, like DBUnit.[12]

- Database containers offer a method to include a script to populate all the databases.

```
public static PostgreSQLContainer postgreSQL =
        new PostgreSQLContainer<>("postgres:14")
                .withUsername("postgres")
                .withPassword("postgres")
                .withInitScript("db/migration/V1.0__init_
                database.sql") //Url of the init script
                .withDatabaseName("catalog");
```

---

[12] https://www.dbunit.org/

- Another strategy is creating a custom image with all the information preloaded in a Docker repository. The main problem with this type of image is the responsibility to maintain the updated structure and the information in this custom image. Still, this approach could help reproduce critical bugs or strange situations.

```
public static PostgreSQLContainer postgreSQL =
        new PostgreSQLContainer<>("custom-postgres:1.0.0")
                .withUsername("postgres")
                .withPassword("postgres");
```

- The last strategy is to execute commands inside the container after the start of the container. This strategy could be useful in the containers that emulate the infrastructure like LocalStack.

Potential Problems

Testcontainers is not a silver bullet that solves all the problems but helps you detect them in your queries.

On the other hand, it introduces other problems that you need to consider.

Each time you start a container, the execution of the tests takes more time. Times differ by database; for example, Cassandra databases take longer to run than MySQL databases. It's essential to reuse the container in the same class methods to prevent each test from creating a new container.

- If you use a fixed port and run the tests in a pipeline, for example, using Jenkins, there is a risk that two or more applications use the same ports, which could conflict with the ports. Also, if an application has an exception and does not stop the containers, the next time you run the pipeline of the same application. In that case, the ports are unavailable, and an exception appears. The best solution is to use a mechanism to obtain a random port for the containers.

  Testcontainers considers that this problem can happen, so offer by default use a random port, but you can set a port, and examples you can find in books or articles appear setting the port. This is an example of a container that has defined the image's port.

```
PostgreSQLContainer postgreSQL = new PostgreSQLContainer("postgres:14")
        .withDatabaseName("integration-tests-database")
        .withUsername("test")
        .withPassword("test")
        .withExposedPorts(5432); //Try to not set this property because by
        default Testcontainers use a random port to run the container
```

- Try using the same database version in production. If you use a custom version of a database like ElasticSearch in AWS, use LocalStack, a container that contains most of the services of AWS to run locally.

- A lot of duplicate code between your integration tests to init the containers. To solve this problem, you can create an abstract class that defines all the containers the application needs to run and all the tests that need to be inherited for that class.

- All the images you use in your test download on the machine, so you need to prune periodically to prevent all the images from using a lot of space.

- One potential problem is having multiple connections with different databases, so it's not simple to write the configuration. To solve this problem, you can create a docker-compose file and execute including the module that allows you to run multiple containers simultaneously.

```
import com.apress.catalog.model.Country;
import org.junit.jupiter.api.AfterAll;
import org.junit.jupiter.api.BeforeAll;
import org.springframework.beans.factory.annotation.Autowired;
import org.springframework.test.context.DynamicPropertyRegistry;
import org.springframework.test.context.DynamicPropertySource;
import org.testcontainers.containers.DockerComposeContainer;
import org.testcontainers.containers.wait.strategy.Wait;

import java.io.File;
import java.util.Optional;
```

```
import static org.junit.jupiter.api.Assertions.*;

@Testcontainers
@SpringBootTest(webEnvironment = SpringBootTest.WebEnvironment.
RANDOM_PORT)
public class CountryRepositoryIntegrationTest {

    //To run a Docker Compose
    private static final DockerComposeContainer environment = new
    DockerComposeContainer(new File("src/test/resources/docker-
    compose.yml"))
                        .withExposedService("postgres", 5432, Wait.
                        forListeningPort())
                        .withLocalCompose(true);

    //The rest of the source code is the same

    @DynamicPropertySource
    static void postgresqlProperties(DynamicPropertyRegistry
    registry) {
        String postgresUrl = environment.getServiceHost
        ("postgres", POSTGRES_PORT)
            + ":" + environment.getServicePort("postgres",
            POSTGRES_PORT);

    registry.add("spring.datasource.url", () ->
"jdbc:postgresql://" + postgresUrl + "/catalog");
        //The rest of the source code is the same
    }
}
```

Testcontainers' problems are a low price to pay given its benefits, and most problems have a potential solution.

Summary

This chapter offers the possibility to create tests that only check one portion of the application without any problem using a real database instead of a memory database, which could not have the same features.

Do not set a specific port to run the containers in Testcontainers to prevent conflicts with other containers or applications. This is important when running this test in a pipeline where many other applications need to use the same ports.

CHAPTER 13

Detecting Performance Issues

Many developers create or modify the logic of applications that accesses a database. In most cases, this does not cause a problem because the modifications are simple, and developers create unit or integration tests to check if everything continues to function properly. Still, most problems related to performance or the application's behavior appear in production when your database has thousands or millions of records. This scenario cannot be replicated in any test environment, including the tools you learned about in the previous chapter.

Many factors affect the performance of a data access layer, including not having the correct type of index in your relational database, not being relational like MongoDB, writing an inefficient query, or using the wrong criteria to filter. Other factors could be directly connected with how you write the business logic that accesses the database layer.

For both types of factors, you can deploy changes in production in a canary deployment,[1] monitor how the changes affect the application's performance, or use a tool to reduce the risk of deploying something wrong in production. In this chapter, you learn two ways to use libraries to execute a performance test or to detect excessive use of the resources in your application.

---

[1]https://semaphoreci.com/blog/what-is-canary-deployment#:~:text=In%20software%20engineering%2C%20canary%20deployment,the%20rest%20of%20the%20users.

© Andres Sacco 2023
A. Sacco, *Beginning Spring Data*, https://doi.org/10.1007/978-1-4842-8764-4_13

Low-Performance Problems

The problems with the performance of your application most of the time do not look connected with the database accesses or with a specific operation because one of the endpoints that do a simple operation starts to take more time than the average cases, so if you don't have the correct metrics or alerts in your application, you take more time to discover the real problem. The time you spend discovering the real problem is unique because there are others.

- In some cases, the use of CPU or memory increases which implies that depending on the strategy of autoscaling in your cloud provider, you spend a lot of money adding a lot of instances to compensate for the excessive use of resources. Most cloud providers require you to pay for resources, so keeping your applications performing is essential.

- In relational databases, the problems with the queries could be that they take a lot of time to do, which implies that one of the pools of connections could be unavailable for a long time.

- Increase the latency between your microservices. Imagine that you have an endpoint that takes one second to respond to a request in normal conditions. Still, when you introduce modifications to the query, the same endpoint takes ten seconds to respond to the same request, so the latency decreases the performance of the entire platform.

- In some extreme cases, when memory use increases so quickly and uses all the available memory, the application could produce an exception and stop suddenly.

- It's difficult to debug and reproduce scenarios when you have many microservices, and the problem randomly appears and disappears.

All these problems, which you can think of as technical situations that developers can solve, can potentially cause companies to lose a lot of money. For example, suppose a big e-commerce company has a problem with the endpoint responsible for users searching for products on their website. If the platform takes a long time to show results, users may go to another website to buy products. You must consider all the possible impacts of developing a bad feature.

Detecting Problems

There is no silver bullet that helps you in all situations, but there are tools that help you minimize and analyze problems, depending on the context. Another thing to consider is not all libraries/tools help you to solve the problems related to access on the database because it could produce that you taking more time to develop a new feature; use it only in situations where access to the database is a risky operation or when you modify an existent repository.

Note   All the tools in this chapter apply to the languages that use the JVM, like Kotlin/Java in the concrete case of Spring Boot, but if you want, it's possible using with other frameworks.

Analyzing Query Performance

There are tools to analyze the problems connected directly with the JVM, like VisualVM,[2] or the other tools in which the responsibility is monitoring the entire application, like APM.

Note   It is not in the scope of this book to show all the alternatives of APM and the pros/cons of each of them. The idea is to give a brief overview and explain how these tools help find clues to solve the problem.

Using VisualVM,[3] you can see what happens to all the applications running on your machine or remoting if the application has opened the ports for JMX. this approach of profiling the application could be used to analyze the use of memory, CPU, or the queries that the application executes but only if your application uses JDBC behind the scenes because this tool does not work for the non-relational databases.

---

[2] https://visualvm.github.io/
[3] https://visualvm.github.io/

To check how it looks in VisualVM with a running application, use **api-catalog** from Parts I and II, which is connected to a relational database, and run the tool. After the application runs, open the tool (you already downloaded it from the official website[4]), and check that the package name and the main class are in VisualVM to analyze any problems (see Figure 13-1).

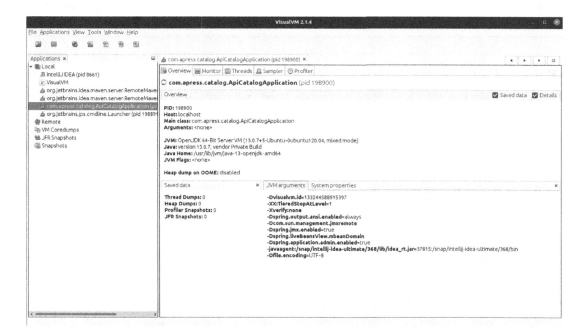

Figure 13-1.   *VisualVM general view*

The Profiler section shows the metrics for executing queries and the framework methods involved. This approach is very useful for detecting where you spend a lot of time. Still, remote debugging could produce extra problems, like the application could become slow because of the need to transfer a lot of information.

To obtain the same result in Figure 13-2, call any endpoints that access the database after enabling the profiling of the operation in the database.

---

[4]https://visualvm.github.io/download.html

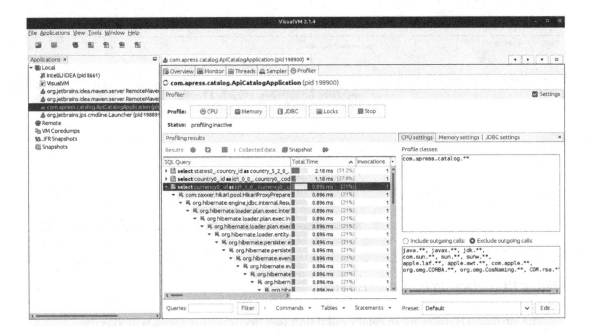

Figure 13-2. *VisualVM JDBC profiling*

In APM, are many free alternatives like the Elastic APM[5] or another, which you need to pay to have all the features, like New Relic.[6] Most of the alternatives have different purposes, like giving you a chance to see the metrics of your microservices with a granularity of the classes that one request passes and how much time takes on each of them. The spirit of these tools is to give you the clues that help you to find where the problem is but not which is the problem in your application; the last part is your responsibility.

For example, in Redis, some APM does not show which operation takes more or less time to execute. One example of this problem appears in Figure 13-3, where New Relic shows you the various operations, but you don't have any information.

[5] https://www.elastic.co/observability/application-performance-monitoring
[6] https://newrelic.com/

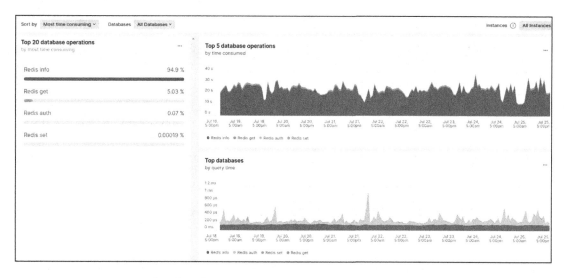

Figure 13-3. *New Relic database view*

The situation is different in relational databases because the agent, which is the application that you add to intercept all the traffic inbound or outbound in your application, gives a lot of detail about the queries that take a lot of time to be executed. For example, Figure 13-4 shows a level of detail of the queries that permit detection where the problem is.

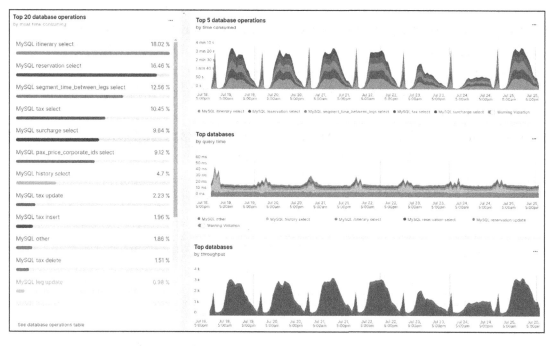

Figure 13-4. *New Relic relational database view*

One of the key points of using the APM is to reduce the number of modifications to the source code, you can include the dependency as part of the Docker image which contains the application.

These tools give you a brief overview of which queries are not performant. Still, perhaps you have a part of the application that does multiple operations, so you need other tools when you don't detect anything.

Another thing to consider is that all these tools are reactive. You need to detect your application's problem and then find the reasons. In the next section, you see alternatives to detect the problems before they appear.

Analyzing Query Complexity

QuickPerf[7] is a library that allows you to analyze the performance of sections of your application by considering different aspects like the use of the JVM or the number of queries the block executed. This library supports versions of JUnit and frameworks like Spring Boot, Quarkus,[8] and Microprofile.[9]

This library's benefits include detecting excessive use of resources in blocks of code, and it's not necessary to write a large number for the new test. You can reuse the previous integration tests you created with Testcontainers in the previous chapter and add annotations to validate the correct behavior of the methods.

Let's add the dependencies in your POM file to analyze whether some of the queries you defined in the repositories in previous chapters work fine (see Listing 13-1).

Listing 13-1. QuickPerf Dependencies

```
<dependencies>
    <dependency>
        <groupId>org.quickperf</groupId>
        <artifactId>quick-perf-junit5</artifactId>
        <version>1.1.0 </version>
        <scope>test</scope>
    </dependency>
```

---

[7] https://quickperf.io/
[8] https://es.quarkus.io/
[9] https://microprofile.io/

```
<dependency>
        <groupId>org.quickperf</groupId>
        <artifactId>quick-perf-springboot2-sql-starter</artifactId>
        <version>1.1.0</version>
        <scope>test</scope>
</dependency>

← Other dependencies ->
</dependencies>
```

Next, let's introduce modifications to the previous integration test, which uses Testcontainers to analyze if the repositories work fine. The first modification is annotating the entire class with **@QuickPerfTest,** which indicates that some of the tests that are inside of the class need to validate something and include the configuration that the library needs to use; in this case, you use the default configuration that exists inside of the class **org.quickperf.spring.sql.QuickPerfSqlConfig,** but you can extend this class and indicate different values.

The last modification is to include the number of operations in the database you want; the previous example is a select operation, but you can analyze how many insert, delete, or update operations are executed (see Listing 13-2).

Listing 13-2. Modifications to the Previous Integration Test

```
import org.quickperf.junit5.QuickPerfTest;
import org.quickperf.spring.sql.QuickPerfSqlConfig;
import org.quickperf.sql.annotation.ExpectSelect;
//Previous imports

@Import(QuickPerfSqlConfig.class) //The configuration of the library
@QuickPerfTest //This annotations indicate that you will analyze the
operations
@Testcontainers
@SpringBootTest(webEnvironment = SpringBootTest.WebEnvironment.RANDOM_PORT)
public class CurrencyRepositoryIntegrationTest {
    //Previous test code

    @Test
    @ExpectSelect(1) //Validate the number of queries that are executed
```

```
public void should_get_a_currency() {
    Optional<Currency> currency = currencyRepository.findById(1L);

    assertAll(
            ()-> assertTrue(currency.isPresent()),
            ()-> assertEquals("ARS", currency.get().getCode())
    );
}
}
```

If you run the tests again using **mvn verify –P IT**, everything continues working as previously. So how can you be sure? Let's change the value of the **@ExpectedSelect** annotation to 10 and run the same test again; if everything is correct, you will see an error in your test with a message like the following on the console.

```
[PERF] You may think that <10> select statements were sent to the database
        But there is in fact <1>...

[JDBC QUERY EXECUTION (executeQuery, executeBatch, ...)]
        Time:1, Success:True, Type:Prepared, Batch:False, QuerySize:1,
        BatchSize:0, Query:["
    select
        currency0_.id as id1_1_0_,
        currency0_.created_on as created_2_1_0_,
        currency0_.updated_on as updated_3_1_0_,
        currency0_.version as version4_1_0_,
        currency0_.code as code5_1_0_,
        currency0_.decimal_places as decimal_6_1_0_,
        currency0_.description as descript7_1_0_,
        currency0_.enabled as enabled8_1_0_,
        currency0_.symbol as symbol9_1_0_
    from
        currency currency0_
    where
        currency0_.id=?"], Params:[(1)]
```

This message indicates that you only executed the following sentence once, so your assertion indicated with the annotation is wrong. The annotation only checks the number of queries executed, not the number of rows impacted during the execution.

Another annotation that can help you to detect problems is **@AnalyzeSql**, which gives metrics on the execution of the query. Let's modify the previous example to include the annotation (see Listing 13-3).

Listing 13-3. Include the Query Analysis

```
//Previous imports
import org.quickperf.sql.annotation.AnalyzeSql;

@Import(QuickPerfSqlConfig.class) //The configuration of the library
@QuickPerfTest //This annotations indicate that you will analyze the
operations
@Testcontainers
@SpringBootTest(webEnvironment = SpringBootTest.WebEnvironment.RANDOM_PORT)
public class CurrencyRepositoryIntegrationTest {
    //Previous test code

  @Test
  @ExpectSelect(1) //Validate the number of queries that are executed
  @AnalyzeSql
  public void should_get_a_currency() {
      Optional<Currency> currency = currencyRepository.findById(1L);

      assertAll(
              ()-> assertTrue(currency.isPresent()),
              ()-> assertEquals("ARS", currency.get().getCode())
      );
  }
}
```

If you execute the same test again, everything continues working, but you have all the analysis information on the console. I recommend saving the test execution output to a file so it's simple to find the metrics.

```
[QUICK PERF] SQL ANALYSIS
                              * * * * *

SQL EXECUTIONS: 1
MAX TIME: 1 ms
                              * * * * *

SELECT: 1
                              * * * * *

QUERY
    Time:1, Success:True, Type:Prepared, Batch:False, QuerySize:1,
    BatchSize:0, Query:["
  select
      currency0_.id as id1_1_0_,
      currency0_.created_on as created_2_1_0_,
      currency0_.updated_on as updated_3_1_0_,
      currency0_.version as version4_1_0_,
      currency0_.code as code5_1_0_,
      currency0_.decimal_places as decimal_6_1_0_,
      currency0_.description as descript7_1_0_,
      currency0_.enabled as enabled8_1_0_,
      currency0_.symbol as symbol9_1_0_
  from
      currency currency0_
  where
      currency0_.id=?"], Params:[(1)]
```

There are many other annotations that can assist your application's operation in a database. Table 13-1 lists some of the most relevant.

Table 13-1. *Annotations*

Annotation	Description
@ProfileConnection	Exposes all the operations that happen with the connection to the database
@ExpectSelect @ExpectInsert @ExpectDelete @ExpectUpdate	Checks the number of queries of one type that executed
@ExpectMaxSelect @ExpectMaxInsert @ExpectMaxDelete @ExpectMaxUpdate	Checks if the number of sentences executed is not up to a certain number
@ExpectMaxQueryExecutionTime	Indicates how much time in milliseconds the query takes to be executed
@ExpectSelectedColumn @ExpectUpdateColumn	Checks the number of columns connected with the query
@DisableSameSelects	Checks if the same query executes two or more times

This solution only works for the relational database. You can check by analyzing if your service or the controller that accesses the repository for a non-relational database has a problem using the JVM annotation that offers QuickPerf. Some examples are **@MeasureHeapAllocation** or **@HeapSize(value = 1, unit = AllocationUnit.GIGA_ BYTE)**, which checks how much memory space is used for a particular method.

Checking the Performance of an Endpoint

The previous approach is the best alternative to check or analyze blocks of code with a certain risk because they do several critical operations. You could spend hours writing a test that verifies that everything works fine. But you may not always have time to do it. An alternative is to create a performance test for the entire microservice or one endpoint providing information for different requests, which could be executed simultaneously, or increase the number of requests each second until you have the final number of requests.

Following this principle of creating a performance test, there are two tools, Gatling[10] and JMeter,[11] that many developers use because they have a simple way to create the load test for the application. You can create complex scenarios that invoke endpoints in a certain sequence. Both tools are free to be used and have many articles or videos that explain in detail the use of each of them. Gatling also offers a paid option where you can create your scenarios and execute them using the company's infrastructure.

This chapter uses Gatling as a tool to create a performance test instead of JMeter because you can create a Maven project to run tests using Karate[12] and reuse the same tests to create a performance test with the idea of not maintaining two tools with all the requests/responses. Karate, in general, is not a popular tool that all developers know. Still, it's powerful because it has great features and integrates with other tools, like Gatling.

Karate is readable because it follows the spirit of BDD Given-When-Then, so anyone can understand what the test is doing and use it to create end-to-end tests for your entire platform, not a set of tests. Figure 13-5 is a simple example of this tool that tests an endpoint of your **api-catalog** application.

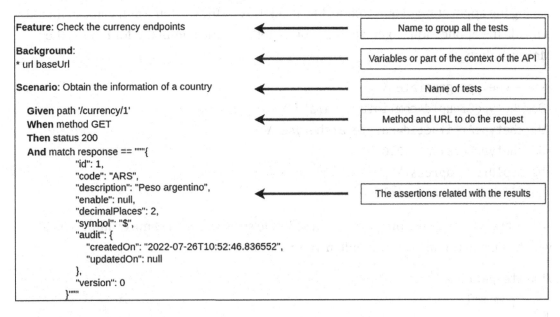

Figure 13-5. Karate test

---

[10] https://gatling.io/

[11] https://jmeter.apache.org/

[12] https://github.com/karatelabs/karate

One thing that you may be thinking when reading the previous block is, "Why is not the entire URL of the API?" the idea is not to define the API host in each of these scenarios so you can define custom variables and refer using the keyword *background*. Each file can have one or more scenarios, and each of them is like one of your methods in the unit/integration test.

Note   This book does not explain all the features related to Karate, but it's not necessary to have the entire JSON of the response in the test; you can put it in an external file and read it before to make the comparison in the test.

Another relevant thing is you can create complex scenarios and put the structure Given/When/Then many times one after another; for example, create a new currency and execute an update operation.

Let's create a new project that is not connected with **api-catalog;** the idea is that you can execute the performance test on your machine or in another environment without having the application's source code, like black-box testing. If you want, you can include it inside the application. To create the project, let's use the command for Karate, the Maven archetype.

```
mvn archetype:generate \
-DarchetypeGroupId=com.intuit.karate \
-DarchetypeArtifactId=karate-archetype \
-DarchetypeVersion=1.2.0 \
-DgroupId=com.apress \
-DartifactId=karate-gatling
```

After that, create the project. Obtain a simple structure with some examples inside, which you can run using the simple **mvn test** command.

```
/karate-gatling
├── pom.xml
└── src
    └── test
        └── java
            ├── examples
            │   ├── ExamplesTest.java
```

```
|     └── users
|           ├── users.feature
|           └── UsersRunner.java
├── karate-config.js
└── logback-test.xml
```

Let's open karate-config.js, which contains all the configuration and supports multiple environments, and introduce the modifications to request your **api-catalog** application (see Listing 13-4). For testing in this book, both environments—dev and e2e—have the same URL.

Listing 13-4. Configuration Modifications

```
function fn() {
  var env = karate.env;
  karate.log('karate.env system property was:', env);
  if (!env) {
    env = 'dev';
  }
  var config = {
    env: env,
    AppUrl: '/api/catalog' //The URL of the API
  }
  if (env == 'dev') { //devlopment
    config.AppUrl = 'http://127.0.0.1:8080' + config.AppUrl //The entire
                                                            URL with
                                                            the host
  } else if (env == 'e2e') { //end to end
    config.AppUrl = 'http://127.0.0.1:8080' + config.AppUrl
  }
  return config;
}
```

Create a new class called **APITest** in **src/test/java** with the idea of finding all the Karate tests in the folder and running it without the need to indicate each feature file (see Listing 13-5).

Listing 13-5. The Main Class That Executes All the Tests

```
import com.intuit.karate.junit5.Karate;

class ApiTest {

    @Karate.Test
    Karate runAllTests() {
        return Karate.run().tags("~@ignore").relativeTo(getClass());
        //This will execute all the test ignoring all the test that have the
        annotation @ignore on the files .features
    }
}
```

After that, drop all the files into the **examples** folder and create a new one called **app/currency** to create a correct structure representing the things you are testing. The next step is to create a file called **get-currency.feature** in **src/test/java/app/currency**, which contains all the scenarios (see Listing 13-6).

Listing 13-6. The Structure of the Scenario

```
Feature: Currency operations

  Background:
    * url AppUrl
    * def get_currency_response = read('./get-currency-response.json')

  Scenario: Get all the information about one currency
    Given path 'currency/1'

    When method GET

    Then status 200
    And match response == get_currency_response
```

The structure of the test is simple and does not have anything strange. AppUrl refers to the variable that you defined in the context of karate-config.js. The **get_currency_response** variable contains all the information in another file. It is created to reduce the number of things that appear because you can have multiple scenarios in one file (see Listing 13-7).

Listing 13-7. The Expected Response of the Endpoint

```
{
  "id":1,
  "code":"ARS",
  "description":"Peso argentino",
  "enable":null,
  "decimalPlaces":2,
  "symbol":"$",
  "audit":{
    "createdOn":"2022-07-26T10:52:46.836552",
    "updatedOn":null
  },
  "version":0
}
```

Now the last thing to check if everything works fine or not is running the **api-catalog,** and in the directory of your new project, run the **mvn test** command. The console displays information about the tests that were executed.

```
--------------------------------------------------------------
feature: classpath:app/currency/get-currency.feature
scenarios:  1 | passed:  1 | failed:  0 | time: 0.2407
--------------------------------------------------------------

Karate version: 1.2.0
==============================================================
elapsed:    2.20 | threads:      1 | thread time: 0.24
features:      1 | skipped:      0 | efficiency: 0.11
scenarios:     1 | passed:       1 | failed: 0
==============================================================
```

All this information is great, but you didn't do a performance test in the application, only once this test, so the next step is adding Gatling support to your application. Let's introduce modifications to the pom file to run the Karate test or the Gatling test on profiles, so drop all the content of the section's dependencies and build to replace the following block (see Listing 13-8).

Listing 13-8. Pom File Modifications

```
<profiles>
    <profile>
        <id>karate</id>
        <dependencies>
            <dependency>
                <groupId>com.intuit.karate</groupId>
                <artifactId>karate-junit5</artifactId>
                <version>${karate.version}</version> <!-- By default
                the version is 1.2.0 -->
                <scope>test</scope>
            </dependency>
        </dependencies>
        <build>
            <testResources>
                <testResource>
                    <directory>src/test/java</directory>
                    <excludes>
                        <exclude>**/*.java</exclude>
                    </excludes>
                </testResource>
            </testResources>
            <plugins>
                <plugin>
                    <groupId>org.apache.maven.plugins</groupId>
                    <artifactId>maven-compiler-plugin</artifactId>
                    <version>${maven.compiler.version}</version>
                    <configuration>
                        <encoding>UTF-8</encoding>
                        <source>${java.version}</source> <!-- By
                        default the version is 8 -->
                        <target>${java.version}</target>
                        <compilerArgument>-Werror</compilerArgument>
                    </configuration>
                </plugin>
```

```xml
            <plugin>
                <groupId>org.apache.maven.plugins</groupId>
                <artifactId>maven-surefire-plugin</artifactId>
                <version>${maven.surefire.version}</version>
                <configuration>
                    <argLine>-Dfile.encoding=UTF-8</argLine>
                </configuration>
            </plugin>
        </plugins>
    </build>
</profile>

<profile>
    <id>gatling</id>
    <dependencies>
        <dependency>
            <groupId>com.intuit.karate</groupId>
            <artifactId>karate-gatling</artifactId>
            <version>${karate.version}</version>
            <scope>test</scope>
        </dependency>
    </dependencies>
    <build>
        <plugins>
            <plugin>
                <groupId>net.alchim31.maven</groupId>
                <artifactId>scala-maven-plugin</artifactId>
                <version>4.5.6</version>
                <executions>
                    <execution>
                        <goals>
                            <goal>testCompile</goal>
                        </goals>
```

```xml
                    <configuration>
                        <args>
                            <arg>-Jbackend:GenBCode</arg>
                            <arg>-Jdelambdafy:method</arg>
                            <arg>-target:jvm-1.8</arg> <!--
                            It's not connected with the version
                            of the application -->
                            <arg>-deprecation</arg>
                            <arg>-feature</arg>
                            <arg>-unchecked</arg>
                            <arg>-
                            language:implicitConversions</arg>
                            <arg>-language:postfixOps</arg>
                        </args>
                    </configuration>
                </execution>
            </executions>
        </plugin>
        <plugin>
            <groupId>io.gatling</groupId>
            <artifactId>gatling-maven-plugin</artifactId>
            <version>${gatling.plugin.version}</version> <!--
            By default the version is 4.1.1 -->
            <configuration>
                <simulationsFolder>src/test/java</
                simulationsFolder>
            </configuration>
            <executions>
                <execution>
                    <phase>test</phase>
                    <goals>
                        <goal>test</goal>
                    </goals>
                </execution>
            </executions>
```

```
            </plugin>
          </plugins>
        </build>
      </profile>
    </profiles>
```

After that, you can execute the Karate scenarios as a common test or a performance
test indicating the profiles. For now, let's continue with the next step is create a file called
CurrencySimulation.scala in the same directory where the **get-currency.feature** file is
located, which is **src/test/java/app/currency**. This file contains the Karate test and the
number of users doing the same action (see Listing 13-9).

Listing 13-9. Gatling Simulation Using the Karate Scenario

```scala
package app.currency

import com.intuit.karate.Runner
import com.intuit.karate.gatling.PreDef._
import io.gatling.core.Predef._

import scala.concurrent.duration._

//Define the simulation which imply the URL, how many request during
a period
class CurrencySimulation extends Simulation {

  def urlPattern = "GET /api/catalog/currency/1"

  val protocol = karateProtocol(
    "/currency/{id}" -> Nil
  )

  protocol.nameResolver = (req, ctx) => req.getHeader("karate-name")

  //Which is the environment to run the test
  protocol.runner.karateEnv("dev")

  //The name of the file and the scenario to run
  val get = scenario("Get all the information about one currency").exec
  (karateFeature("classpath:app/currency/get-currency.feature"))
```

319

```
setUp(
  //The number of users that receive the endpoint for a period of time
  get.inject(rampUsers(10) during (5 seconds)).protocols(protocol)
).assertions(
  //The conditions that you want to validate
  details(urlPattern).responseTime.percentile3.lte(3000)
)
}
```

This simulation is basic, but you can combine various scenarios, like creating multiple currencies at the same time, which is defined in rampUsers in Listing 13-8, so that you obtain the information for another one. The definition of the complexity of the situation is your decision and depends on the complexity of the actions that do one endpoint.

The last step is to run the performance test using the **mvn test -P gatling** command, which uses only the simulation classes that you defined previously. If everything works fine, you see on the console the results of the execution of the test. The Gatling profile was defined in Listing 13-7, so the Maven command works fine.

```
Generating reports...


================================================================================
---- Global Information ---------------------------------------------------------
> request count                                                  10
(OK=10      KO=0     )
> min response time                                              4
(OK=4       KO=-     )
> max response time                                              27
(OK=27      KO=-     )
> mean response time                                             15
(OK=15      KO=-     )
> std deviation                                                  10
(OK=10      KO=-     )
> response time 50th percentile                                  8
(OK=8       KO=-     )
```

```
> response time 75th percentile                              27
(OK=27      KO=-     )
> response time 95th percentile                              27
(OK=27      KO=-     )
> response time 99th percentile                              27
(OK=27      KO=-     )
> mean requests/sec                                           2
(OK=2       KO=-     )
---- Response Time Distribution ----------------------------------------
> t < 800 ms                                            10 (100%)
> 800 ms < t < 1200 ms                                   0 (  0%)
> t > 1200 ms                                            0 (  0%)
> failed                                                 0 (  0%)
========================================================================

Reports generated in 0s.
Please open the following file: /home/apress-spring-data/chapter 13/karate-
gatling/target/gatling/currencysimulation-20220727184940969/index.html
GET /api/catalog/currency/1: 95th percentile of response time is less than
or equal to 3000.0 : true
```

These reports could not be the best option to understand well what happened during the execution. Gatling generated a report in the target folder containing an entire webpage with the same information but a different look and feel.

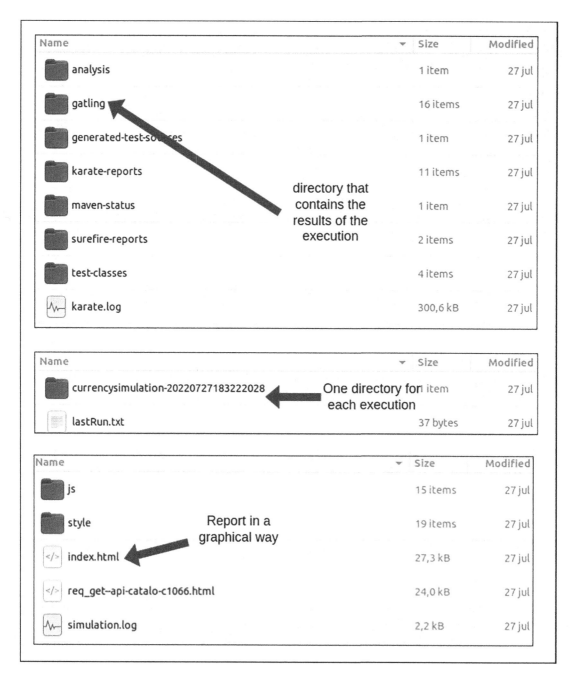

Figure 13-6. *The structure of the output of the reports*

Figure 13-7 graphically shows all the results so you can see each endpoint, the time of the executions, and other relevant information.

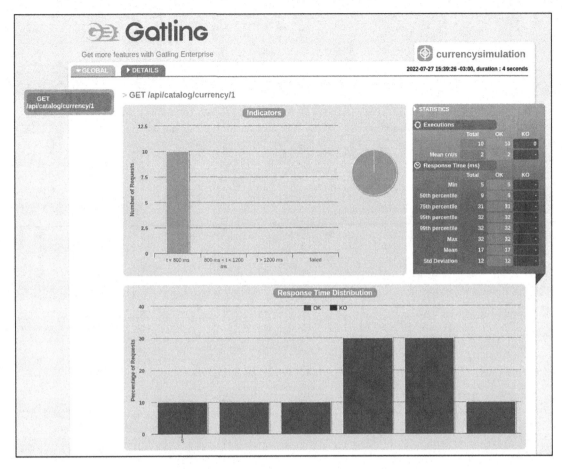

Figure 13-7. *The metrics for the execution times*

In this chapter, you saw mechanisms to analyze problems in your repositories that access the database. Still, there are many ways to find problems.

Summary

There are many ways to detect problems related to your application's performance. The tool you use always depends on the problem because some problems only appear in production instead of other ones that you can reproduce in the same way using tools like Gatling.

I recommend creating a test in Gatling that simulates the situation when problems occur after modifications are made to your application.

CHAPTER 14

Best Practices

Developers frequently implement a solution that accesses a database, but problems appear months later. These problems may or may not relate to the solution's implementation because many factors can affect performance (e.g., a significant number of requests or the need to save a lot of information within a short period of time).

Best practices minimize the impact or reduce the size of the information you save in your database. This chapter covers many of the most common practices. Some of them are simple, while others require changes to your application.

Compressing Information

Sometimes, you need to save a sizeable, complex object in Redis, which is not a problem. Still, if you need to save thousands of them within a short period, this could impact performance or the cost of memory usage.

Redis allows you to define custom serializers, giving you the power to serialize or deserialize information. Let's create a serializer that compresses and then decompresses an object to save space in your database.

This process implies modifying the code you implemented in Chapter 7 but let's start to create a class that has the responsibility to transform an array of bytes into a compressed object. This task is not complex because you can use this class to compress something before persisting the information in a file. Listing 14-1 shows a possible implementation of a class that compress all the values of the object.

Listing 14-1. The Compression Class

```
package com.apress.catalog.util;

import java.io.BufferedReader;
import java.io.ByteArrayInputStream;
import java.io.ByteArrayOutputStream;
```

325

© Andres Sacco 2023
A. Sacco, *Beginning Spring Data*, https://doi.org/10.1007/978-1-4842-8764-4_14

```java
import java.io.IOException;
import java.io.InputStreamReader;
import java.util.zip.GZIPInputStream;
import java.util.zip.GZIPOutputStream;

public class CompressionUtil {

    private CompressionUtil() {
        // just to avoid create instances
    }

    // This method will receive an array of bytes and try to decompress
    // the information using GZIPInputStream
    public static String decompress(byte[] compressed) throws IOException {
        ByteArrayInputStream bis = new ByteArrayInputStream(compressed);
        GZIPInputStream gis = new GZIPInputStream(bis);
        BufferedReader br = new BufferedReader(new InputStreamReader(gis,
        "UTF-8"));
        StringBuilder sb = new StringBuilder();
        String line;
        while ((line = br.readLine()) != null) {
            sb.append(line);
        }
        br.close();
        gis.close();
        bis.close();
        return sb.toString();
    }

    // This method will receive a String and try to compress the
    // information using GZIPOutputStream
    public static byte[] compress(String data) throws IOException {
        ByteArrayOutputStream bos = new ByteArrayOutputStream(data.length());
        GZIPOutputStream gzip = new GZIPOutputStream(bos);
        gzip.write(data.getBytes());
        gzip.close();
        byte[] compressed = bos.toByteArray();
```

```
        bos.close();
        return compressed;
    }
}
```

The next step is to create a class with custom methods that transform an object into an array of bytes and vice versa (see Listing 14-2). The idea is to use the **T** object to delegate into another class, which is the particular type of object to compress and decompress, without creating a specific class for each class that needs to be serialized.

Listing 14-2. The Serializer That Transforms an Array of Bytes in an Object

```
package com.apress.catalog.util;

import com.apress.catalog.exception.SerializeException;
import com.fasterxml.jackson.databind.DeserializationFeature;
import com.fasterxml.jackson.databind.MapperFeature;
import com.fasterxml.jackson.databind.ObjectMapper;
import com.fasterxml.jackson.databind.PropertyNamingStrategy;
import com.fasterxml.jackson.datatype.jsr310.JavaTimeModule;
import org.slf4j.Logger;
import org.slf4j.LoggerFactory;

import java.io.IOException;

public class JsonGzipSerializerUtil {

    private static final Logger LOGGER = LoggerFactory.getLogger(JsonGzip
    SerializerUtil.class);
    private static final ObjectMapper OBJECT_MAPPER;

    private JsonGzipSerializerUtil() {
        // just to avoid create instances
    }

     //General definition about how transform the information into a String
     or an Object
    static {
        OBJECT_MAPPER = new ObjectMapper()
                .configure(MapperFeature.USE_GETTERS_AS_SETTERS, false)
```

```
            .configure(DeserializationFeature.FAIL_ON_UNKNOWN_PROPERTIES,
            false)
            .setPropertyNamingStrategy(PropertyNamingStrategy.SNAKE_CASE)
            .registerModule(new JavaTimeModule());
    }

    //Transform an object into an array de bytes which is compressed
    public static byte[] serialize(Object object) {
        byte[] compressedJson;
        try {
            String json = OBJECT_MAPPER.writeValueAsString(object);
            compressedJson = CompressionUtil.compress(json);
        } catch (IOException e) {
            LOGGER.error("Error serializing object: {}", e.getMessage());
            throw new SerializeException("Can't serialize object", e);
        }
        return compressedJson;
    }

    //Transform an array de bytes which is compressed into a specific
    object define it on the <T>
    public static <T> T deserialize(byte[] raw, Class<T> reference) {
        if (raw == null)
            return null;

        T object;
        try {
            String json = CompressionUtil.decompress(raw);
            object = OBJECT_MAPPER.readValue(json, reference);
        } catch (IOException e) {
            LOGGER.error("Can't deserialize object: {}", e.getMessage());
            throw new SerializeException("Can't deserialize object.", e);
        }
        return object;
    }
}
```

As a suggestion, create a custom Exception class to represent all the possible problems associated with this transformation of the objects (see Listing 14-3).

Listing 14-3. A Custom Exception to Express the Problems in the Serialization

```
package com.apress.catalog.exception;

public class SerializeException extends RuntimeException {
    public SerializeException(String message, Throwable cause) {
        super(message, cause);
    }
}
```

The next step is to create a custom serializer to transform a specific object into a compressed object in the database. The **JsonGzipSerializerUtil** class only needs to pass an object to serialize. If you want to deserialize, you only need to pass an array of bytes with type of class as you can see on Listing 14-4.

Listing 14-4. Custom Serializer for the Country Entity

```
package com.apress.catalog.serializer;

import com.apress.catalog.model.Country;
import com.apress.catalog.util.JsonGzipSerializerUtil;
import org.springframework.data.redis.serializer.RedisSerializer;
import org.springframework.stereotype.Component;

@Component
public class CountrySerializer implements RedisSerializer<Country> {

    public byte[] serialize(Country country) {
        return JsonGzipSerializerUtil.serialize(country);
    }

    public Country deserialize(byte[] raw) {
        return JsonGzipSerializerUtil.deserialize(raw, Country.class);
    }
}
```

Now that you have a specific serializer for the entity, you need to declare it as a new Redis template in the RedisConfiguration class (see Listing 14-5).

Listing 14-5. Declaration of the New Template

```
import com.apress.catalog.model.Country;
import com.apress.catalog.serializer.CountrySerializer;
import com.apress.catalog.serializer.LongSerializer;
import io.lettuce.core.ReadFrom;
import org.springframework.context.annotation.Bean;
import org.springframework.context.annotation.Configuration;
import org.springframework.data.redis.connection.RedisConnectionFactory;
import org.springframework.data.redis.connection.
RedisStaticMasterReplicaConfiguration;
import org.springframework.data.redis.connection.lettuce.
LettuceClientConfiguration;
import org.springframework.data.redis.connection.lettuce.
LettuceConnectionFactory;
import org.springframework.data.redis.core.RedisTemplate;
import org.springframework.data.redis.repository.configuration.
EnableRedisRepositories;

@Configuration
@EnableRedisRepositories
public class RedisConfiguration {

    final RedisSettings settings;
    final LongSerializer longSerializer;

    final CountrySerializer countrySerializer;

    public RedisConfiguration(RedisSettings settings, LongSerializer
    longSerializer, CountrySerializer countrySerializer) {
        this.settings = settings;
        this.longSerializer = longSerializer;
        this.countrySerializer = countrySerializer;
    }
```

```
@Bean
public RedisTemplate<Long, Country> countryRedisTemplate(RedisConnection
Factory connectionFactory) {
    RedisTemplate<Long, Country> template = new RedisTemplate<>();
    template.setConnectionFactory(connectionFactory);
    template.setKeySerializer(longSerializer);
    //Declare the serializer which will be responsible to the
    compression and decompression
    template.setValueSerializer(countrySerializer);
    return template;
}

//Previous source code
}
```

The last modification implies modifying the **CustomCountryRepositoryImpl** class, replacing the general RedisTemplate with a new one on the same way that appears on Listing 14-6.

Listing 14-6. Declaration of the New Template

```
public class CustomCountryRepositoryImpl implements
CustomCountryRepository {

    private static final Object COUNTRY_KEY = "country";
    final RedisTemplate<Long, Country> countryRedisTemplate;
    private HashOperations hashOperations;

    @Autowired
    public CustomCountryRepositoryImpl(RedisTemplate
    countryRedisTemplate) {
        this.countryRedisTemplate = countryRedisTemplate;
        this.hashOperations = countryRedisTemplate.opsForHash();
    }

    //Previous source code
}
```

This solution is an approach to solve a memory use problem in Redis for object size. There are various ways to implement the same, but this approach makes it impossible to read the information in Redis because it is compressed. You need a tool or mechanism to decompress manually to check what is inside this database row.

Other databases like Cassandra offers the possibility to declare explicitly which compression mechanism the database uses. When you insert something, Cassandra compresses and stores the information. It follows the same process when you try to obtain information.

Reducing Transferred Information

One of the key problems related to the performance and the latency of the microservices has endpoints that retrieve everything for a collection which is great if you have a short number of elements and the number of requests to that endpoint each day. Still, when you have many elements to transfer across the network, this could be a problem, so return only a small number of elements.

Spring Data offers an interface called **PagingAndSortingRepository<T, ID>**, which extends from the **CrudRepository<T, ID>**. This interface offers the **findAll** method, which receives an interface called **Pageable**. It contains the number of elements and the offset to obtain from the database.

Using Optional in Custom Queries

Many frameworks or libraries use the Optional class as a "silver bullet" to prevent NullPointerException in an application. Spring Data uses this approach to prevent developers from committing a mistake, so when you write a custom query in your repository, return Optional.

Using Lazy in Relationships

Depending on the number of elements in the collection of the relationship that one entity has could be a good option explicitly indicate that all have **FetchType.Lazy** to reduce the number of elements in memory, and only when you need the information explicitly indicate that load it.

Persisting Multiples Elements

Another problem that it's common to see is having a list of elements that need to be persisted in the database, so developers create an iteration and persist each of them one at a time. The alternative is to pass the list of elements and delegate it to Spring Data using the best to persist the information.

```
public void save(List<Country> countries) {
    //Not use this approach
    for (Country entity: countries) {
        countryRepository.save(entity);
    }

    //Use this approach
    countryRepository.saveAll(countries);
}
```

Using Master/Slave or Replicas

One of the most relevant problems that appear when you have a database with many operations which only access to obtain certain information without modifying anything could affect the performance of other operations that need to introduce modifications like inserting/updating/deleting rows in tables. The correct approach for this problem is to have a master/slave configuration in your database and configure the application to consider these things, like in Chapter 7 with the configuration of Redis.

In relational databases, Spring Data does not offer a default method to do the same, so the alternatives imply that you must define two data sources. One is exclusive for the operations that imply modifications in the database, and the other is for reading the information. This approach implies creating custom classes to indicate to Spring Data that when the operations are read-only, use one data source in particular.

Mongo is another database where you can indicate all the configurations of the replicas in **application.yml**, reducing the problems associated with creating custom classes to support.

Using Cache to Reduce Access

Spring Framework allows you to use a cache mechanism that you can use on another level, not just the repositories. You need to use the **@Cacheable** annotation and define a specific name for each type of object you save.

There are two ways to use this mechanism. One option is to save the elements in the application's memory, which implies that if you have multiple instances of the same application, each has different elements in the cache. The other option is to use Redis as a mechanism of cache, so you have a mechanism of cache in a distributed mode, so all the instances have the same information. Each approach has pros and cons. The second option implies that you need to make an external request to check if the information exists or not in the cache. If you want to reduce the number of operations that your application does in the database without the need to access an external resource like a Redis, the best alternative is to use the first approach, which reduces a smaller number of operations that go directly to the database.

Let's implement the mechanism of cache in memory in **api-catalog,** which uses a relational database to persist the information. Since Spring Boot 2.x.x, the default dependency has been Caffeine.[1] It has a good performance with saving and retrieving information from the cache. Add the dependencies related with the cache on the pom file on the same way that appears on Listing 14-7.

Listing 14-7. Cache Dependencies

```
<dependency>
    <groupId>org.springframework.boot</groupId>
    <artifactId>spring-boot-starter-cache</artifactId>
</dependency>

<dependency>
    <groupId>com.github.ben-manes.caffeine</groupId>
    <artifactId>caffeine</artifactId>
</dependency>
```

---

[1] https://github.com/ben-manes/caffeine

The next step is adding the @Cacheable annotation with a name and when you want to save the information. In the case of the api-catalog application, a possible approach is to include it on the Service in the same way that it appears on Listing 14-8.

Listing 14-8. Service Modifications

```
//Previous imports
import org.springframework.cache.annotation.Cacheable;

@Service
public class CountryService {

    //The annotation will obtain the information from the cache CATALOG_
    COUNTRY before invoking the real implementation if the information
    does not exist try to obtain the information and saved unless  that
    the result is null
    @Cacheable(cacheNames = "CATALOG_COUNTRY", unless = "#result == null")
    @Transactional(readOnly = true)
    public CountryDTO getById(Long id) {
        //Previous source code
    }
}
```

You can store information using an annotation. Still, there are problems with this approach; for example, you can store a lot of values for an infinite period which implies that your application uses a lot of memory. The best approach is to create a configuration to restrict the number of elements and the time your explication stores the information.

Consider adding a cache to the service, not the repository, because your repository does not have custom methods. To use the cache in the repositories, you must declare all the methods again and use the **@Cacheable** annotation.

Let's improve the previous example by adding logic to expire the content in the cache. The modifications to **application.yml** imply that you can have a fine-grained configuration for each type of element, which in Listing 14-8 is **Country**. Still, you can have other methods that obtain information about a city. You need a way to differentiate both caches.

Listing 14-8. Cache Configuration

```
cache:
  configuration:
    CATALOG_COUNTRY:
        refreshAfterWriteTime: 1 #Minutes that the information exist until
        need to be refresh it
        expireAfterWriteTime: 1 #MINUTES
        maxSize: 180 # Number of elements to save on memory
```

The next step is to create a class that maps all the configurations, which is a map with the idea of becoming the extensible solution (see Listing 14-9).

Listing 14-9. Class to Load the Configuration

```
public class CacheSettings {

    private Integer refreshAfterWriteTime;
    private Integer expireAfterWriteTime;
    private Integer maxSize;

    private static final Integer DEFAULT_REFRESH_AFTER = 10;
    private static final Integer DEFAULT_EXPIRE_AFTER = 15;
    private static final Integer DEFAULT_MAX_SIZE = 180;

    public static final CacheSettings DEFAULT_CACHE_SETTINGS = new
    CacheSettings(DEFAULT_REFRESH_AFTER,
            DEFAULT_EXPIRE_AFTER, DEFAULT_MAX_SIZE);

    public CacheSettings() {
    }

    public CacheSettings(Integer refreshAfterWriteTime, Integer
    expireAfterWriteTime, Integer maxSize) {
        this.refreshAfterWriteTime = refreshAfterWriteTime;
        this.expireAfterWriteTime = expireAfterWriteTime;
        this.maxSize = maxSize;
    }

    //Define setters and getters
}
```

You need a class that loads the configuration to **application.yml** in the Spring context. To do this, create a class with the name CacheConfiguration which loads the configuration of "cache" node in the same way that appears on Listing 14-10.

Listing 14-10. Load the Configuration

```
import org.springframework.boot.context.properties.ConfigurationProperties;
import org.springframework.context.annotation.Configuration;

import java.util.Map;

@Configuration
@ConfigurationProperties("cache") //Only load the information of the
"cache" key on the application.yml
public class CacheConfiguration {
    private Map<String, CacheSettings> configuration;

     //You can obtain the configuration of one specific cache with the name
     like how many elements could exist on the cache
    public CacheSettings getCacheSettings(final String cacheName) {
        return configuration.getOrDefault(cacheName, CacheSettings.DEFAULT_
        CACHE_SETTINGS);
    }

    public Map<String, CacheSettings> getConfiguration() {
        return configuration;
    }

    public void setConfiguration(Map<String, CacheSettings> configuration) {
        this.configuration = configuration;
    }
}
```

The last step is to create a class that manages everything about the cache, like the names and how to obtain the information (see Listing 14-11).

Listing 14-11. Load the Configuration

```
package com.apress.catalog.cache;

import com.apress.catalog.repository.CountryRepository;
import com.github.benmanes.caffeine.cache.Caffeine;
import com.google.common.collect.Lists;
import org.springframework.beans.factory.annotation.Autowired;
import org.springframework.cache.CacheManager;
import org.springframework.cache.annotation.EnableCaching;
import org.springframework.cache.caffeine.CaffeineCache;
import org.springframework.cache.support.SimpleCacheManager;
import org.springframework.context.annotation.Bean;
import org.springframework.context.annotation.Configuration;

import java.util.concurrent.TimeUnit;
import java.util.function.Function;

@Configuration
@EnableCaching //Enable the mechanism of cache on the application
public class CacheManagerConfiguration {

    //The name of one cache that will exist on the application
    public static final String CATALOG_COUNTRY = "CATALOG_COUNTRY";

    private final CacheConfiguration cacheConfiguration;

    private final CountryRepository countryRepository;

    @Autowired
    public CacheManagerConfiguration(final CacheConfiguration
    cacheConfiguration, final CountryRepository countryRepository) {
        this.cacheConfiguration = cacheConfiguration;
        this.countryRepository = countryRepository;
    }

    // Define the names and which type of cache use it.
    @Bean
```

```java
public CacheManager cacheManager() {
    CacheSettings cacheCitySettings = cacheConfiguration.
    getCacheSettings(CATALOG_COUNTRY);

    SimpleCacheManager simpleCacheManager = new SimpleCacheManager();
    simpleCacheManager.setCaches(Lists
            .newArrayList(buildCaffeineCache(CATALOG_COUNTRY,
            cacheCitySettings, countryRepository::findById)));

    return simpleCacheManager;
}

// Define the cache, the expiration and the number of elements
// that exist in the cache. Also, define the mechanism to obtain the
// information
public static CaffeineCache buildCaffeineCache(String cacheName,
CacheSettings settings, Function<Long, Object> serviceCall) {

    return new CaffeineCache(cacheName,
            Caffeine.newBuilder().refreshAfterWrite(settings
            .getRefreshAfterWriteTime(), TimeUnit.MINUTES)
                    .expireAfterWrite(settings
                    .getExpireAfterWriteTime(), TimeUnit.MINUTES)
                    .maximumSize(settings.getMaxSize()).build(key ->
                    serviceCall.apply((Long) key)));
    }
}
```

The main problem with this solution is if you have a lot of elements to include in the cache, you have a problem related to memory use.

These solutions are a general rule for all the databases, but relational databases could be an excellent option to use the levels of cache that offer Hibernate.

Summary

Best practices improve the quality of your applications. Many could be best for your application. It depends on the context, such as how critical your application is and how many requests are received daily.

Spring Boot 3 introduces many features to improve an application's performance, like support for compiling a native way using GraalVM[2] and refactoring projects related to Spring Data. I suggest reading the official documentation and checking the forum to find the solution to strange problems because the last version of the framework is not stable, and bugs could appear, which could affect your platform.

---

[2] https://www.graalvm.org/

Setting up Environment Tools

This book used tools that are required to run all the examples. In this appendix, I show you how to install the most relevant of them, excluding the tools and databases you saw in the chapters.

Installing Java

Java JDK is the first thing you need to install before starting to try something. There are several JDK editions, but you must install version 17 in all cases.

- **OracleJDK:**[1] This version was free until Java 11. After this version, you can use it for development/test environments, but you need to pay a license to use it in production. This version of the JDK offers the most recent patches of bugs and new features because Oracle is the owner of the language.

- **OpenJDK:**[2] When Oracle bought Sun Microsystems created this as an open source alternative that all developers can use in any environment without restrictions. The main problem with this version is the patches of the bugs take time to appear in a case that is not critical.

---

[1] `https://www.oracle.com/java/technologies/`
[2] `https://openjdk.org/`

© Andres Sacco 2023
A. Sacco, *Beginning Spring Data*, https://doi.org/10.1007/978-1-4842-8764-4

- **Others**: There are many other alternatives to JDK (e.g., AWS (Amazon Web Services) have Amazon Corretto[3] which extends from OpenJDK and optimizes the performance of the applications in the environments of this cloud provider.

OpenJDK was used throughout this book, but you can choose any alternative. Depending on the operating system, there are many ways to install the JDK.

For macOS and Linux, you can use Homebrew,[4] a tool for installing/updating.

➜ ~ brew install openjdk

Another possibility is to use SDKMAN[5] which is similar to Homebrew and has multiples versions and implementations of the JDK

➜ ~ sdk install java 17.0.35-ms

For Windows platforms, you have two possibilities. The first option is installing SDKMAN and running the same macOS/Linux command. The second option is to install Adoptium[6] which allows you to download the OpenJDK for various platforms. You can download a file MSI in Windows, making the installation easy.

After installing the JDK, check if the version of Java is available on your system. To do this, type the following.

```
➜  ~ java -version
openjdk 17.0.4 2022-07-19 LTS
OpenJDK Runtime Environment Microsoft-38107 (build 17.0.4+8-LTS)
OpenJDK 64-Bit Server VM Microsoft-38107 (build 17.0.4+8-LTS, mixed
mode, sharing
```

To execute all the examples, there are no limitations between which version of Java you need to have installed on your machine, but all the examples were written using JDK 17, the version required to use Spring Boot 3.0. Still, only a few developers use this version in production. According to Snyk,[7] about 61% of developers use version 11 in production environments.

---

[3] https://aws.amazon.com/corretto/

[4] https://brew.sh/

[5] https://sdkman.io/

[6] https://adoptium.net/

[7] https://snyk.io/jvm-ecosystem-report-2021/

Installing Maven

The second thing you need to have on your machine to run all the examples or follow the examples is Maven. This tool provides a good way to manage and solve the conflict between versions of the dependencies in your projects.

Depending on the operating system, there are many ways to install Maven. Some involve doing it manually, so you need to download it from the official website[8] and configure the environment variables to recognize the mvn command. Let's look at how to install Maven using package manager tools.

For macOS and Linux, you can use Homebrew,[9] a tool for installing/updating.

➜   ~ brew install maven

Also, you can install it using SDKman [10] which follows the same approach as Homebrew and provides a simple way to install libraries or tools.

➜   ~ sdk install maven

Another way to do it is only available in specific Linux distributions.

- Ubuntu

  ➜   ~ sudo apt install maven

- Fedora

  ➜   ~ sudo dnf nstall maven

For Windows platforms, there are two possibilities. The first option is to install SDKMAN! and run the same commands as in macOS and Linux. The second option involves downloading manually, unzipping all the content in one directory, and creating an environment variable named M2_HOME with the root directory's location inside the Maven folder you created.

---

[8] https://maven.apache.org/download.cgi
[9] https://brew.sh/
[10] https://sdkman.io/

After finishing the Maven installation, check the version available in your system. To do this, type the following.

```
➜  ~ mvn --version
Apache Maven 3.8.1
Maven home: /usr/share/maven
```

Installing Git

Git is a version control system tracking all the modifications people can introduce. This tool is not required for using the source code in this book because GitHub allows you to download all the repositories. I included it in case you want to introduce modifications to the repository.

To install this tool, you can use packager manager tools.

- Homebrew

  ```
  ➜  ~ brew install git
  ```

- SDKman

  ```
  ➜  ~ sdk install git
  ```

If you want another option, check the official Git[11] website, where you can download an executable that installs everything in Windows.

After you install the tool, you need to check which version is on your system. To do this, type the following.

```
➜  ~ git --version
git version 2.37.1
```

As a suggestion to not need to write in every commit information like your username and email, you can configure globally using these commands.

```
➜  ~ git config --global user.name "John Doe"
➜  ~ git config --global user.email "johndoe@example.com"
```

---

[11] https://git-scm.com/downloads

Installing IntelliJ

The instructions to install IntelliJ are on the official JetBrains webpage,[12] which mentions the minimum resources and operating system. There are two versions of the IDE. The Community edition is free, and you can use and install several plugins. The Ultimate edition has a fee and offers extra features that are unnecessary for this book.

Figure A-1 shows the official webpage with all the differences between both versions.

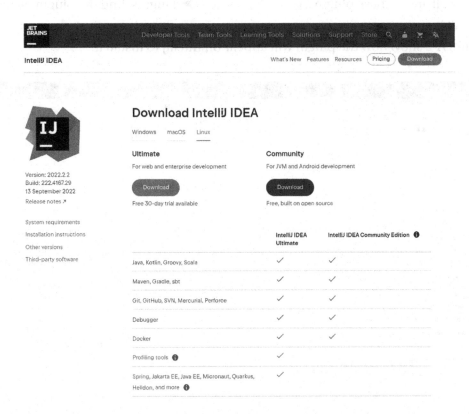

Figure A-1. *Official site to download the IDE*

---

[12] https://www.jetbrains.com/idea/download/#section=linux

The following plugins could be helpful to install on this IDE.

- Maven Helper[13]

- GitToolBox[14]

- Docker[15]

- Spring Tools[16]

To install any of these plugins, go to Preferences ➤ Plugins, find the plugin by name, and install it.

Figure A-2 show how the plugin will appear on Intellij to install it.

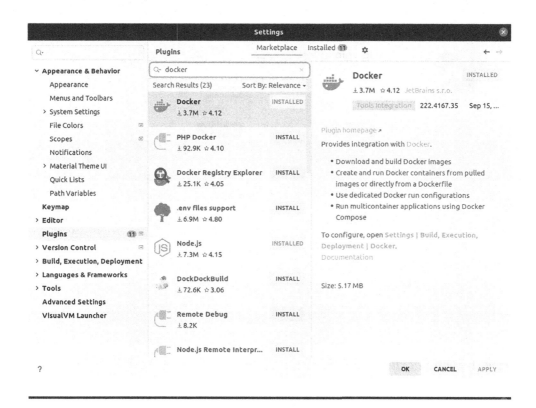

Figure A-2. *IntelliJ plugins installation*

---

[13] https://plugins.jetbrains.com/plugin/7179-maven-helper

[14] https://plugins.jetbrains.com/plugin/7499-gittoolbox

[15] https://plugins.jetbrains.com/plugin/7724-docker

[16] https://plugins.jetbrains.com/plugin/14279-spring-tools

Installing Docker

Docker is one of the most popular options for running a container engine based on Linux. In this book, you can use it to reduce the complexity of installing databases on your system. using Docker. You can run it easily and remove it to stop the container.

Note This book does not explain all the pros and cons of using Docker. Many other books, articles, and videos explain all the concepts related to this technology in a lot of detail.

Installing Docker depends on your operating system because there are a few ways to install it natively in a Linux distribution. In Windows/macOS, Docker Desktop introduces a layer between the operating system and Docker to provide the capacity to run containers. For details, follow the instructions on the official website.[17]

After you install this tool, the only thing that you need to do is check which version is on your system. To do this, you type the following.

```
→  ~ docker --version
Docker version 20.10.12, build 20.10.12-0ubuntu2~20.04.1
```

To run a container, you can find on the official webpage of Docker Hub[18] all the images that exist. For the examples, run the hello-world images to test that everything works.

```
→  ~ docker pull hello-world:latest
→  ~ docker run hello-world:latest
Hello from Docker!
This message shows that your installation appears to be working correctly.

To generate this message, Docker took the following steps:
1. The Docker client contacted the Docker daemon.
2. The Docker daemon pulled the "hello-world" image from the Docker Hub.
```

---

[17] http://docs.docker.com/install
[18] https://hub.docker.com/

    (amd64)

3. The Docker daemon created a new container from that image which runs the executable that produces the output you are currently reading.

4. The Docker daemon streamed that output to the Docker client, which sent it to your terminal.

To try something more ambitious, you can run an Ubuntu container with:
$ docker run -it ubuntu bash

Share images, automate workflows, and more with a free Docker ID:
https://hub.docker.com/

For more examples and ideas, visit:
https://docs.docker.com/get-started/

   For more information on the commands, you can check this blog[19] which explains the most relevant commands and components.

---

[19] https://michaelhaar.dev/my-docker-compose-cheatsheet

APPENDIX B

Recommended and Alternative Tools

This appendix discusses the tools used in the book and alternative options.

IDEs

IntelliJ[1] is the most widely used IDE for Java development. IntelliJ IDEA Community Edition provides everything you need to start with Java and Spring. The Ultimate version contains extra features and other plugins. Figure B-1 shows how IntelliJ looks like.

---

[1] https://www.jetbrains.com/idea/

© Andres Sacco 2023
A. Sacco, *Beginning Spring Data*, https://doi.org/10.1007/978-1-4842-8764-4

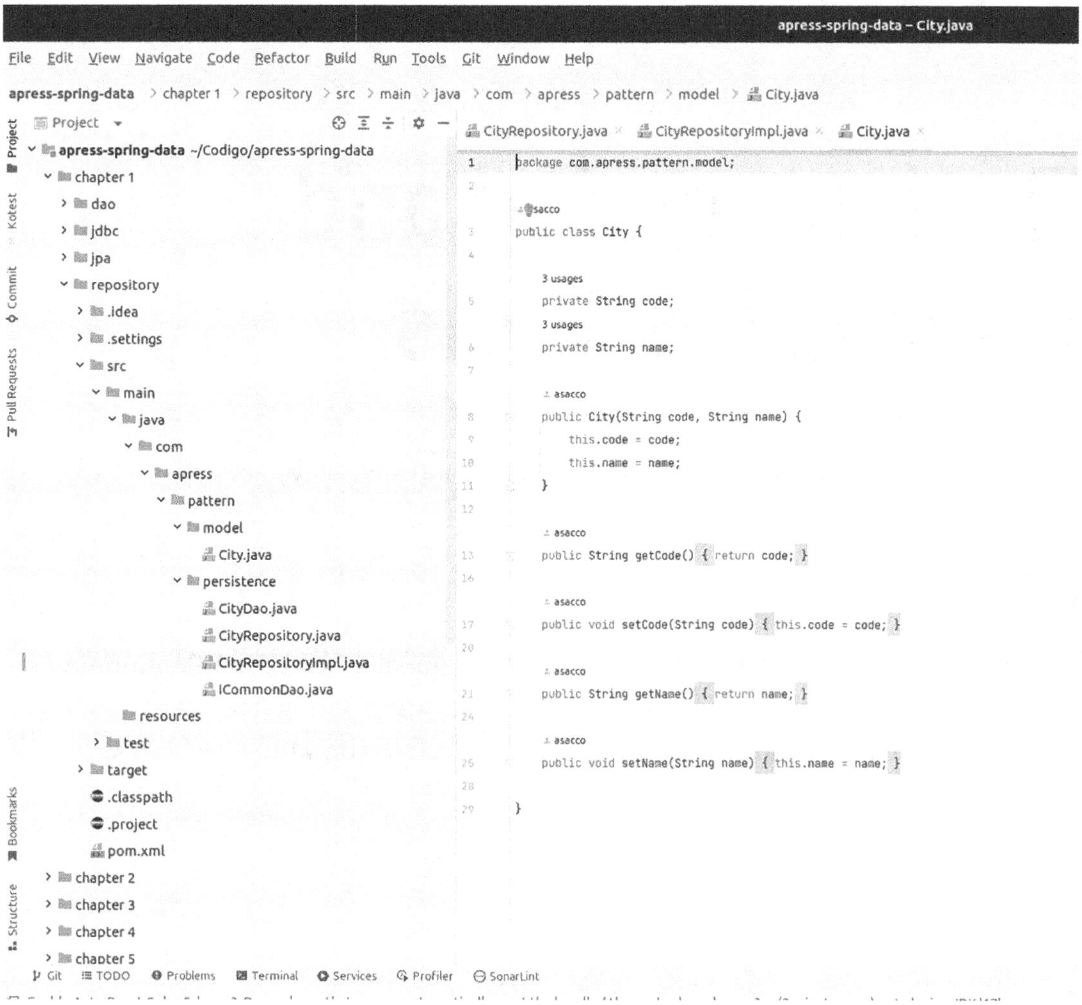

Figure B-1. *IntelliJ with an imported project*

Eclipse[2] is another IDE option for Java development that most old developers know. Most plugins are free and have a vast community of developers who frequently update them and a large number of Spring's plugins. The most relevant ones appear on the Spring website.[3] If you use this tool, please follow the instructions to install the plugins. Figure B-2 shows how Eclipse looks like.

---

[2] https://www.eclipse.org/downloads/
[3] https://spring.io/tools

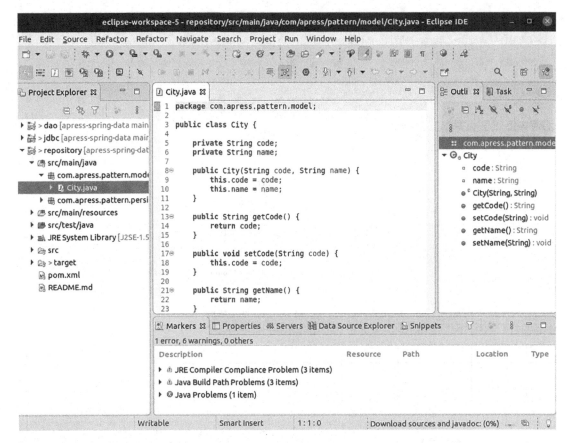

Figure B-2. *Eclipse with an imported project*

NetBeans[4] develops applications using various programming languages. There is no longer a large community of users because other options cover most developers' needs. Some developers use it as they start to learn their first language. Figure B-3 shows how Netbeans looks like.

---

[4] https://netbeans.apache.org/

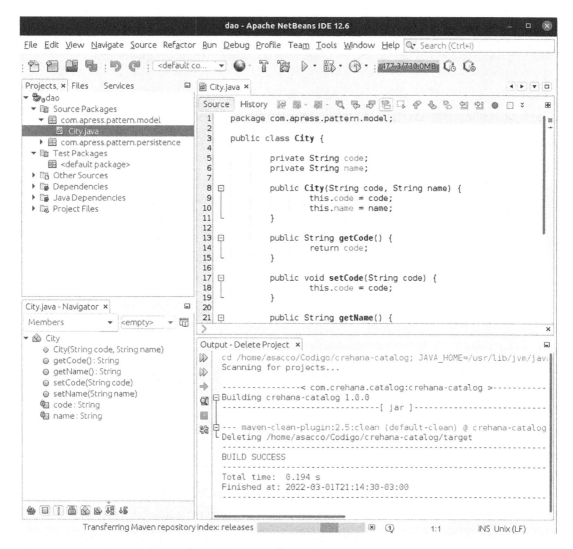

Figure B-3. *NetBeans with an imported project*

REST Tools

Postman[5] is a tool that tests REST endpoints where you can have variables representing environments or another thing like the actual date. You can use it to execute tests at a specific time. Figure B-4 shows a little overview of what the tool looks like.

---

[5] https://www.postman.com/

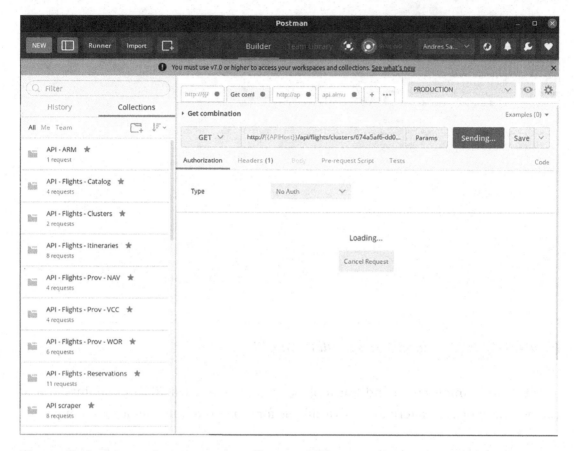

Figure B-4. *Insomnia executes a call to an API*

Insomnia[6] is a tool for requests in REST endpoints. One of the biggest difference with Postman is this tool support multiple protocols like REST, gRPC, SOAP, and GraphQL. The feature is similar to Postman and the user interface but can have at least two themes. Figure B-5 shows a little overview of what the tool looks like.

_____

[6] https://insomnia.rest/

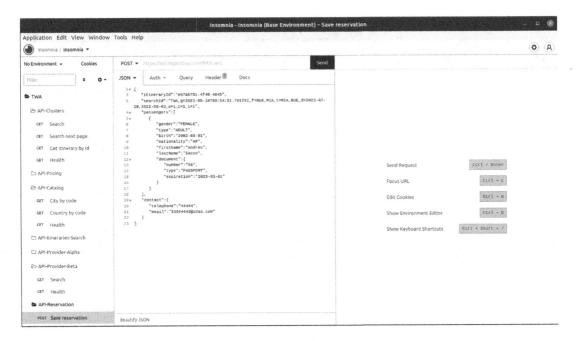

Figure B-5. *Insomnia executes a call to an API*

cURL[7] is a simple command-line tool that you can use to call REST endpoints. You can use this tool as an alternative. It's available for most common operating systems.

Databases

An example of each type of database was covered in this book; the approach is similar.

Cassandra[8]

DataStax Studio[9] was created and is maintained by developers who created Cassandra and provide the chance to install it on all the operating systems or use Docker. This tool's features include exporting information in multiple formats, exporting the queries or the process to import in another machine, and an intelligent editor that validates the queries. Figure B-6 shows a little overview of what the tool looks like.

---

[7] https://curl.se/download.html

[8] https://cassandra.apache.org/_/index.html

[9] https://downloads.datastax.com/#studio

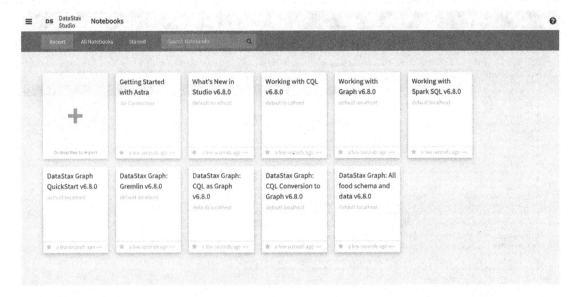

Figure B-6. *DataStax configuration page*

MongoDB[10]

Compass[11] is the official solution to connect, query, optimize, and analyze the performance in MongoDB. It offers the possibility to install on multiple operating systems and has a simple user interface. It also provides a good interface for seeing the impact of executing each query.

Studio 3t[12] is an alternative to Compass, which many beginning developers use. The interface looks similar to tools like MySQL Workbench or pgAdmin III. You can run queries without blocking the UI. Figure B-7 shows a little overview of what the tool looks like.

---

[10] https://www.mongodb.com/

[11] https://www.mongodb.com/products/compass

[12] https://studio3t.com/

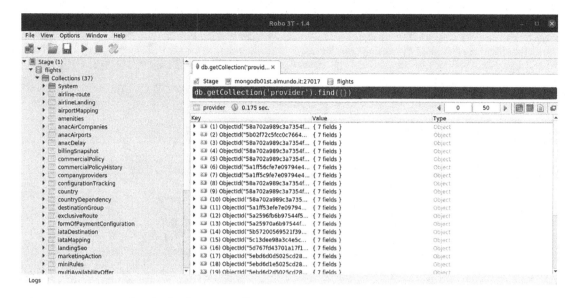

Figure B-7. *Studio 3t finding a collection*

MySQL[13]

MySQL Workbench[14] is one of the most used interfaces to execute queries and do a certain level of administration of MySQL databases. Using this tool, you can see the use of the resources for each database, model the tables and the relationship between them, and explain each query. Figure B-8 shows a little overview of what the tool looks like.

---

[13] https://www.mysql.com/

[14] https://www.mysql.com/products/workbench/

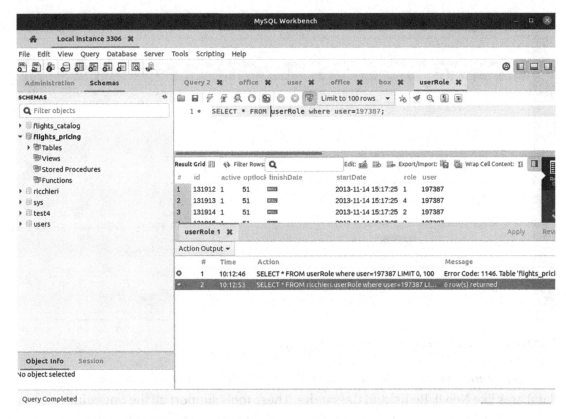

Figure B-8. MySQL Workbench with the results of one query

Neo4j[15]

Neo4j Browser[16] is the default way to connect with any Neo4j database. By default, tools include Neo4j Browser. One of the pros of this tool is that it is free and created and supported by the company that created Neo4j. Figure B-9 shows a little overview of what the tool looks like.

---

[15] https://neo4j.com/

[16] https://neo4j.com/developer/neo4j-browser/

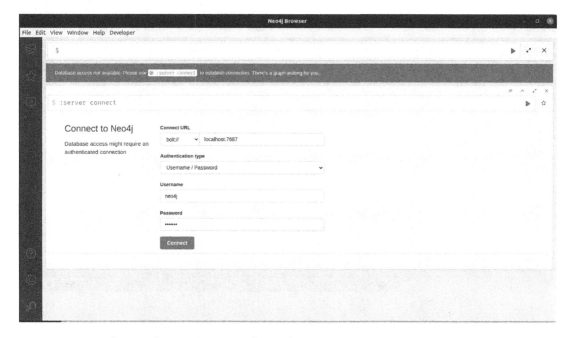

Figure B-9. *The configuration window of Neo4j*

Graphileon[17] is a fee-based tool to connect with different types of non-relational databases like Neo4j, Redis, and Cassandra. These tools support all the operating systems and provide some features that do not exist in Neo4j Browser, like creating libraries to visualize the information like diagrams or images. Figure B-10 shows a little overview of what the tool looks like.

---

[17] https://graphileon.com/

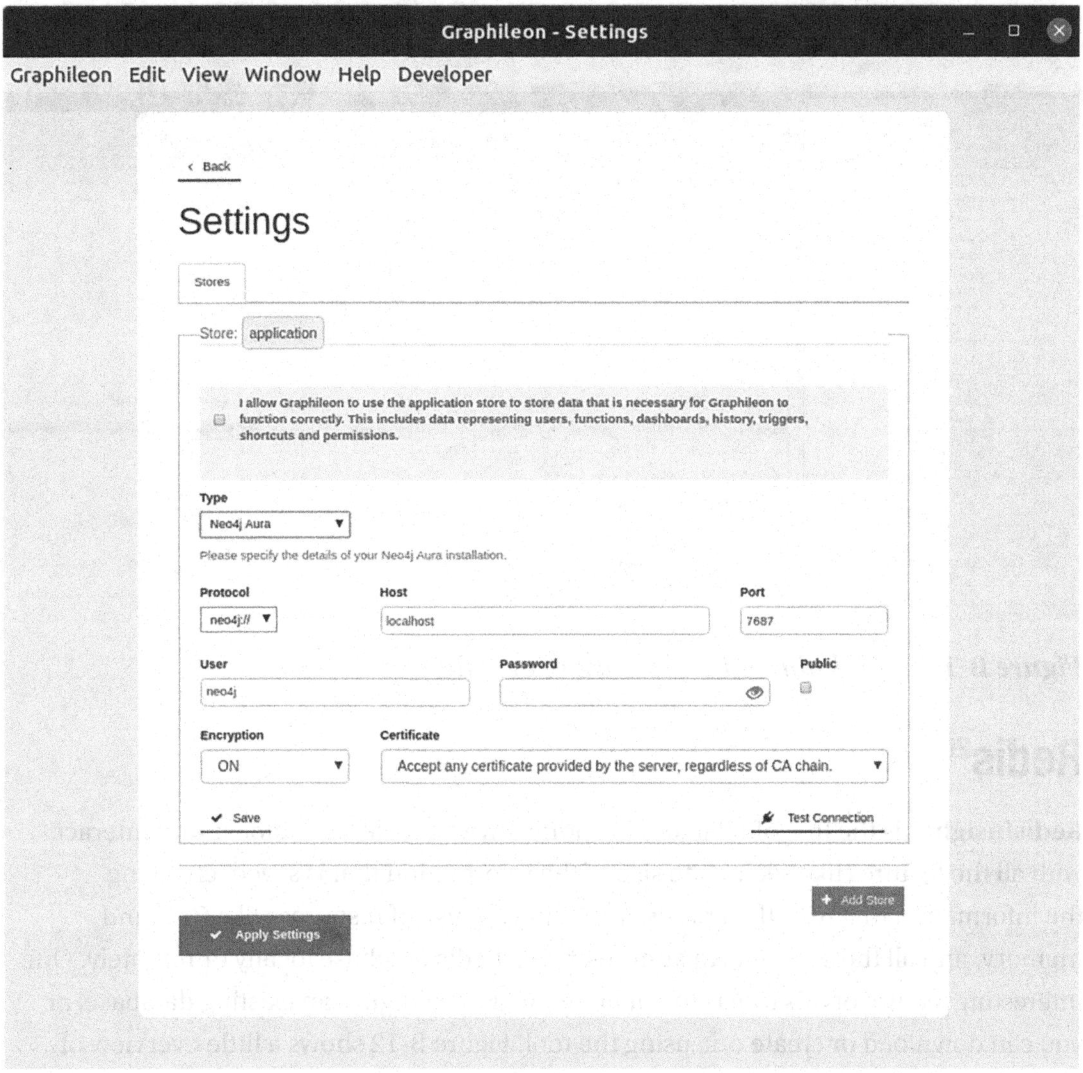

Figure B-10. *Settings windows of Neo4j*

PostgreSQL[18]

pgAdmin[19] is the most popular tool to connect with PostgreSQL databases. It provides a set of features to check the use of the memory/CPU and explain the queries graphically. Figure B-11 shows a little overview of what the tool looks like.

---

[18] https://www.postgresql.org/

[19] https://www.pgadmin.org/

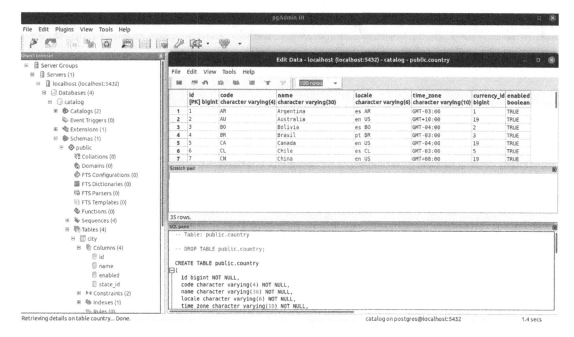

Figure B-11. *pgAdmin with the results of one query*

Redis[20]

RedisInsight[21] is the free official tool to connect with the Redis database and interact with all the features like seeing the size of the information that is saved, checking the information that uses the graphs, analyzing the use of resources like CPU and memory, and all the elements to administrate a Redis database locally or remotely. One interesting feature of this tool is that it allows you to configure an existing database, or you can download or create one using the tool. Figure B-12 shows a little overview of what the tool looks like.

---

[20] https://redis.io/

[21] https://redis.com/redis-enterprise/redis-insight/

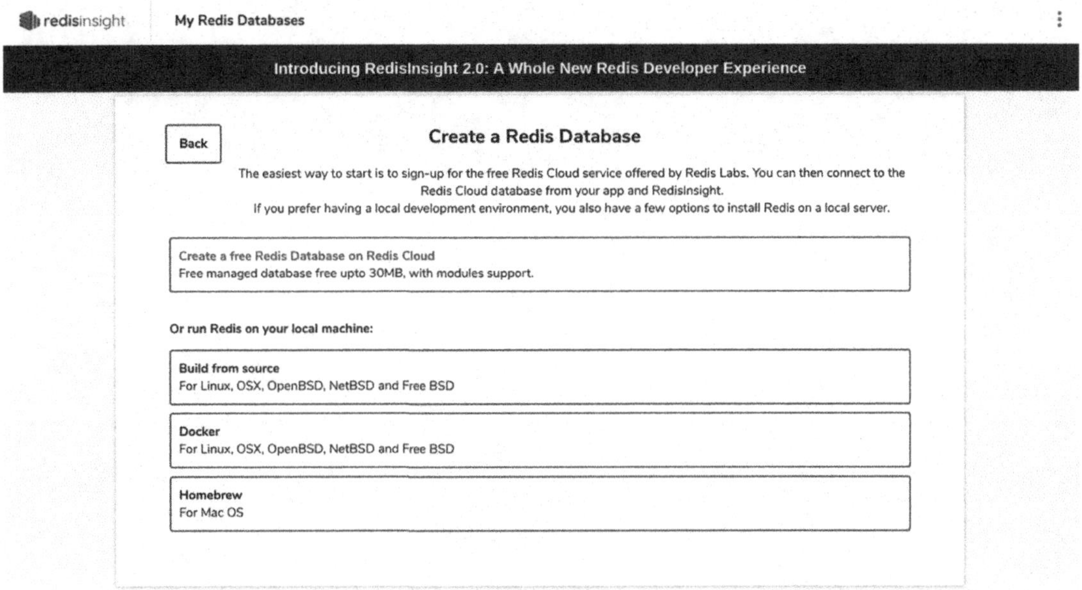

Figure B-12. *Configuration page of RedisInsight*

SQLYog[22] is a powerful alternative to MySQL Workbench and pgAdmin, offering other features like comparing data between databases or tables, giving the possibility to synchronize the schema from a SQL file or another database, and the possibility to create a backup at a certain time each day.

Dbeaver[23] is a free, open source tool for accessing multiple relational databases like MariaDB, PostgreSQL, and others. Offers an interface user friendly and similar to MySQL Workbench.

---

[22] https://webyog.com/product/sqlyog/
[23] https://dbeaver.io/

APPENDIX C

Opening a Project

This book shows examples of projects which use different types of databases. You can create following the instructions in the chapters or download it from the official source code. You can follow the instructions in this appendix if you want to download and import it to your IDE.

Note   The IDE suggested for this book is IntelliJ, so all the instructions are related to this IDE.

JDK 17 or higher must be installed on your machine to run all the projects in this book. There is no restriction about which distribution you need to have. Appendix A has more information about the tools you need to install.

Figure C-1 shows how to open a file or an existing project in IntelliJ IDEA. To select the project you want to open, choose **File ➤ Open**.

© Andres Sacco 2023
A. Sacco, *Beginning Spring Data*, https://doi.org/10.1007/978-1-4842-8764-4

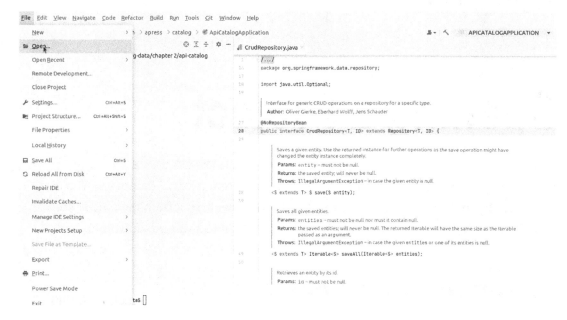

Figure C-1. *Menu option to open a project*

When you click the Open button, a pop-up window lets you select the project's location to import into the IDE, as shown in Figure C-2.

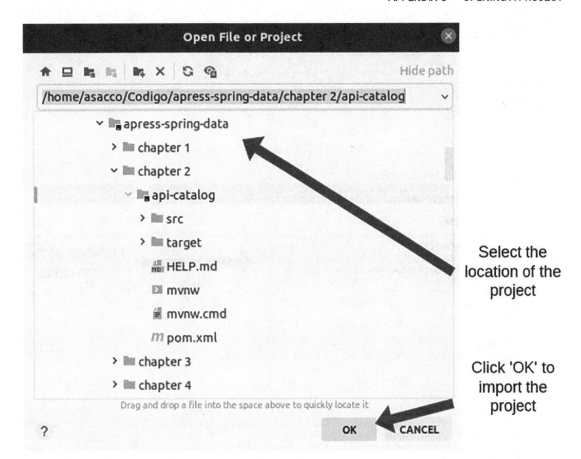

Figure C-2. *Pop-up window to select the project to import*

After you import the project to your IDE, you can open the packages to find the main class, which is usually located in the root package. Figure C-3 shows all the project structures that appear in Chapter 2.

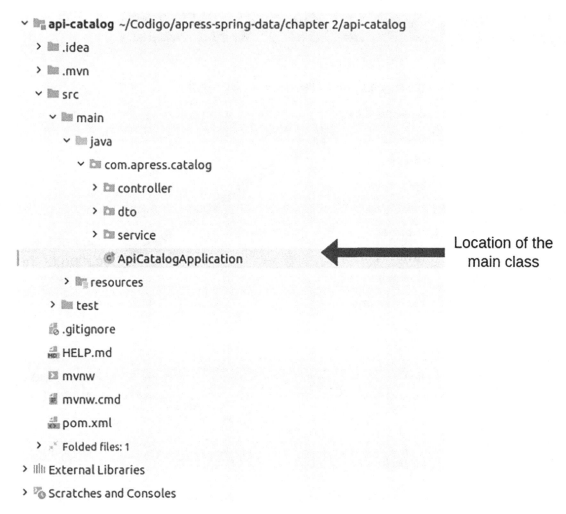

Figure C-3. *Location of the main class to execute the application*

To run the application, you only need to click the main class and choose the option Run Application or run it using the terminal.

Install and Configure a Relational Database

This appendix explains how to install MySQL and PostgreSQL databases in Parts I and II of this book. There is no restriction to using one database instead of another; this appendix shows the two most popular free databases. If you can use another one, you can do it because Spring Data supports at least all the existing relational databases.

Each section finds the steps you need to execute to load a functional database with a good data set to use in your microservice.

1. Install the database on your local machine.

2. Install the client to access the database.

3. In the client application, configure the connection with the database.

4. Create the schema.

5. Load the data.

You can choose not to install the database and run it using Docker. See Appendix F for more information about how Docker works on each database.

MySQL

MySQL is a relational database that was published in 1994 by Sun Microsystems. The following are some of the features that make this database popular among developers.

- It's free to use.

- Have a great performance with a considerable number of operations.

367

- According to a 2021 StackOverflow survey,[1] 50% of developers use this database in an application, which is important because many people can detect any problem and report it.

Step 1: Install the Database on Your Local Machine

The first step of the process is to download the database installer and run the process. MySQL supports multiple operating systems, including Windows, macOS, and many distributions of Linux. You can download the installer from the official website[2] and follow the instructions[3] for each operating system. Define a username/password for the root which you use to connect with the database in step 3.

Step 2: Install the Client to Access the Database

To work with MySQL, you need a client that helps you to do certain operations like creating a schema, inserting data, and checking if everything works fine. There are many options to install on your machine; some are free, and another has a trial for a short period of time. This book uses MySQL Workbench, the suggested and the most popular tool to use in MySQL, but there are other options, as discussed in Appendix B.

To download the installer according to your operating system, you can check the official documentation of MySQL Workbench.[4] If you want to check the system requirements for installation, you can check the MySQL installation webpage.[5]

Step 3: Configure the Connection

After you install the database and the client accesses it, the next step is open the MySQL Workbench and create a new connection with the credentials that you set up in step 1. If the installer didn't request to set up a username and password, perhaps the database has *root* as a default username and an empty password.

---

[1] https://insights.stackoverflow.com/survey/2021#technology

[2] https://dev.mysql.com/downloads/mysql/

[3] https://dev.mysql.com/doc/refman/8.0/en/installing.html

[4] https://dev.mysql.com/downloads/workbench/

[5] https://dev.mysql.com/doc/workbench/en/wb-installing.html

Figure D-1 shows the plus icon in MySQL Workbench, which you click to make a new connection.

Figure D-1. *Client to access the database*

Figure D-2 shows the screen where you complete all the information related to the new connection. In this window, you only need to complete the information about the username. This hostname is localhost or 127.0.0.1, the port in all cases is 3306, and a name to the connection, which could be anything because there is no restriction with the name.

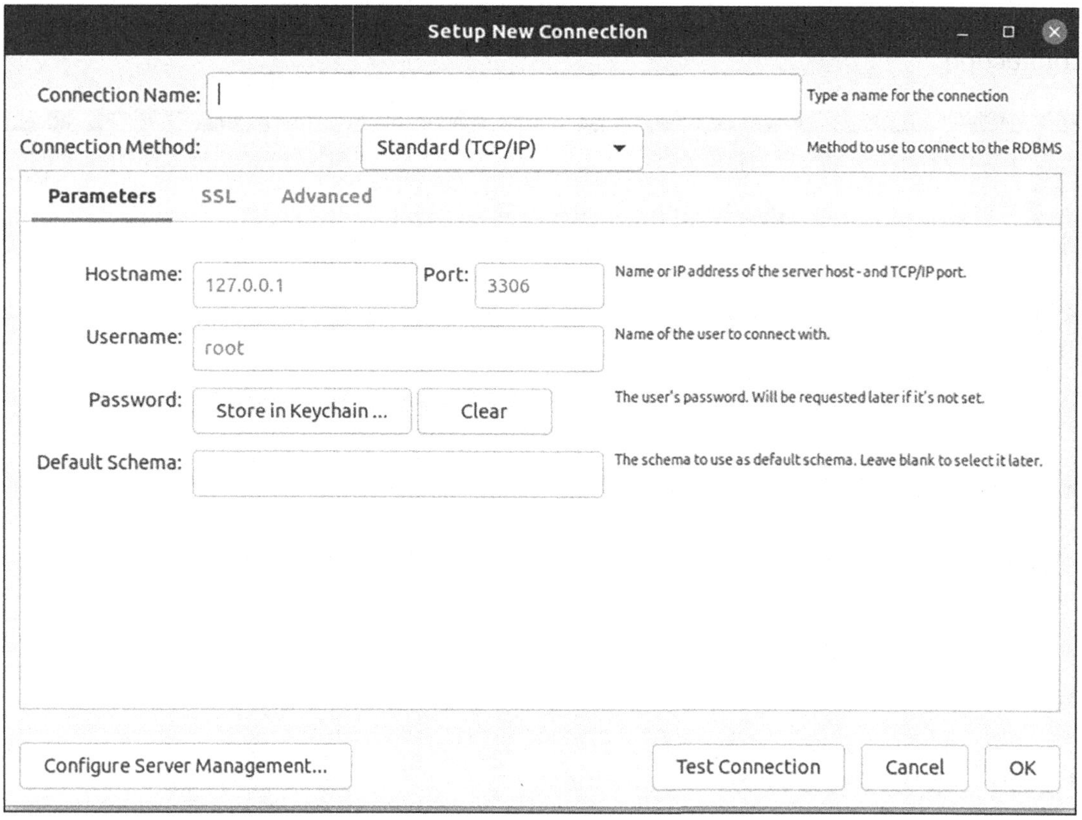

Figure D-2. *Create a new connection*

If you want to check if everything works fine, you can click the Test Connection button, and a pop-up window completes the connection's password. If you want to set the password and never complete the pop-up, you need to click the Store in Keychain… button, which asks for the password and saves the value in a secure place on your machine.

After you test the connection, click the OK button to save all the information about the connection.

Step 4: Create the Schema

Double-click to access this database and execute the operations you want when you have a connection created in MySQL Workbench (see Figure D-3).

Figure D-3. *Active connections in MySQL Workbench*

The first thing that you need to do is create a new schema that contains all the tables. Click the plus icon plus. When the form appears, enter the name of the database. Finally, click the Apply button to create an empty schema, which you populate with different tables in the next step.

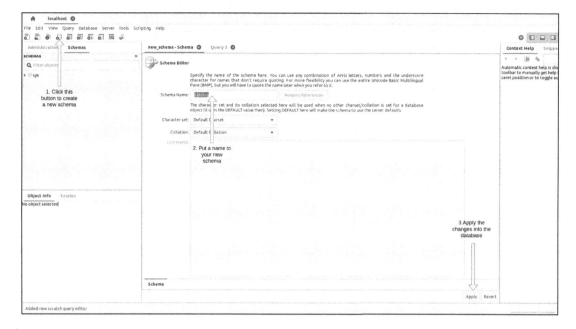

Figure D-4. *Create a new schema*

Step 5: Load the Data

The last step of this process is to create the structure of the schema and populate it with the information you use in the chapters on relational databases. It is in the code repository folders (github.com/apress/beginning-spring-data). Each of them is associated with one chapter. The databases folder is where you can find all the scripts to execute (see Figure D-5).

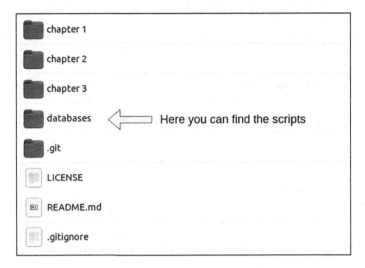

Figure D-5. *Source repository with the scripts of the database*

There are several files inside this folder. Execute each of them by version number (see Figure D-6). The first script to execute is V1.0_init_database.sql.

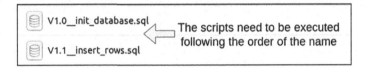

Figure D-6. *Scripts that need to be executed in the database*

The final step is to open each script and execute it. You can drag and drop the file inside the MySQL Workbench to do this. The application opens the file, showing the content. After that, you only need to click the button to run all the scripts into the database and repeat this process for each script (see Figure D-7).

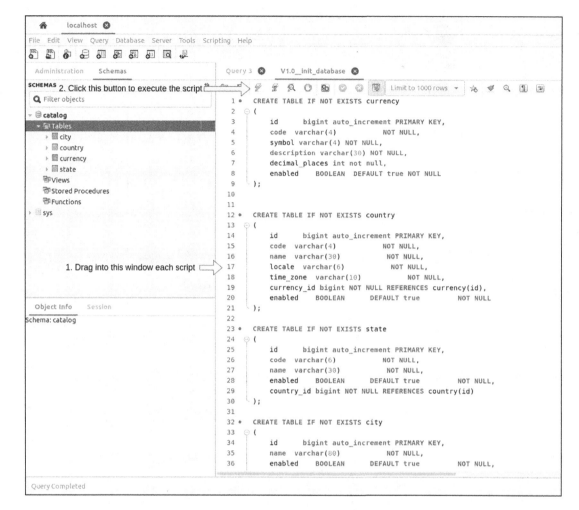

Figure D-7. *Loading the script in MySQL Workbench*

PostgreSQL

PostgreSQL is a relational database created in 1996 as an alternative to MySQL. The following are some of the features that make this database popular among developers.

- It's free to use.

- It's an optimized database for a huge volume of reads and writes.

- Supports more datatypes than MySQL, such as enumerated values.

- According to StackOverflow's 2021 survey, [6] PostgreSQL is the second most used database after MySQL, which means that if something does not work well, many people report the bug.

Step 1: Install the Database on Your Local Machine

The first step of the process is to download the database installer and run the process. PostgreSQL supports multiple operating systems, including Windows and macOS, and many distributions of Linux, such as Debian, Ubuntu, Red Hat, and Suse. You can download the installer from the official website[7] and follow the instructions after clicking your operating system. The instructions webpage includes the prerequisites for using each database version.

Define a username/password for the root which you use to connect with the database in step 3.

Step 2: Install the Client to Access the Database

To work with PostgreSQL, you need a client that helps you do certain operations like creating a schema, inserting data, and checking if everything works fine. There are several options for all the relational databases; some are free, and another has a trial for a short time. This book uses pgAdmin, one of the most popular options.

Find and download the installer according to your operating system by checking the official documentation.[8] A great difference between this client to access the database and others is the possibility to run using Docker, so if you don't want to install it for this book, you can run it using Docker.

When you select your operating system, you see the prerequisites and instructions to install it on your local machine.

---

[6] https://insights.stackoverflow.com/survey/2021#technology
[7] https://www.postgresql.org/download/
[8] https://www.pgadmin.org/download/

Step 3: Configure the Connection

After installing the database and the client accesses it, the next step is to open pgAdmin and log in using the credentials you defined in step 2 (see Figure D-8).

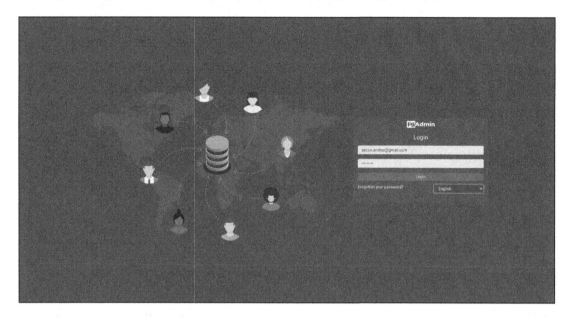

Figure D-8. *Login webpage*

Figure D-9 shows the pgAdmin dashboard. Click the icon to add a new connection.

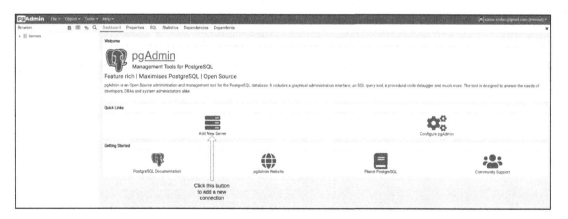

Figure D-9. *Add a new server*

Next, you see the window with all the information related to the database, such as username/password, the hostname (localhost or 127.0.0.1), the port (5432), and the connection name, which could be anything because there are no restrictions with the name.

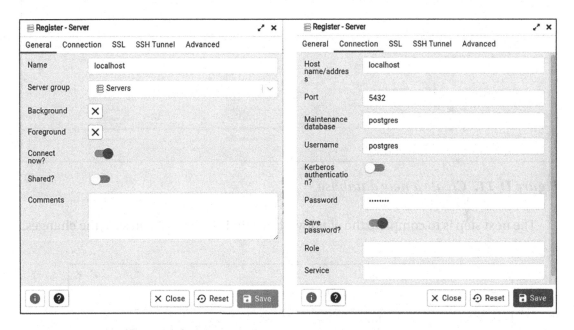

Figure D-10. *Connection configuration*

If everything is okay, click the Save button. You create the schema in the next step.

Step 4: Create the Schema

When you connect to a server created in pgAdmin (see Figure D-11), left-click the server, select Create in the menu, and then select the Database option.

Figure D-11.   *Create a new database*

The next step is to complete the window shown in Figure D-12 and save the changes.

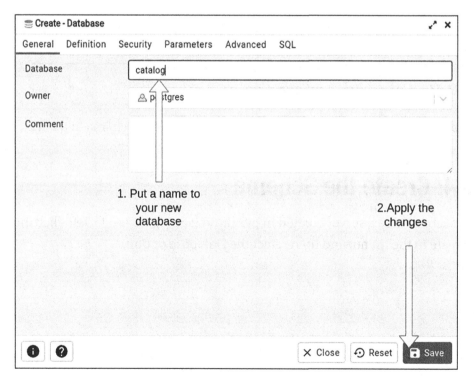

Figure D-12.   *Window to create a new database*

Step 5: Load the Data

The last step of this process is to create the schema structure and populate it with the information you used in the chapters on relational databases. Inside the source code folder are several files. You execute each of them by version number, so the first script to execute is V1.0_init_database.sql.

Finally, you need to double-click the Schemas section in the database that you created and click the database icon to open the connection to execute queries. After that, you need to copy and paste the content of each file into the query editor and press the Play button to execute the queries. You need to repeat this process with each file in the scripts folder.

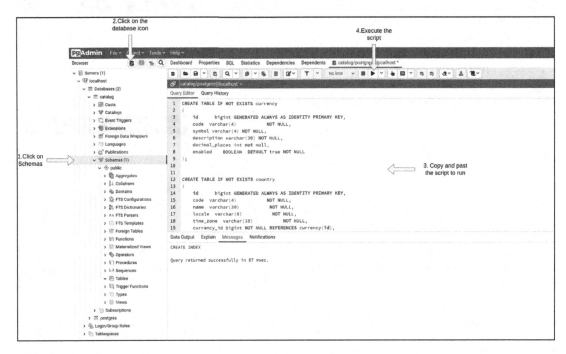

Figure D-13. *Window to create a new database*

Databases Using Docker

Many developers don't want to install databases on their machines because they consume resources and are not always used. For example, to do the exercises in this book, you must have a database running on your machine. After you complete the book, you won't want to use MySQL or PostgreSQL any longer. Use Docker for a database that runs easily.

You must check the Docker Hub site for a particular version of MySQL[9] or PostgreSQL.[10] I recommend that you not use the latest version but instead the last version that exists in Docker Hub.

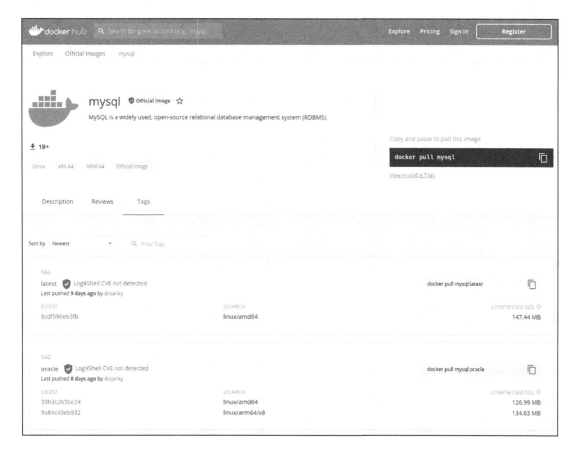

Figure D-14. *Docker Hub's webpage*

---

[9] https://hub.docker.com/_/mysql?tab=tags
[10] https://hub.docker.com/_/postgres?tab=tag

When you decide which database you want to run, the next step is downloading the image to use locally.

```
asacco@asacco:~/$ docker pull mysql/mysql-server: 8.0.30
8.0.30: Pulling from mysql/mysql-server
221c7ea50c9e: Pull complete
d32a20f3a6af: Pull complete
28749a63c815: Pull complete
3cdab959ca41: Pull complete
30ceffa70af4: Pull complete
e4b028b699c1: Pull complete
3abed4e8adad: Pull complete
Digest: sha256:6fca505a0d41c7198b577628584e01d3841707c3292499baae8703
7f886c9fa2
Status: Downloaded newer image for mysql/mysql-server:8.0. 30
docker.io/mysql/mysql-server: 8.0.30
```

The last step is to run the database image you downloaded moments ago.

```
asacco@asacco:~/$ docker run mysql/mysql-server:8.0.30  -e MYSQL_ROOT_
PASSWORD: muppet
[Entrypoint] MySQL Docker Image 8.0.30-1.2.7-server
[Entrypoint] No password option specified for new database.
[Entrypoint]   A random onetime password will be generated.
[Entrypoint] Initializing database
.........
[Entrypoint] MySQL init process done. Ready for start up.

[Entrypoint] Starting MySQL 8.0.30-1.2.7-server
2022-04-08T03:01:52.053869Z 0 [System] [MY-010116] [Server] /usr/sbin/
mysqld (mysqld 8.0.30) starting as process 1
2022-04-08T03:01:52.061845Z 1 [System] [MY-013576] [InnoDB] InnoDB
initialization has started.
2022-04-08T03:01:52.208388Z 1 [System] [MY-013577] [InnoDB] InnoDB
initialization has ended.
2022-04-08T03:01:52.411922Z 0 [Warning] [MY-010068] [Server] CA certificate
ca.pem is self signed.
```

```
2022-04-08T03:01:52.411987Z 0 [System] [MY-013602] [Server] Channel mysql_
main configured to support TLS. Encrypted connections are now supported for
this channel.
2022-04-08T03:01:52.433058Z 0 [System] [MY-010931] [Server] /usr/sbin/
mysqld: ready for connections. Version: '8.0.30'  socket: '/var/lib/mysql/
mysql.sock'  port: 3306  MySQL Community Server - GPL.
2022-04-08T03:01:52.433067Z 0 [System] [MY-011323] [Server] X Plugin ready
for connections. Bind-address: '::' port: 33060, socket: /var/run/mysqld/
mysqlx.sock
```

When the database is running, you can use it in the same port as the database installed on your local machine.

APPENDIX E

Installing and Configuring Non-Relational Databases

This appendix explains how to install the non-relational databases in Part III of this book.

The main problem with this type of database depends on which database you use; the installation process takes time and executes instructions. I recommend that you use Docker to run the images. You can use the UI console with Docker too.

Redis

Redis is a high-performance non-relational database with various installation options.

Using the popular Homebrew installation tool is an option that implies the database is installed and running on your machine. After reading this book, you need to remove it if you don't use it. Listing E-1 shows how to install using Homebrew.

Listing E-1. Installation Using Homebrew

```
$ brew install redis
==> Installing redis
==> Pouring redis--7.0.4.x86_64_linux.bottle.tar.gz
==> Caveats

To restart redis after an upgrade:
  brew services restart redis
Or, if you don't want/need a background service you can just run:
  /home/linuxbrew/.linuxbrew/opt/redis/bin/redis-server /home/linuxbrew/.
linuxbrew/etc/redis.conf
```

383

© Andres Sacco 2023
A. Sacco, *Beginning Spring Data*, https://doi.org/10.1007/978-1-4842-8764-4

```
==> node
Bash completion has been installed to:
  /home/linuxbrew/.linuxbrew/etc/bash_completion.d
```

When this installation process is finished, you have the database running on port 5432, and if you want not to use it or remove it call the remove or stop command in Homebrew.

If you want to check which version of Redis is installed on your machine, you can use the following command to check it. Also, this command helps you clarify if the installation was successful.

```
$ redis-server --version
Redis server v=7.0.4 sha=00000000:0 malloc=jemalloc-5.2.1 bits=64
build=5aabc73c47c29d1e
```

The second option is to create a docker-compose file that runs the database and RedisInsight, one of the tools to access and interact with Redis. Listing E-2 shows the structure of a Docker-compose file to run a Redis database using RedisInsight.

Listing E-2. Docker-compose File to Run Redis

```
version: '3.1'

services:
  redis-db:
    image: redis:6.2
    restart: always
    ports:
      - 6379:6379

  redisinsight:
    image: redislabs/redisinsight:1.12.1 #This version refers to the
    version 2.0 of the tool
    ports:
      - '8001:8001'
```

After creating a file, run it using the docker-compose up command. Then, go to the browser and enter **localhost:8001** which is the port that uses **RedisInsight**. Figure E-1 shows how RedisInsight looks like the first time that you enter the webpage.

Figure E-1. *RedisInsight home page*

The next step is to connect this tool with your database, which is running, so you need to press the "I already have a database" button. You see a webpage where you have multiple connection options because a database is hosted in different places, such as on your machine, on a dedicated server, or by cloud providers like AWS. Figure E-2 shows the different options that exist to configure access to the database.

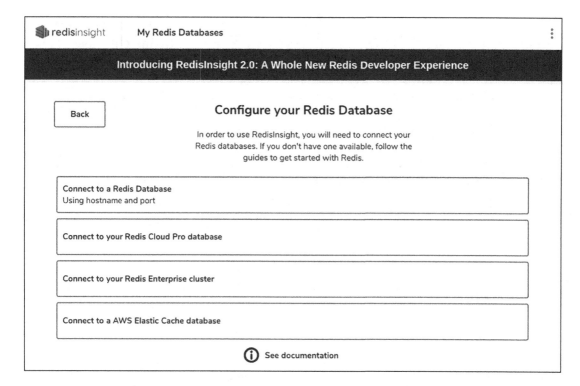

Figure E-2. *Configuration of the database*

The next step is to click the Connect to a Redis Database button and complete the modal with the information on the connection.

- **host**: redis-db

- **port**: 6379

- **name**: catalog (or anything that you want to use)

When you confirm all the information, RedisInsight connects to validate if all the information that you provided is correct or not before adding the database. If everything works fine you will see a screen like the Figure E-3 with the databases that you have configured on the tool.

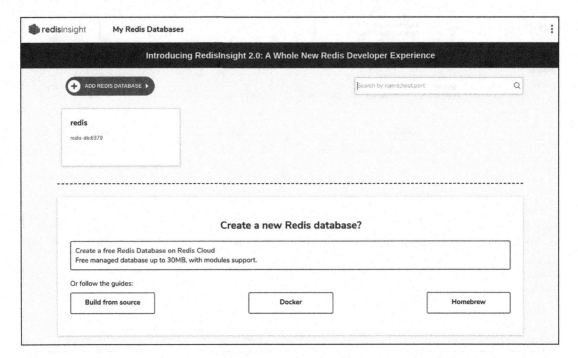

Figure E-3. *The connection with the database*

If you double-click the database, you access a new page containing all the operations you can execute for this particular database and check the status. The operations could be performed from your application using the command line or the CLI tool on RedisInsight (see Figure E-4).

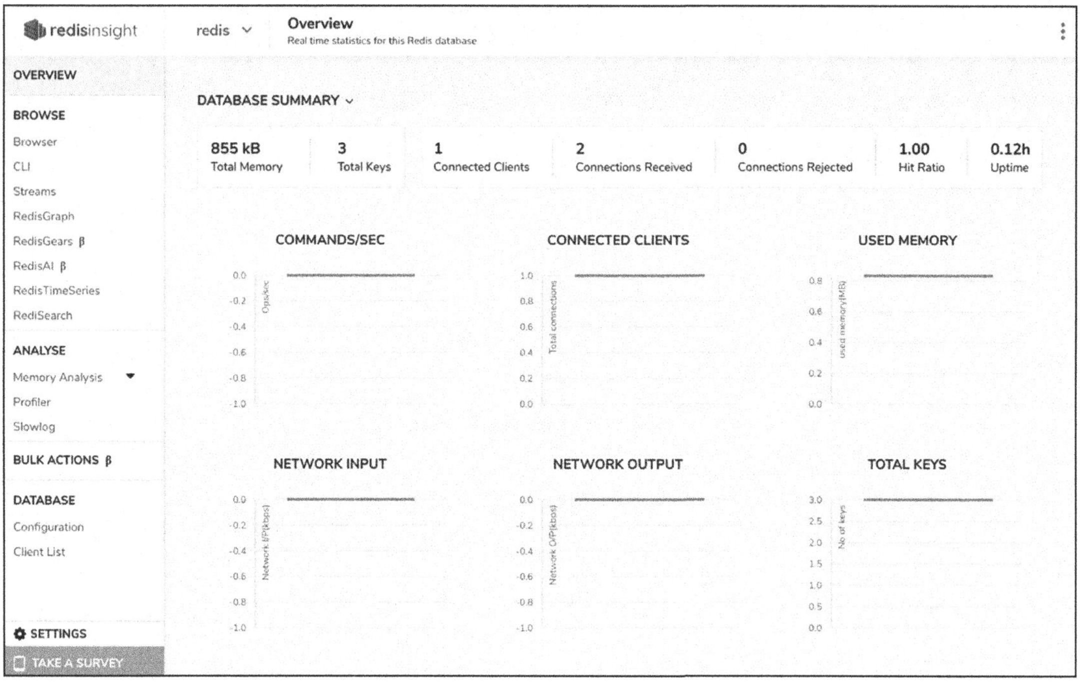

Figure E-4. *Active database*

The last thing that you can do is open the "Browser" option to add new elements to the database or check the existing one, which could be helpful to check if the TTL of the key is okay or not (see Figure E-5).

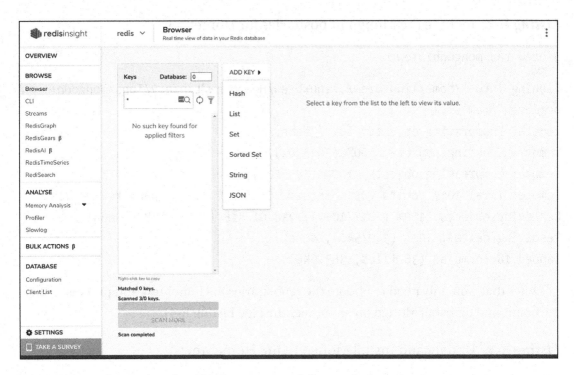

Figure E-5. Browser tab, which permits adding new keys

MongoDB

MongoDB is a non-relational database that persists information, like a document, with some of the features offered by relational databases. This database offers installation options.

This database has documentation[1] on installing it using different packages according to your operating system. However, the process could take extra steps depending on your operating system.

Homebrew reduces the complexity of the installation process. The first step is to include the repositories related to Mongo in Homebrew, which by default does not include it (see Listing E-3).

---

[1]https://www.mongodb.com/docs/v6.0/administration/install-on-linux/

Listing E-3. Include the Mongo Repositories for Homebrew

```
$ brew tap mongodb/brew

Cloning into '/home/linuxbrew/.linuxbrew/Homebrew/Library/Taps/mongodb/
homebrew-brew'...
remote: Enumerating objects: 1017, done.
remote: Counting objects: 100% (302/302), done.
remote: Compressing objects: 100% (105/105), done.
remote: Total 1017 (delta 245), reused 208 (delta 196), pack-reused 715
Receiving objects: 100% (1017/1017), 218.01 KiB | 1.79 MiB/s, done.
Resolving deltas: 100% (540/540), done.
Tapped 18 formulae (36 files, 363.6KB).
```

After that, you only need to update the repositories in Homebrew and proceed with the command to install Mongo on your machine (see Listing E-4).

Listing E-4. Update and Install Mongo Using Homebrew

```
$ brew update
Already up-to-date.

$ brew install mongodb-community@6.0
Warning: mongodb-community provides a launchd plist which can only be used
on macOS!
You can manually execute the service instead with:
  mongod --config /home/linuxbrew/.linuxbrew/etc/mongod.conf
```

The last option is to use Docker commands to run the database or a docker-compose file. Listing E-5 show the basic configuration of the MongoDB using Docker-Compose.

Listing E-5. Docker-compose File to Run Mongo

```
version: '3.1'

services:
  mongo-db:
    image: mongo:6.0
    container_name: mongo-db
    restart: always
```

```
environment:
  MONGO_INITDB_ROOT_USERNAME: root
  MONGO_INITDB_ROOT_PASSWORD: rootpassword
ports:
  - 27017:27017
```

After running MongoDB on your machine, the next step uses the tool to access the database graphically. Install Mongo Compass, an official Mongo tool, by following the steps of the official documentation[2] according to your operating system.

When you have Mongo Compass on your machine, the first time you open see a screen like Figure E-6, which allows you to configure the first connection.

Figure E-6. *Mongo Compass first page*

The next step is to click Advanced Connection Options to introduce the username and password of the Mongo Server running on your machine. If you use the docker-compose file, the username is **root,** and the password is **rootpassword**. Figure E-7 shows how the advanced configuration on the Mongo Compass looks like.

---

[2] https://www.mongodb.com/try/download/compass

Figure E-7. *Configure the connection with MongoDB server*

If you introduce all the information correctly, you see a screen with all the databases available on your MongoDB server. By default, there are three databases that try not to remove it (see Figure E-8).

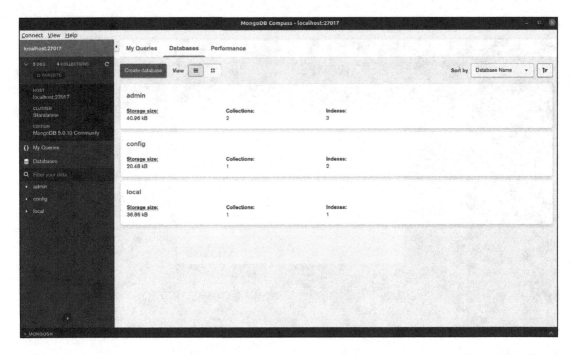

Figure E-8. *The available database on your machine*

The last step implies creating a new database to save the information related to your application that contains the catalog information. To do this, you only need to press the Create Database button and complete the fields as you can see on Figure E-9.

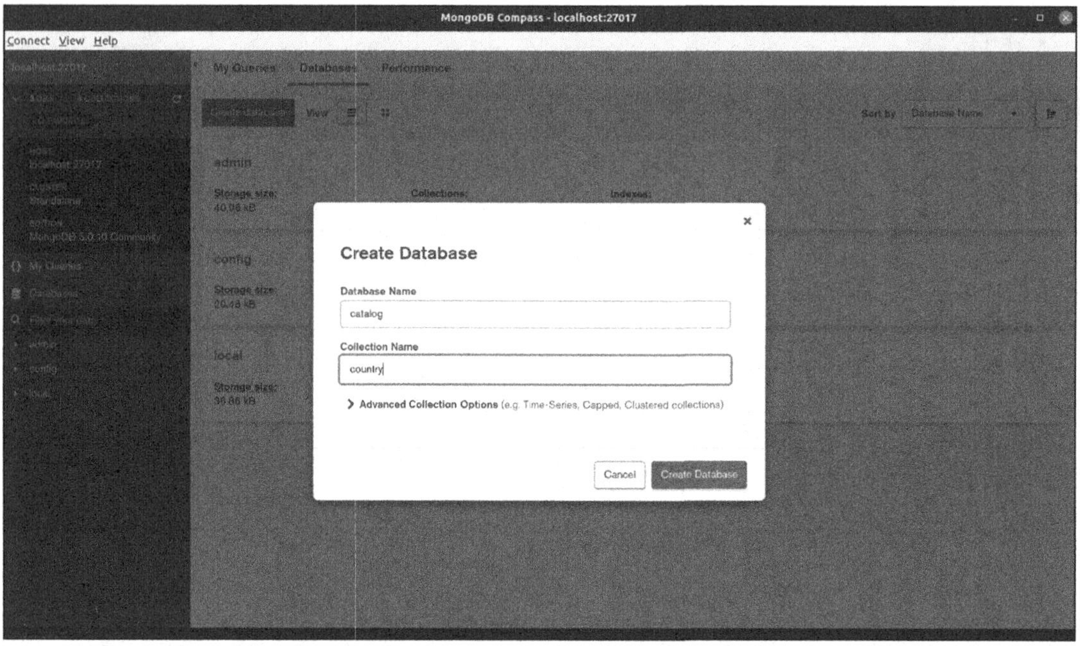

Figure E-9. *Creating a new database on your Mongo server*

Cassandra

The Cassandra database's official documentation includes instructions on installing it.[3] The best options are to use Docker commands or a docker-compose file. Listing E-6 shows how to configure different instances of Cassandra using Docker-Compose.

Listing E-6. Docker-compose File to Run Cassandra with Multiple Nodes

```
version: "2.1"

services:
  cassandra-1:
    image: cassandra:3.11.1
    container_name: cassandra-1
    environment:
      CASSANDRA_CLUSTER_NAME: twa
      CASSANDRA_DC: TDC1
```

---

[3] https://cassandra.apache.org/doc/latest/cassandra/getting_started/installing.html

```
      MAX_HEAP_SIZE: 600M
      HEAP_NEWSIZE: 100M
    ports:
      - '9042:9042'
      - '9160:9160'
    networks:
      cassclus:
        ipv4_address: 10.0.75.11

  #Other nodes of cassandra

  cassandra-web:
    image: dcagatay/cassandra-web
    environment:
      CASSANDRA_HOST_IPS: 10.0.75.11,10.0.75.12,10.0.75.13
      CASSANDRA_PORT: 9042
    ports:
      - "3000:3000"
    restart: always
    depends_on:
      - cassandra-1
      - cassandra-2
      - cassandra-3
    networks:
      cassclus:
        ipv4_address: 10.0.75.15

networks:
  cassclus:
    driver: bridge
    ipam:
      driver: default
      config:
        - subnet: 10.0.75.0/24
          gateway: 10.0.75.1
```

To simulate a real scenario, you use three different instances connected with limited resources to abuse the use of resources on your machine. The docker-compose file includes Cassandra Web,[4] a visual tool based on Ruby to work with the database.

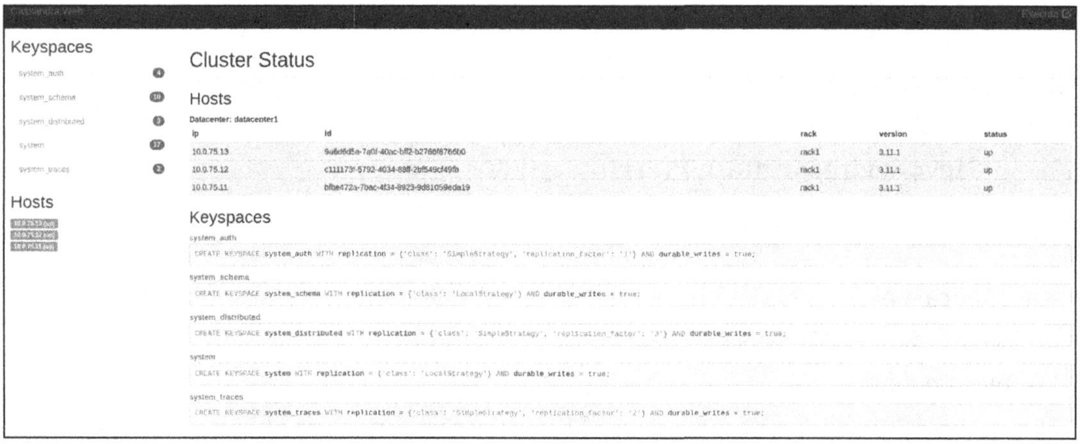

Figure E-10. *Cassandra Web with the status of the nodes*

After executing the docker-compose file and ingressing it to localhost:3000 in your browser, you see the result shown in Figure E-10 with the available nodes and the keyspaces. I recommend creating a new keyspace indicating the replication factor because if you do not indicate it, the database assigns a default value which could not be the best option. Figure E-11 shows how looks like the page to create a new keyspace.

---

[4]https://github.com/avalanche123/cassandra-web

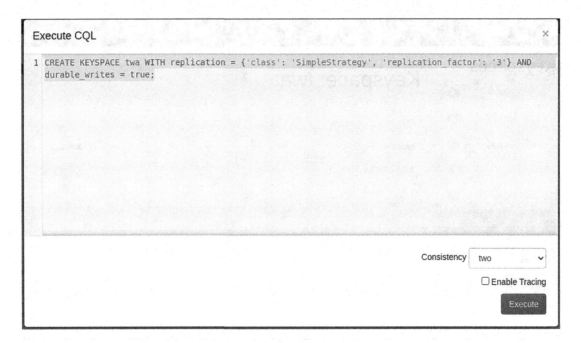

Figure E-11. *Create a keyspace to contain all the tables*

When you have the new keyspace created, you see the tables. In this case, there are no tables because this structure is new. You only need to click the twa keyspace in the left menu and you will see the detail of the keyspace like the Figure E-12.

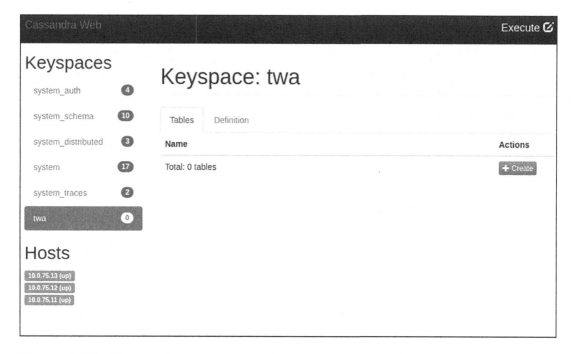

Figure E-12. *The new keyspace created*

To create a table, you only need to click the Create button and complete the sentence. Indicate the right type of consistency that appears at the bottom of the modal. Figure E-13 show you the editor looks like with the creation of a table.

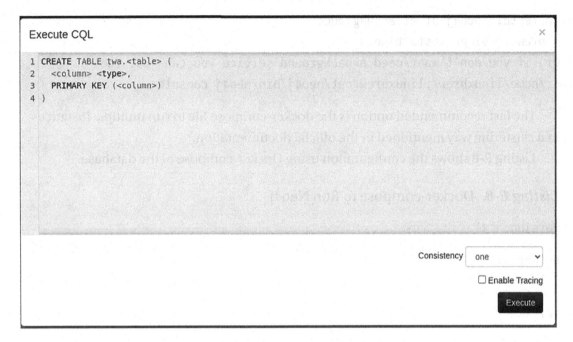

Figure E-13. *How to create a table*

Neo4j

Neo4j offers various methods of installation; some of them have more complexity. One of the basics implies following the instructions for each operating system.[5]

There is another option covered in the official documentation. **Homebrew** reduces the complexity of the installation process which you see the steps on the Listing E-7.

Listing E-7. Install Neo4j

```
$ brew install neo4j

==> Checking for dependents of upgraded formulae...
==> No broken dependents found!
==> Caveats
==> neo4j
```

---

[5] https://neo4j.com/docs/operations-manual/current/installation/ ·

To restart neo4j after an upgrade:
  brew services restart neo4j
Or, if you don't want/need a background service you can just run:
  /home/linuxbrew/.linuxbrew/opt/neo4j/bin/neo4j console

The last recommended option is the docker-compose file to run multiple instances in a clustering way mentioned in the official documentation.[6]

Listing E-8 shows the configuration using Docker-compose of the database.

Listing E-8. Docker-compose to Run Neo4j

```
version: '3'

networks:
  lan:

services:

  core1:
    image: neo4j:3.5-enterprise
    networks:
      - lan
    ports:
      - 7474:7474
      - 6477:6477
      - 7687:7687
    volumes:
      - $HOME/neo4j/neo4j-core1/conf:/conf
      - $HOME/neo4j/neo4j-core1/data:/data
      - $HOME/neo4j/neo4j-core1/logs:/logs
      - $HOME/neo4j/neo4j-core1/plugins:/plugins
    environment:
      - NEO4J_AUTH=neo4j/changeme
      - NEO4J_dbms_mode=CORE
      - NEO4J_ACCEPT_LICENSE_AGREEMENT=yes
```

---

[6] https://neo4j.com/docs/operations-manual/current/docker/clustering/

- NEO4J_causal__clustering_minimum__core__cluster__size__at__
  formation=3
- NEO4J_causal__clustering_minimum__core__cluster__size__at__
  runtime=3
- NEO4J_causal__clustering_initial__discovery__members=core1:5000,co
  re2:5000,core3:5000
- NEO4J_dbms_connector_http_listen__address=:7474
- NEO4J_dbms_connector_https_listen__address=:6477
- NEO4J_dbms_connector_bolt_listen__address=:7687

Next, run the database on your local machine. The next step is to download the Neo4j Browser, an application to manage and see the representation of the information in the database. The official documentation[7] explains how to install depending on your operating system.

When you finish installing Neo4j Browser and opening the application, the first step implies the terms and conditions with the key that appear on the site where you downloaded the tool (see Figure E-14).

---

[7]https://neo4j.com/download-center/#community

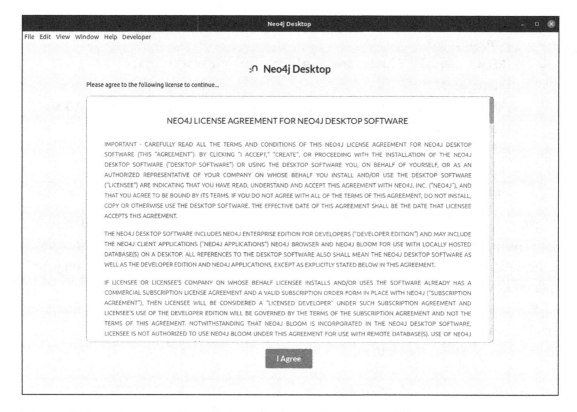

Figure E-14. *Terms and conditions that must be accepted*

After you load your license key, you need to create a project containing connections to a particular database. To do this, click the New button and select the Create Project option as you can see on Figure E-15.

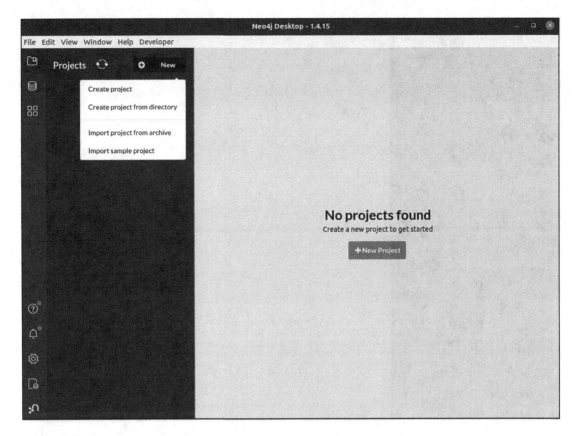

Figure E-15. *Create a new project*

Now that you have a project, the next step is to connect the project with a database. If you have an instance running locally, choose the correct option. Figure E-16 shows how the connection with the database looks like.

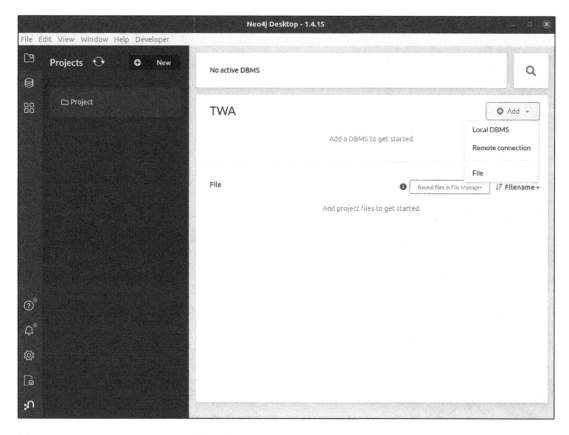

Figure E-16. *Connect to a database*

When you load the username/password associated with your instance of Neo4j, you see the database's name and the active connections. The username/password is defined in the docker-compose file. Using Homebrew, you must set the password by following the official documentation instructions.[8] Figure E-17 shows how the active database looks like on the tool.

---

[8] https://neo4j.com/docs/operations-manual/current/configuration/
set-initial-password/

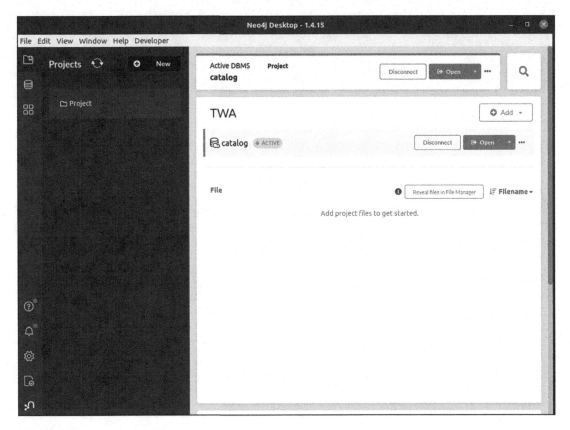

Figure E-17. *The active database*

APPENDIX F

Further Reading

This book covers frameworks and libraries, technologies, and databases but it does not cover advanced topics. This appendix offers lists of books and other resources that you can explore to learn advanced topics more in-depth. There are three groups of resources: general, relational databases, and non-relational databases.

General

- **Beginning IntelliJ IDEA** by Ted Hagos (Apress, 2021).[1] This book covers all the aspects of using IntelliJ, like the installation process, how you can debug the application, and the most relevant elements to acquiring the basic skills of the IDE.

- **Learn Microservices with Spring Boot 3.0** by Moisés Macero García (Apress, 2020).[2] Suppose you want to understand all the aspects of a microservice, like how to create a new one or the philosophy of using microservices instead of monoliths. This book helps you understand these concepts and how to implement them using Spring Boot.

- **Docker in Action** by Jeff Nickoloff and Stephen Kuenzli (Manning, 2019).[3] This book extensively explains all the aspects of Docker and how it interacts with the layers of the operating system. Also, you learn how to create an image or run an existing one.

---

[1] https://link.springer.com/book/10.1007/978-1-4842-7446-0

[2] https://link.springer.com/book/10.1007/978-1-4842-6131-6

[3] https://www.manning.com/books/docker-in-action-second-edition?query=Docker%20in%20Action

© Andres Sacco 2023

A. Sacco, *Beginning Spring Data*, https://doi.org/10.1007/978-1-4842-8764-4

- ***Spring Boot Persistence Best Practices*** by Anghel Leonard (Apress, 2020).[4] This book covers the most relevant topics to improve the quality and the performance of the persistence of relational databases. Most of the concepts relate to relational databases, but there are aspects that you can apply to non-relational databases.

- ***Learning Spring Boot 3.0*** by Greg L. Turnquist (Packt, 2023).[5] This book covers most of the relevant topics in the new version of Spring Boot, such as messaging and reactive applications.

- **Laurentiu Spilca's channel on Youtube**.[6] This channel features videos on relevant Spring topics, like security, performance, and basic tutorials. Laurentiu is one of the most recognized speakers and authors on Spring.

Relational Databases

- ***Beginning SQL Queries*** by Clare Churcher (Apress, 2008).[7] This book covers all the basic aspects of SQL, from how to write operations (insert, update, select, and delete) to the efficiency or performance of queries.

Non-Relational Databases

- ***Cassandra: The Definitive Guide, 3rd Edition*** by Jeff Carpenter, Eben Hewitt (O'Reilly, 2020).[8] The author shows all the advantages this database provides instead of other non-relational databases. Also, this book covers topics that are not common, like monitoring, maintenance, and scaling.

---

[4] https://link.springer.com/book/10.1007/978-1-4842-5626-8
[5] https://www.amazon.com/Learning-Spring-Boot-3-0-production-grade/dp/1803233303
[6] https://www.youtube.com/c/laurentiuspilca
[7] https://link.springer.com/book/10.1007/978-1-4842-1955-3
[8] https://learning.oreilly.com/library/view/cassandra-the-definitive/9781098115159/

- ***Beginning Neo4j*** by Chris Kemper (Apress, 2015).[9] This book is a basic introduction to Graph databases and how to implement them in Neo4j.

- ***Redis in Action*** by Josiah Carlson (Manning, 2013).[10] This book explains the basic use of Redis, building examples of information you can save into the database. The book also covers other aspects related to performance and scalability.

- ***MongoDB Performance Tuning*** by Guy Harrison and Michael Harrison (Apress, 2021)[11]. This book covers the basic aspects of queries and how to improve performance. There are other topics, like creating a cluster with different instances and monitoring the use of the resources of the database.

---

[9] https://link.springer.com/book/10.1007/978-1-4842-1227-1
[10] https://www.manning.com/books/redis-in-action?query=Redis
[11] https://link.springer.com/book/10.1007/978-1-4842-6879-7

Index

A

A/B testing, 179, 180
ACID, 85, 146, 147, 234
Actuator, 40, 44, 46, 53
Adoptium, 342
Amazon Document DB, 215
Apache Cassandra, 249, 264
Apache OpenJPA, 17
api-catalog application, 177, 195, 213, 236, 253, 275, 311–313, 315, 334
APITest in src/test/java, 313
Application architectures types
    hexagonal, 27, 28
    layer, 24, 26
Azure Cosmos DB, 216

B

BEGIN_TRANSACTION keyword, 145

C

@Cacheable annotation, 334, 335
Cassandra, 269, 354, 355, 394, 396, 397, 399
    benefits, 250, 251, 264
    CAP theorem, 252
    configuration
        custom repositories, 260–262
        database/connection
            settings, 253–260

TTL, 263, 264
    definition, 249
    node architecture, 250
    relational database, 249
    structure, 252, 253
Cassandra Query Language (CQL), 252, 263
CassandraTemplate, 260–262
CloudWatch, 60
@Column annotation, 94, 256
    binary types, 101
    character types, 99
    date/time types, 99, 100
    default value, 96
    definition, 94
    primitive types, 96–98
    properties, 94
    types, 102
@ColumnDefinition annotation, 96
columnDefinition property, 95
COMMIT keyword, 145
Consistency and integrity, 143
Couchbase, 19, 216
CountryRepository, 181, 281
CountryService DELETE method, 154
Create, retrieve/read, update, delete (CRUD), 15, 19, 29, 32, 40, 54, 62, 64, 67, 73
CrudRepository, 19, 73, 74, 224
cURL, 354
CurrencyRepository, 75

411

© Andres Sacco 2023
A. Sacco, *Beginning Spring Data*, https://doi.org/10.1007/978-1-4842-8764-4

D

E

F

Feature flags
    A/B testing, 179
    implementation, 181–185
    non-relational databases, 180
    roll back, 179
    toggle options, 180
findById method, 261, 287
Flyway, 103, 167–169, 175

G

Gatling, 311, 315, 320, 321, 323
@GeneratedValue annotation, 104,
       107, 238
GenerationType.SEQUENCE, 105
GET method, 114, 116, 160, 161, 247
Git, 344
GraalVM, 340
Gradle/Maven, 42, 48, 57, 167
GraphBLAS, 233
Graph database
    definition, 231
    implementations, 233
    nodes/links, 232
    use cases, 232
Graphileon, 358

H

HashCode and equals methods, 91, 93

I

@Id annotation, 92, 93, 198, 223, 238
@Indexed annotation, 211, 223
Inherence
    base class, 121

duplicate code, 120
    embeddable class, 129–132
    listing/auditing events, 132–135
    mapped superclass, 121, 122
    table per class, 127, 129
    table per class hierarchy, 123, 124
    table per class, joins, 125, 126
@Inheritance annotation, 123, 127
Insomnia, 353, 354
IntelliJ, 170, 345, 346, 349
IntelliJ IDEA, xix, 349, 363, 407

J

jakarta.persistence package, 88
Java Database Connectivity (JDBC)
    components/layers, 5, 6
    databases, 9–11
    definition, 5
    driver, 7
        client-based, 8
        ODBC access, 8
        two-tier architecture, 8
        types, 7
        wire protocol/native protocol
          driver, 8
    EJB, 12
    structure, 5
Java JDK, xix, 341
Java/Kotlin application, 278, 301
Java Message Service (JMS), 15
Java Persistence API (JPA), 4
    database, 17, 18
    definition, 16
    layers, 17
    SQL statement, 16
JavaScript, 268
JMapper, 35, 69

Printed in the United States
by Baker & Taylor Publisher Services

Printed in the United States
by Baker & Taylor Publisher Services